"ONE OF THE BEST COOKBOOKS . . . WITH AN ACCENT ON HEALTH." —Working Mother

This extraordinary collection of tempting dishes offers the best of everything, from good health to great food. So whether you are watching cholesterol, salt, sugar, calories—or just the clock— these are the good-tasting, nutritious, diet-conscious recipes you've been looking for. Just think, in practically no time at all, you'll be able to whip up such delectable treats as Crabmeat-Stuffed Pepper Rings, Quick Barbecued Chicken Drummettes, Mandarin Waldorf Salad, Luscious Lobster Cacciatore, and Lemony Cheese Pie.

Deliciously Simple

"Loaded with gourmet-quality, nutritious recipes . . . it's like taking private lessons from one of America's premier cooks."
—Michael F. Jacobson, Ph.D.,
Executive Director of the Center
for Science in the Public Interest

HARRIET ROTH, mother of two, has a B.S. in nutrition from Carnegie Mellon University and extensive training in haute cuisine. A former student of Simone Beck and Roger Vergé, she taught French and Italian cookery for 18 years, until her appointment as Director of the Pritikin Longevity Center Cooking School. She now runs a private dietary consulting service in Los Angeles, California, where she lives with her husband and family. Author of the bestselling cookbook *Deliciously Low*, Mrs. Roth frequently consults with chefs around the world who share her dedication to good health and good eating in the gourmet tradition.

Deliciously Simple

QUICK-AND-EASY
LOW-SODIUM, LOW-FAT,
LOW-CHOLESTEROL,
LOW-SUGAR MEALS

---

by

Harriet Roth

A PLUME BOOK

NEW AMERICAN LIBRARY

A DIVISION OF PENGUIN BOOKS USA INC., NEW YORK
PUBLISHED IN CANADA BY
PENGUIN BOOKS CANADA LIMITED, MARKHAM, ONTARIO

NAL BOOKS ARE AVAILABLE AT QUANTITY DISCOUNTS WHEN
USED TO PROMOTE PRODUCTS OR SERVICES. FOR
INFORMATION PLEASE WRITE TO PREMIUM MARKETING
DIVISION, NEW AMERICAN LIBRARY, 1633 BROADWAY,
NEW YORK, NEW YORK 10019.

NOTE TO THE READER

The information contained in this book is not intended as a
substitute for consulting with your physician. All matters
regarding your health require medical supervision. Please
note also that many of the products mentioned in this book
are registered trademarks.

A hardcover edition was published by New American Library
and simultaneously in Canada by The New American Library
of Canada Limited.

PLUME TRADEMARK REG. U.S. PAT. OFF. AND FOREIGN COUNTRIES
REGISTERED TRADEMARK–MARCA REGISTRADA
HECHO EN HARRISONBURG, VA., U.S.A.

SIGNET, SIGNET CLASSIC, MENTOR, ONYX, PLUME, MERIDIAN
and NAL BOOKS are published *in the United States* by
New American Library, a division of Penguin Books USA Inc.,
1633 Broadway, New York, New York 10019,
in Canada by Penguin Books Canada Limited,
2801 John Street, Markham, Ontario L3R 1B4

LIBRARY OF CONGRESS CATALOGING IN PUBLICATION DATA

Roth, Harriet.
  Deliciously simple.
  Includes index.
  1. Salt-free diet—Recipes. 2. Low-fat diet—
Recipes. 3. Low-cholesterol diet—Recipes. 4. Sugar-free
diet—Recipes. 1. Title.
RM237.8.R66 1986   641.5′632   86-12423
ISBN 0-453-00522-5
ISBN 0-452-25984-3 (pbk)

First Plume Printing, February, 1988

4 5 6 7 8 9

PRINTED IN THE UNITED STATES OF AMERICA

This book is dedicated to the memory
of Nathan Pritikin,
whose pioneering spirit and concern
for the health and longevity
of mankind will affect
generations to come.

Acknowledgments

Here I am, the second time around. After writing *Deliciously Low*, I received many requests for a book about healthy foods that can be easily and quickly prepared. *Deliciously Simple* is the result. I would like to thank those who contributed to its conception and completion. The enthusiasm, encouragement, and love of my family and friends were essential. Carole Hall, a consummate professional, my editor for the second time, helped with her intelligence and guidance. Molly Allen and Irene Pink provided various suggestions and much of the fine tuning that make the recipes so wonderfully workable.

My endless gratitude and thanks go to all my readers for their overwhelming response to *Deliciously Low* and to the following for caring: Suzie Arensburg, Irene Baron, Sharon Berryhill, John Farquhar, M.D., Harriet Friedman, Karen Gillingham, Julian Hamer, Dorothy Hartstein, R.D., Freda Hermann, Annette Korbin, R.D., Barrett S. Litt, Greg Mowery, Nanette Nathanson, Harriet Root, Larry Roth, Sally Roth, Penny Saltsburg, Eva Silver, Gerald Silver, David Sobel, M.D., Irvin Q. Sobel, M.D., Isabel Sobol, and my friends and the participants at the Pritikin Longevity Centers and Computrition Inc.

My acknowledgments could never be complete without thanks to my husband, Harold, my love, my friend, and my inspiration.

—H. R.

Contents

Introduction

A Delicious Difference

Meals of steamed brown rice and vegetables are healthful and most certainly easy to prepare, but *what a bore!* My delight in cooking comes from creating interesting flavors and dishes that tempt a healthy gourmet's palate and make dining a pleasure.

I'm sure yours does, too.

In my previous book, *Deliciously Low*, I proved that we don't have to be nutritionally deprived in order to enjoy gourmet satisfaction. Each recipe showed how nutritious foods can be exotically flavored and beautifully presented. But sometimes we not only want our meals to be tasty and healthful; we also want them to be ready right away.

Now, delicious and nutritious food, simply and conveniently prepared, need not be the impossible dream. It is all here for your culinary enjoyment: more than 300 healthful recipes to delight your family and friends. Meanwhile, back in the kitchen, you will still have the energy to enjoy them.

Quick Alternatives

Half of the recipes in this book will take only 30 minutes to prepare, start to finish. The rest, with few exceptions, take no more than 30 minutes advance preparation time. Recipes that are especially for entertaining may indicate advance preparation time of up to one hour, but I assume your guests are worth a little extra effort! Most days, however, speed counts.

The Mushroom, Bean, and Barley Soup in *Deliciously Low* is one of my favorite recipes, but you may need a rainy day at home to prepare this special brew. So what would I cook if I had thoughts of a nice warm bowl of soup after a day of shopping? *Deliciously Simple's* alternative of

1

Quick Vegetable-Barley Soup, on page 87. It takes only 30 minutes from the moment of your first thought to savor a comforting mouthful. "The same taste?" you ask. Of course not, but delicious, with a special quality of its own.

Now, what about that tough day at work when everything demanded your total attention? All you can think of is a quiet evening at home with the phone off the hook and a light meal with something sweet, something special, maybe even a cheese pie. Oh, but you don't have time for that healthy, Luscious Lemony Cheese Pie in *Deliciously Low*. It takes about 1½ hours to bake and at least 30 minutes more to chill before serving. *Deliciously Simple* provides an exquisite compromise. On page 321 is a cheese pie that takes less than half the time from beginning to end. No whipping of egg whites, no oven, just sheer gustatory enjoyment.

These are just two samples of nutritious but convenient recipes in *Deliciously Simple*. They will be time-savers and palate-pleasers to fit into the busiest of life-styles.

Eating Well

Because of both my personal and professional commitment to good health, all of my recipes adhere to the sound nutrition principles put forth by the United States Department of Agriculture and the National Institutes of Health. But within those guidelines you will have many options.

Life is a series of choices: deciding to turn right or left, to stop or go. Everything, however, is not black or white. There are shades of gray, as in the choices you make when cooking and eating.

Researchers point to a low-cholesterol, low-fat diet as a preventive measure regarding cancer and cardiac problems. A low-sodium diet is advised for people with hypertension, kidney problems, a tendency toward fluid retention, or P.M.S. (Pre-Menstrual Syndrome). Authorities suggest that sugar should be limited to natural sources, and recommend a low-sugar diet without adding sugar or artificial sweeteners.

You notice that these advisories stipulate low-cholesterol, low-fat, low-sodium, low-sugar eating, not *no*. That being the case, my recipes will recommend you use either nonfat or low-fat dairy products, no-cholesterol or low-cholesterol foods, no-salt or salt-reduced products, and use limited polyunsaturated fats (cold-pressed safflower, corn, or soy oil) and extra-virgin olive oil if your health permits.

The ultimate nutritional decisions are yours, depending on whether you are concerned with treatment of a specific condition establishing a healthy eating pattern, or simply staying well. Remember, it is the foods that you eat on a daily ongoing basis, not the exceptions, that help to determine the state of your health.

Here, then, are the guidelines to help you make your choices.

Five Easy Guidelines

1. Limit Fat and Cholesterol

Both the American Cancer Society and American Heart Association are recommending that fat consumption be limited to 30 percent of your total calories per day. The low-fat content of my recipes will help you go a step further by cutting fat to a safer 20 percent of your total calories.

Nonfat milk products are certainly preferable, but if they are too hard to find or if the change from whole milk is too difficult for you, at least you can use low-fat products such as low-fat milk, yogurt, cottage cheese, and other low-fat cheeses. That will reduce your fat consumption from dairy products alone by 50 percent.

The National Institutes of Health have conclusively linked high blood cholesterol levels with heart disease. Since this is no longer conjecture, it behooves us to continue to limit our consumption of foods high in cholesterol. That is to say, my recipes will avoid egg yolks, butter, traditional mayonnaise and salad dressings, lard, chicken fat, organ meats, ice cream, whole-milk products, sour cream, high-fat cheeses, fatty meats, and too much of any red meats or seafood.

If there is an infrequent addition of oil, it will, of course, be one that is highly polyunsaturated (safflower, soy, corn oil); or monosaturated, *preferably olive oil* which current research indicates helps lower cholesterol levels in the blood.

Skin and visible fat will be removed from poultry. Especially high-cholesterol foods such as egg yolks, organ meats, and animal fat will all be avoided. Suggested cholesterol levels will be held to a maximum of 300 milligrams per day.

If you have a blood cholesterol level of 185 milligrams or under, certainly the prudent preparation of a very lean red meat such as flank steak, first-cut brisket, top round, or lean veal, lamb, or pork served occasionally should not encourage higher cholesterol levels. Of course, the cooked portion of protein you serve should be kept to a 4-ounce serving. Large portions of animal protein are no longer fashionable. In fact, they inhibit the absorption of calcium and may contribute to osteoporosis.

2. Keep Your Diet High in Fiber and Complex Carbohydrates

High-fiber diets have become increasingly important in the prevention of some types of cancer, particularly colorectal concer. Fiber also helps lower blood cholesterol and aids in the regulation of hypoglycemia and diabetes.* Former Health and Human Services Secretary Margaret Heckler has spoken of the importance of increasing dietary fiber while reducing fat. This type of high-fiber (40 grams per day) diet could help reduce the incidence of colon cancer by 30 percent.

There are two types of fiber—insoluble and soluble. Wheat bran and vegetables contain insoluble fiber that is valuable in speeding food through the digestive tract. Oat bran (a tasty cereal that may also be added in baking), pears, apples, prunes, dried peas, and beans and corn are good sources of soluble fiber, which current research shows may help lower blood cholesterol levels and regulate blood sugar levels.

In the beginning of this century, the average American diet contained about 40 grams of fiber each day. Potatoes, hearty bean soups, and main courses, and wonderfully fresh garden vegetables and fruits held important places in the diet. Instead of all the exotic fruits, maybe an apple a day did indeed help keep the doctor away.

Americans' average fiber consumption is now only approximately 15 to 20 grams per day, as a result of eating highly processed and refined foods that are overcooked. If your present daily eating pattern is less than generous in whole grains, dried beans, and fresh vegetables and fruits, my recipes will give it a boost.

I also suggest that you try to obtain 60 to 70 percent of your total calories from complex carbohydrates. These are foods like whole-grain cereals and breads; brown rice; barley; pasta; dried peas, beans, and lentils; fresh fruits and vegetables, especially corn, peas, lima beans, and potatoes. There are dozens of recipes here to help you turn back the clock to the time when complex carbohydrates constituted a major and valuable part of the American diet.

3. Limit Sodium and Salt

We all should be concerned about our consumption of sodium, whether found naturally in our food and water, in commercially added preserva-

* Research by Dr. James Anderson, Director of High Carbohydrate-Fiber Diabetes Foundation in Lexington, Kentucky.

tives (i.e., sodium benzoate, sodium nitrate, sodium nitrite, or, amazingly enough, still MSG), or in the salt we so thoughtlessly add ourselves. We should opt for a maximum of 3,000 milligrams of sodium per day, unless, of course, our physician's guidance or the state of our health indicates lower levels.

Maybe a desire for just a touch of added salt in food preparation haunts you, particularly in some soups. If that is the case and there are no contraindications, go ahead and add a bit, but remember that each ¼ teaspoon of added salt contains about 500 milligrams of sodium. As a rule, my recipes have marginal sodium content.

4. Limit Sugar

Excess sugar is still the culprit in many diets. Foods high in sugar are still being consumed in quantities that replace foods with much-needed essential nutrients. The average American consumes approximately 125 pounds of sugar a year. Soft drinks contain up to 14 teaspoons of sugar in each can. A teaspoon of sugar has 16 calories but *no vitamins, minerals, or protein.*

My recipes rely on healthful alternatives to refined sugar, molasses, honey, and syrup. You'll notice that I sometimes recommend date sugar, made from pulverized dried dates. While it does contain fructose, it is low in glucose, which is more readily absorbed by the body. Judicious amounts may be used in baking; however, unsweetened frozen apple juice concentrate or white grape juice are still my preferred sweeteners. I have avoided artificial sweeteners. Diabetics may use aspartame in small amounts. It has been approved by the FDA, but there are still some questions, as noted on its label. The more natural our ingredients in food preparation, the better.

My recipes will give you hundreds of fresh suggestions for preparing whole foods simply and creatively.

5. Keep Your Ideal Weight in Mind

Lots of people want an easy answer to weight control—a pill a day or a powdered solution that will melt pounds. Actually, it is easy to lose weight. Even on a diet of buttermilk and bananas you could lose pounds. The trick, though, is to keep it off and stay healthy. My *Deliciously Simple* recipes will help limit calorie-laden fatty foods and sugars and limit your fluid-retaining sodium intake. If you remember to serve reasonably-sized portions, you stand an extraordinary chance of reaching and keeping your ideal weight.

Convenience Without Compromise

Obviously, we can be healthy without making the preparation of the right foods our life's work. We live in a changing world. Most of us work and have limited time to put into cooking for ourselves or others. However, we know that a steady diet of commercial fast food neither contributes to good health nor satisfies a food lover's fancy.

As a professional, I am always looking for shortcuts to cooking without sacrificing good nutrition and delicious flavors. My sincere hope is that *Deliciously Simple* will provide the tools you need in fulfilling this goal of good food simply prepared, and a long, healthy life to enjoy it.

Helpful Hints and Basic Pantry List

First, Consider a Microwave

If time and convenience are important considerations for you as a cook, a microwave may be your answer.

There is no significant nutritional difference between foods cooked in a microwave oven or by traditional means. Contrary to what many believe, there is no radiation left in food. Microwave cooking is moist-heat cooking resulting from friction or heat transfer from the outside of food continuing to the center. Foods that give best results are those with a high percentage of water, such as vegetables, casseroles, stews, fish, and soups. I also prefer the moistness of a turkey breast prepared in a microwave oven.

Microwave oven pluses are many: They are energy-efficient and generally cook faster than other types of ovens. Since they don't require preheating, they don't heat up the kitchen while in use. Reheated leftovers don't taste reheated, since they don't dry out. Vegetables are wonderful; they do have considerable color, texture, and taste if cooked properly. Of course, steaming is great also. Fish cooks up with an unusually moist texture.

There is always the down side. Microwave ovens do not crisp; they do not cook as evenly. You may have to stir once or twice or turn the dish during cooking.* Meats don't brown well unless you have a browning unit or use a browning dish, or unless the meat is fatty. Even then, they are not done to my satisfaction. There are combination convection and microwave ovens now, however, that do a better job, particularly the built-in units. All utensils must be microwave safe—no metal unless specified by individual manufacturers.

Of course, there is the ever-present fear of radiation. A properly

* Microwave turntables that help avoid hot spots are available from Nordic Ware and Rubbermaid.

functioning microwave oven does not give off as much radiation as a color television set. Reduce the risk from any possible leakage by keeping a reasonable distance (about 4 feet) from the oven when it is operating. Do not make a habit of continually peering into the window to see if your cooking is completed. Make certain that you keep the door seal clean and clear of food residue buildup. *Children, pregnant women,* and *sick people* should be particularly aware of these guidelines. I check periodically for an improper seal around the perimeter of the oven with a Microwave Leakage Detector by Micronta. If it points to the red, there is leakage. Stop using the oven and have it checked.

Here are some microwave techniques, tricks, and hints:

1. To test china and glassware for microwave use: Fill a 1-cup Pyrex measure with cool water. Place the dish you are testing and cup in microwave oven on high for 1 minute, or until water in cup is very hot. Touch the dish you are testing. If it is hot or even warm, *do not use* it for microwave cooking.

2. Cooking time in the microwave oven is always *approximate.* Always remember it is easier to add time to an undercooked product. Once food is overcooked nothing can be done.

3. Standing time in microwave cooking is also important. Most foods will continue to cook by conduction after the microwave oven is turned off. This standing time is necessary to allow foods to complete cooking in the center without overcooking the edges.

4. Using the right dish or casserole is important in microwaving. Size and shape affect the way foods cook.

Round or oval shapes microwave more evenly than squares or rectangles. Shallow casseroles expose more food surface to microwave energy. Deeper ones take longer to cook and do not cook as evenly. Avoid casseroles with sloping sides; food is less deep in the areas which receive most energy and can overcook. A straight-sided casserole is the most efficient.

5. Covering foods prevents spatters and holds in heat or steam. This speeds up cooking time. White paper toweling or waxed paper may be used. Using plastic wraps (marked suitable for microwave) holds in substantial heat and steam. *Make sure to vent a corner of plastic wrap to allow steam to escape.*

6. Rotate dish or stir foods during cooking to promote even cooking.

7. To get more juice from lemons, limes, or oranges, just heat fruit on high for 15 seconds. Don't forget to let it stand 3 minutes before squeezing.

8. Make your own croutons or dried breadcrumbs—7 minutes on high for 4 cups spread in a shallow glass pan.

9. Plump raisins by adding ½ cup of water or juice. Cover and heat for 20 seconds on high, then drain.

10. Heat crêpes or tortillas by wrapping (up to 12) in a cloth or napkin, and heating on high for 1 to 2 minutes.

11. Microwave cooking dried beans saves time. To do so, place 1 cup of beans and 8 cups of water in a 5-quart casserole (plus any seasonings). Microwave 10 minutes on high or until boiling. Cover and let stand 1 hour. Stir several times and add water if necessary to cover beans. Cook beans again on high for 10 minutes, reduce power and cook on medium 20 minutes or until tender. This technique saves about 1½ hours cooking time.

12. To warm bread or rolls in a microwave, cover loosely with dry white paper towel and heat for 15–20 seconds on medium power. *Be conservative.* You can always add more time if necessary.

13. To cook chicken, cook 10 minutes per pound on medium. Remove skin and bones from meat. Store in refrigerator or freezer for future use.

14. Lightly brush chicken, meat, or fish with mild soy sauce or Worcestershire sauce to promote browning. (There is a no-salt seasoning available called Micro-Shake. It is sprinkled on fish, chicken, or meat before cooking to give it a golden brown color.)

15. To speed up barbecuing chicken—cook 10 to 15 minutes on medium and finish cooking over hot coals.

16. Toast shelled nuts on a glass pie plate or paper towel, 3 to 6 minutes per cup on high. Stir during cooking.

17. If you like to serve hot towels to your guests before or after a meal, soak washcloths or napkins in water and lemon juice. Squeeze dry, place in basket, and heat on high for 3 to 5 minutes or so. What a great finale to al fresco dining! (Not bad for the children, either, when you call them in to dinner from play.)

As with all appliances, you do have a studied choice to make, and, of course, you will have to learn how to use the microwave oven properly in order to receive optimum performance. *Be certain to read the owner's manual* of your particular microwave oven before using.

Cooking Tips

To Peel Garlic Quickly

Smash garlic clove with flat side of knife. Skin of garlic will be loosened and removed from clove—no painstaking, time-consuming peeling of garlic.

To Remove Fat from Liquid

Use coffee filter and pour liquid through filter; fat will be removed easily and quickly. Of course you may also use a gravy strain or chill to let the fat harden before removing.

To Store Fresh Strawberries

Place unwashed fresh strawberries in clean, airtight jar. They will remain fresh and flavorful for up to 1 week in the refrigerator.

For a Naturally Sweet, Healthful Snack

Freeze washed and thoroughly dried seedless grapes or pitted cherries on nonstick tray in freezer and flash-freeze. Store in plastic bags for a quick, sweet snack nature's way. (Do not defrost completely before eating.)

To Prevent Watery Tomato Sauce

If sauce is a bit watery, add 1 tablespoon cornstarch mixed with ¼ cup water to 4 cups tomato sauce. Cook till shiny and slightly thickened, stirring occasionally.

Chicken Broth

Remember to spoon fat off top of canned broth (or any other broth) before using. A few recipes call for a very small amount of poly-unsaturated cold-pressed safflower oil or extra-virgin olive oil. If desired, the oil may be omitted and chicken broth substituted without sacrificing flavor.

Bananas

May be frozen in their skins. The peel discolors, but the inside of the fruit remains the same color.

Brown Rice

Because of the oils remaining in brown rice, it has a shorter shelf life. If kept a long time, it should be stored in the refrigerator. One cup of brown rice yields about 3 cups cooked. Because of its bran coating it also requires more time and liquid in cooking than white rice. Rice should be added to rapidly boiling water to shorten cooking time and preserve optimum nutrition. Do not stir during cooking. It results in clumping of rice instead of separate grains.

Short-Grain Brown Rice

Requires less cooking time.

Pasta
When serving pasta, I like to blend a few spoonfuls of sauce into the drained pasta before serving with additional sauce.

Pilaf
Mix leftover cooked lentils, macaroni, and rice with tomato sauce for a quick pilaf. Serve hot or cold.

Brussels Sprouts
Never cook fresh Brussels sprouts longer than 10 minutes—overcooking results in an undesirable strong flavor and soggy texture.

Frozen Fish
Frozen fish is sometimes processed by dipping it into a brine prior to freezing. If you are on a low-sodium diet, avoid frozen and use fresh fish only.

Potatoes and Onions
Should be stored at room temperature (or slightly lower). However, they should not be stored together. Onions shorten the storage life of potatoes.

Commercial Fruited Yogurt
Although high in sugar, they are not high in either Vitamin A or C. Enrich plain, nonfat yogurt by adding 2 tablespoons chopped sun-dried apricots or ½ cup chopped peaches for Vitamin A and ½ cup strawberries or papaya for Vitamin C, or 1 tablespoon raisins to increase iron. You may also lower the calorie content of fruited yogurt by buying those yogurts that have the fruit on the bottom as opposed to premixed. Simply remove one half to two thirds of the sugary fruit mixture on the bottom before mixing it through a plain yogurt. The result will be a decrease of at least 50 to 75 calories.

Cereal Cooking for Busy People
Fill a quart thermos (wide mouth) with boiling water to heat it. Wash whole-grain cereal, such as wheat berry, barley, rye, or triticale. Empty water from thermos, add 1 cup grain and 3 cups boiling water to within 1½ inches of top. Seal and turn on side. Let remain overnight. In the morning, stir; then cereal is ready to serve. Oatmeal or seven-grain cereals may be prepared similarly, but change proportions according to manufacturer's directions.

Dried Herbs
Crush all dried herbs before using. Store all dried herbs in containers with tight-fitting lids in a cool, dark place. Label with date and discard after 6 months or when spice is weak. (If you store herbs in freezer, they will keep much longer.) Do not buy in bulk. Fresh herbs may be chopped and frozen in plastic bags or microwaved on paper towels on high for 2 minutes before freezing in order to dry.

To Freeze Leafy Herbs
(Celery, parsley, basil, thyme, rosemary, dill, oregano, etc.) Place herbs on a paper towel in microwave oven on high for 2 minutes. They will be crisp, dry, and retain their green color. Freeze in jars for future use. They may also be kept at room temperature, but they stay fresh longer in the freezer.

To Store Fresh Tarragon in White Wine Vinegar
It seasons the vinegar as well as preserving the herb, which can be used directly from the bottle. (Rinse with cold water before using.)

To Supply a Salty Taste
Add dehydrated onion flakes or powder, garlic flakes or powder, celery seed, parsley, lemon juice, chili, or hot pepper sauce.

To Supply a Sweet Flavor
Add natural extracts, such as vanilla, almond, orange, banana, raspberry, etc. Cinnamon, nutmeg, and allspice also contribute to a sweet taste.

For a Healthy Carbonated Drink
Mix unsweetened fruit juice such as apple, cranberry, or papaya with Perrier or low-sodium club soda.

To Defrost Frozen Peas Quickly
Place peas in colander under hot water from the tap.

To Thaw Other Frozen Vegetables
Place in strainer under cold running water until completely thawed; drain well. Use in salads or as cold marinated vegetables.

To Extend Shelf Life of Milk 7 to 10 Days
Microwave 1 cup of milk for 2 minutes on high. Make sure milk heats to 160°. This destroys bacteria responsible for spoilage.

To Clean Sharp Knives
Scrub with moistened cork dipped in cleanser. This method is quick and safe.

Mushroom Stems
Chop and save in freezer for use in soups, stews, or sauces.

To Freeze Egg Whites
Place egg whites in ice cube tray or Styrofoam egg carton. Freeze and pop out into plastic bags for storage. If whites are to be beaten to peaks, they must be brought to room temperature first.

Salt-Reduced Canned Tomato Products
Fifty percent salt-reduced tomatoes and other vegetable products are now available in cans in markets. If not available in your market, and you have a hypertensive problem or are concerned with your sodium consumption, use salt-free products instead.

Baking Soda as a Deodorizer
Place open box of baking soda in refrigerator or freezer. It absorbs odors and prevents flavor transfer between foods. Replace box or soda periodically and pour used contents down drain or disposal to freshen or remove garbage odors. Baking soda is also desirable to use when washing the inside of a refrigerator or freezer.

Powdered Buttermilk
Avoid waste by using shelf-stable powdered buttermilk instead of liquid buttermilk for baking or cooking. It is made from churned buttermilk, unlike most liquid buttermilks today, which are made by adding bacteria to skim milk.

Liquid Buttermilk
If liquid buttermilk is not homogenized, you can remove particles of fat by straining with a tea strainer.

Whole-Wheat Bread Crumbs
Whole-wheat bread crumbs made from Pritikin bread are preferable because they have no fat, sugar, honey, molasses, or preservatives added. If you have a local whole wheat bread that is suitable, use it.

Cold-Pressed Oils
Use cold-pressed oils that are extracted naturally, not by adding chemicals.

Salad Dressings
Low-calorie oil-free dressings are frequently a little higher in sodium than the usual bottled dressings. If your sodium requirements are fairly rigid, dilute the dressing with fruit juice, salt-free chicken broth, or salt-free tomato juice.

Lemons
A bowl of fresh lemons in a room imparts a fragrant aroma as well as a colorful appearance. Grind a used lemon in your garbage disposal as a freshener. Add a wedge of lemon to low-sodium bottled soda or mineral water to add a little zip. As always, lemon juice is a dependable flavor enhancer to be used on fish, chicken, turkey, or game.

Ginger Root
Ginger root may be peeled, then grated and stored in freezer for future use.

Three Different Salad Dressings from One Bottle of Pritikin Vinaigrette Dressing or Other Low-Sodium Dressing
   1. ½ cup dressing plus ¼ cup orange juice and 1 tablespoon lemon juice.
   2. ½ cup dressing plus ¼ cup salt-free tomato sauce and a dash of hot pepper sauce.
   3. ½ cup dressing plus ¼ cup nonfat yogurt, ½ cup peeled and grated cucumber, and ½ teaspoon dried dill or 2 teaspoons chopped fresh dill.

Ricotta Spread
In blender or food processor, puree *very fresh* (look at the date) ricotta until smooth. Add chopped chives and use in small servings as a spread on bagels or as a sandwich filling with alfalfa sprouts, romaine lettuce, tomato, and thinly sliced red onion on toasted whole-wheat bread.

Pancake Syrup
To make a delicious pancake syrup, combine ⅔ cup water with 1 cup frozen unsweetened apple juice concentrate. Bring to a boil and simmer for 5 minutes. Add 2 teaspoons maple flavoring or pure raspberry or vanilla extract. Store in tightly covered jar in refrigerator for future use.

Chocolate Syrup
Mix 1 cup frozen unsweetened apple juice concentrate with 1 cup carob powder and bring to a boil. Simmer for 5 minutes. Add 2 teaspoons pure

vanilla extract and 1 teaspoon chocolate flavoring. Cool and store in tightly covered container in refrigerator. Use as topping on Special Strawberry Ice Cream (page 331).

Basic Pantry List

Nothing is more frustrating than not having all the ingredients you need when you start to cook. It would be impossible, of course, to list everything needed in all the recipes. However, in order to make things easier for you, I have listed some basic pantry supplies that will help complete many of the recipes. The wisest thing to do, of course, is to read your recipe ahead of time, check your pantry, make a market list, and purchase the supplies a day before or on the way home. The following is a list of basic pantry products to help start you on the road to healthful eating.

Dry Storage

Salt-free canned chicken broth
50 percent salt-reduced canned tuna in water
Canned red salmon
Canned sliced or chopped pimiento
Nonfat evaporated milk
Nonfat powdered milk
Powdered buttermilk
Canned fruit cocktail in unsweetened juice
Canned fruits in unsweetened juice
Canned salt-reduced tomato sauce
Canned salt-reduced stewed tomatoes
Canned salt-free tomato juice
Canned salt-free tomato paste
Canned Italian plum tomatoes
Salt-free marinara sauce
Canned salt-free corn
Canned green chili salsa
Nonstick cooking spray
Dried beans, lentils, and peas

Brown rice, bulgur, quick-cooking barley, and other whole grains
Pasta
Unsweetened whole-grain cereal flakes
Whole-grain hot cereal
Whole-grain pasta
Oat bran
Wheat bran
Rapid-rise yeast
Low-sodium baking powder
Baking soda
White wine or brown rice vinegar
Red wine vinegar
Dijon mustard
Mild soy sauce
Worcestershire sauce
Salt-free vegetable seasoning
Herbes de Provence
Italian herb blend*
Crushed red pepper flakes

* A mixture of oregano, rosemary, and thyme or basil.

Dry Storage (continued)

Dried dill	Garlic powder
Dried thyme	Salt-free Micro-Shake
Dried bay leaves	Hungarian paprika
Dehydrated onion flakes	Nutmeg, grated or whole
Dehydrated garlic flakes	Cinnamon, ground
Dehydrated vegetable flakes	Pure vanilla extract
Vegetable broth powder	An acceptable pilaf mix
Onion powder	Onions and potatoes

Refrigerator Storage

Nonfat milk
Nonfat or low-fat yogurt
Low-fat or 1 percent fat cottage cheese or skim-milk ricotta cheese
Light mayonnaise
Low-calorie Italian or vinaigrette dressing
Chopped or crushed garlic
Sugar-free preserves (no honey, either)
Extra-virgin olive oil
Cold-pressed safflower oil
Large eggs (using whites only)
Fruits (apples, oranges, lemons, etc.)
Vegetables (salad greens, green pepper, carrots, tomatoes, celery, etc.)
Corn tortillas (flour tortillas have lard added)

Freezer Storage

Frozen unsweetened juice concentrates (apple, orange, etc.)
Frozen vegetables (corn, peas, chopped spinach, chopped broccoli, carrots, cauliflower, French-cut green beans, mixed beans for salad, mixed vegetables, etc.)
Grated fresh ginger
Freshly grated Parmesan cheese
Shredded mozzarella cheese
Almonds
Whole-wheat bread crumbs, preferably Pritikin
Whole-wheat flour
Whole-grain bread (preferably Pritikin whole-wheat bread and whole-wheat muffins)
Natural juice bars

Note: Throughout the recipes where I call for whole green onions (scallions), both the white and green parts should be used.

Simple Menus for Memorable Occasions

Good cooks are not born; they are made through experience and creativity. Many capable cooks have difficulty putting the right combination of foods together. Novices are often timid or lacking in self-confidence or judgment. As an aid to both groups of cooks, I have prepared a group of menu suggestions to help remove some of the stress and mystique from entertaining. In 500 B.C., Aeschylus said, "The pleasantest of ties is that of host and guest." Here, near the end of the twentieth century, this quote is still appropriate.

The recipes marked with an asterisk appear in this book. All recipes may be doubled or tripled as needed.

AL FRESCO DINING
*Easy Gazpacho
Celery, Carrot, and Fennel Sticks
*Teriyaki Chicken Kebabs
Corn on the Cob
*Oriental Coleslaw
Sliced Assorted Fresh Melon Platter
*Hazelnut Meringue Cookies

LUNCHEON BUFFET FOR THE LADIES (OR GENTLEMEN)
*Cauliflower, Crabmeat, and Pea Salad on a Bed of Fresh Greens
*Pasta Primavera (cold)
*Blueberry Corn Mini-Muffins
Assorted Fresh Fruit Platter
*Strawberry-Banana-Yogurt Pie

SUPPER OR LUNCH
*Fresh Artichoke with Tomato Vinaigrette
*Three Vegetable Pasta
Crisp Italian Bread
*Sherried Orange Gelatin with Fruit

*Harriet F's Albondigas Soup with Warm Tortillas
*Kidney Bean Salad
*Tapioca with Mango

*False Alarm Chili
*Corn Bread
Crisp Mixed Green Salad with *Cucumber-Dill Dressing
Fresh Fruit

*Speedy Tomato-Rice Soup
*Warm Sliced Chicken Salad on a Bed of Greens
*Pineapple Parfait

*Quick Vegetable-Barley Soup
*Hot Tuna Salad Sandwich
Seasonal Fresh Fruit

*Nanette's Skillet-Baked Pasta with Salmon and Vegetables
Crisp Green Salad
*Harriet's Quick and Crusty Multi-Grain Bread
Pineapple Chunks with Blueberries

*E-Z-Time Pizza
*Almost Santo Pietro's Salad
Fresh Fruit Cup

*Stuffed Whole-Wheat Pita Pockets with
Tuna Salad and Vegetables
Fresh Fruit

*Fast-Food Chicken Burger on a Whole-Wheat Bun with Romaine
and Tomato Slice
*Larry's Oven-Fried Potatoes
*Mandarin Waldorf Salad

LATE BREAKFAST OR BRUNCH
*Whole-Wheat Cheese Puffs
Fresh Orange Slices and Fresh Pineapple Wedges

½ Papaya with Lime
*French Toast with Raisins, *Country Whole-Wheat Pancakes,
or *Waffles with Unsweetened Preserves
*Red Raspberry and Cottage Cheese Salad

½ Grapefruit with Prune Garnish
*Harold's Choice: Bread Pudding

*Chilled Cantaloupe Soup
*My Favorite Frittata
*Rapid-Rise Oatmeal Bread, Toasted
Fresh Berries with Vanilla Yogurt

Poached Salmon with *Green Sauce
Toasted Bagels with *Julie's Farmer's Pâté
*Almost Ken's Salad
*Sally's Cottage Cheese Swedish Pancakes
Assorted Fresh Fruit Slices
Assorted Sweet Breads or Muffins

PICNIC SUPPERS FOR THE BOWL,
PARK, OR BACK YARD
*Cold Carrot Soup with Whole-Wheat Bread Sticks
*Cold Sliced Meat Loaf with Creole Sauce
*Harriet F's Potato Salad Vinaigrette
*Red and Green Slaw
Fresh Fruit Basket
*Always Delicious Zucchini Bread

*Cold Curried Broccoli Bisque with Italian Breadsticks
*Deviled Drumsticks
*Sweet Potato Salad
*Sweet and Sour Cucumbers
Fresh Fruit Cup
*Banana-Nut Muffins

DINNER FROM LEFTOVERS
*Hot Curried Broccoli Bisque
*Leftover Chicken Casserole
*Peas à la Française
Mixed Fruit Cup

NEW YEAR'S DAY BUFFET
*Salmon-Leek Bisque
*No-Crust Broccoli Quiche
*Black-Eyed Pea and Bean Salad
*Rapid-Rise Oatmeal Bread
Bagel Chips with *Julie's Farmer's Pâté
Fresh Fruit Basket
—or—
*Microwaved Fresh Fruit Coupe
*Freda's Pecan/Carob Macaroons

SIMPLY SUPER MENU FOR FRIENDS
*Minted Pea Soup in Minutes
*Scallops with Tomato-Garlic Sauce
*Jan's Microwaved Rice with Vegetables
*Artichoke and Mushroom Salad
*Harriet's Blueberry Coffee Cake

ALL-AMERICAN BARBECUE
*Diet Watcher's Barbecued Chicken
*Baked Beans Bravo
Crisp Mixed Green Salad with *Pear Vinaigrette Dressing
*Corn Bread
Watermelon

UNEXPECTED GUESTS FOR SUPPER
*My Mother's Salmon Patties
*Corn Pasta Noodles and Cottage Cheese
*All-Seasons Freezer Vegetable Salad
Chilled Canned Fruit in Juice

TWO COMPANY DINNERS
*Sea-Fruit Salad
*Chicken Marengo
(with Snow Peas, Tomatoes, and Rice)
Hot Whole-Wheat French Bread
*Company Apricot Chiffon Torte

*Hot and Cold Mixed Green Salad
*Barbecued Butterflied Lamb
*Twice-Baked Potatoes
*Broccoli-Stuffed Tomatoes
Crisp Rolls
*Orange-Baked Alaska

A NATURALLY GOOD COCKTAIL PARTY
Sparkling Apple Juice
Perrier with Lime
*Harriet's Crispy Cocktail Snacks
*Asparagus Dip with Garden Fresh Vegetables
*Hot Bean Dip with Warm Corn Tortillas
*Eggplant Caviar with Crisp Pita Bread
*Texas-Style Meatballs
*Fresh Tuna Tartare and Cherry Tomatoes with Dark Bread Squares
*Chicken Salad Spread with Assorted Whole-Grain Crackers
Basket of Seasonal Fresh Fruit

SEASONAL MENUS

Spring
*Fish Bundles in Swiss Chard
Steamed Baby Carrots, Asparagus, and Red Potatoes in Their Jackets
*Fresh Strawberries with Sabayon Sauce

Summer
*Fresh Tomato Soup with Toasted Pita Bread
*Piquant Broiled Salmon
Corn on the Cob
*Marinated Vegetable Platter
*California Fresh Fruit Bowl

Fall
*Quick Corn Soup
*Apricot-Glazed Cornish Game Hens
*Helen's Celery Amandine
*Singaporian Waldorf Salad
*Harold's Choice: Bread Pudding

Winter
*Almond-Broccoli Bisque
*Penny's Simply Perfect Veal Stew
*Best-Ever Zucchini-Corn Casserole
Crisp Sourdough Bread
*Truly Delicious Baked Apple

INTERNATIONAL MENUS

Chinese
*Whole Steamed Fish with Ginger and Spring Onions
Assorted Steamed Vegetables: Broccoli, Bok Choy,
Snow Peas, and Mushrooms
*Chinese Stir-Fried Brown Rice
*Chicken Sub Gum Soup
Mandarin Orange Segments
—or—
Fresh Orange Wedges

American
*Black-Eyed Pea and Bean Salad
*Oven-Fried Chicken
*Scalloped Potatoes and Corn
Steamed Spinach
*Special Strawberry Ice Cream

Mexican
*Yogurt-Salsa Dip with Assorted Vegetables
*Fajitas with Warm Corn Tortillas
*Mexican Red Rice
*Kidney Bean Salad
*Papaya Custard

Russian
*Best Beet Borscht (cold)
*Mother Mollie's Cheese Blintzes with *Special Sour Cream Topping
*Red Russian Salad
Sliced Fresh Fruit
*Carrot Cake

French
*French Onion Soup with Garlic Croutons
*Paula's Salmon Papillote
*Ratatouille
Radicchio, Chicory, and Bibb Lettuce Salad Vinaigrette
*Fresh Strawberry Tart with *Almost Crème Anglaise

Hungarian
*Goulash Soup
Hearty Rye and Pumpernickel Breads
*Sarah's Hungarian Wilted Salad
Seasonal Fresh Fruit

Italian
*Antipasto Salad
*Perfect Chicken Cacciatore with *Baked Polenta
Steamed Zucchini Circles
Crusty Italian Bread
*Amaretto Peach Crème

N O T E

Ⓠ indicates recipe may be prepared in 30 minutes or less.

Ⓜ indicates recipe may be prepared in a microwave oven.

Back to Basics

A LITTLE KNOWLEDGE ISN'T A DANGEROUS THING

Sometimes a little advanced preparation really speeds up a recipe. The following basics may be prepared at your leisure and refrigerated or frozen for future use. I'm certain you have some ideas of your own that you would like to add.

Before You Start to Cook:
1. Read the *entire* recipe.
2. Familiarize yourself with its ingredients, procedures, and time commitment.
3. Check to see if you have the ingredients. (There's nothing more frustrating than finding a vital ingredient is missing.)

Basic Béchamel or White Sauce
Busy Day Baking Mix
Steamed Brown Rice
Chicken Bouillon Cubes
Basic Crêpes (A Baker's Dozen)
Special Sour Cream Topping
Speedy Soup Mix

Basic Tart Crust
Onion Magic
Steamed Turkey or Chicken
Meatball Mania
Marinated Roast Turkey or Chicken
Toast Tartlets
Simply Delicious Tomato Sauce

Basic Béchamel or White Sauce Ⓠ

Yield: 2½ cups (2 tablespoons = 1 serving)

In my home economics class in junior high school, I can remember cringing when we *had* to make a béchamel, white sauce, or cream sauce, as it is sometimes known. Servicemen had a much less flattering name for creamed chipped beef on toast. Béchamel is actually a basic French sauce with many variations, whose calories and cholesterol content, depending on which ingredients you add, are endless. When used with a little creativity, béchamel can be a delicious addition to your pantry. My basic recipe that follows is very simple to prepare. It may be refrigerated for up to a week or frozen for future use. Its various possibilities include uses as a soup base, in casseroles, crêpes, or as a topping on vegetables. Though easy enough to prepare, it is convenient to have some already available for immediate use.

¼ cup whole-wheat flour
¼ cup nonfat powdered milk
2 cups nonfat milk
2 slices onion or 1 sliced shallot
1 bay leaf
½ teaspoon white pepper

1 teaspoon salt-free vegetable
 seasoning
⅛ teaspoon freshly grated nutmeg
2 tablespoons dry sherry or
 vermouth (optional)

1. Mix flour and powdered milk together in 1-quart nonstick saucepan.
2. Add milk gradually, while stirring with wire whisk. Add remaining ingredients.
3. Place over low heat and stir constantly until mixture coats whisk or wooden spoon. (Sherry may be added at this time and simmered for a few minutes more to evaporate alcohol.) Remove bay leaf and onion or shallot before serving.

Variations:
1. Two tablespoons cornstarch may be substituted for the flour and 1 tablespoon yogurt added as enrichment at the end of the cooking time.
2. A velouté sauce may be prepared with 1 cup chicken, vegetable, or fish broth being substituted for 1 cup milk, depending on the dish in which you are using the sauce. Spices may be changed; that is, with fish, add 1 tablespoon chopped fresh dill; with chicken, add 1 tablespoon chopped fresh tarragon.

3. Curried sauce: 2 to 3 teaspoons of your favorite curry powder mixture may be added after sauce thickens.

4. A few drops of hot pepper sauce may be added to give your sauce a little extra zip.

5. I could go on and on, but I'll leave a few unknowns for you to discover yourself.

Per serving: 20 calories; 1.6 gm protein; 0.1 gm fat; 3.3 gm carbohydrate; 0.1 gm fiber; 1 mg cholesterol; 21 mg sodium

Busy Day Baking Mix Ⓠ

Yield: 7 cups

7 cups whole-wheat flour
½ cup oat bran
⅓ cup powdered buttermilk
  or nonfat dry milk

1½ teaspoons baking soda
3 tablespoons low-sodium baking
  powder
1 envelope rapid-rise yeast

1. Place all ingredients in food processor bowl and process thoroughly to blend. If you do not have a food processor, place in a large bowl and stir well with slotted spoon.

2. Place in tightly closed plastic bag or airtight container and store in the freezer or refrigerator. Remember to mix with fork before using.

Helpful Hint: This baking mix may be used in preparing Busy Day Griddle Cakes (page 334), Waffles (page 336, see Note below), Everyday Muffins (page 340), or quick coffee cake, as in Harriet's Blueberry Coffee Cake (page 337, see Note below).

Note: If you do not have mix on hand for *Waffles*, use 1¾ cups whole-wheat flour, 2 tablespoons oat bran, 2 teaspoons low-sodium baking powder, and ½ teaspoon baking soda; for *Coffee Cake*, use 1½ cups whole-wheat flour, ½ cup unbleached white flour, 3 tablespoons oat bran, 1 tablespoon low-sodium baking powder, and ½ teaspoon baking soda.

Per ½ cup: 224 calories; 9.2 gm protein; 1.4 gm fat; 44 gm carbohydrate; 5 gm fiber; 1 mg cholesterol; 56 mg sodium

Steamed Brown Rice

Yield: 6 cups (½ cup = 1 serving)

While consulting in Asia, I observed that mostly white rice was eaten. "What happens to all the bran?" I asked. "Oh, we feed it to the pigs," was the answer. What lucky pigs, to have such a healthy diet! While white rice is a highly desirable complex carbohydrate, it does lack the fiber and nutrients found in brown rice. Because of its bran coating, brown rice needs to cook a bit longer. For added convenience, place 1-cup portions in sealed plastic bags, flatten, and freeze. To defrost, place bag in microwave oven on medium for 2 minutes or in boiling water for about 4 minutes.

4½ cups salt-free chicken broth, defatted, vegetable broth, or water
1 tablespoon mild soy sauce
1 teaspoon dehydrated onion flakes

Few flakes crushed red pepper
1 tablespoon dehydrated vegetable flakes (optional)
2 cups brown rice, washed

1. Combine first 5 ingredients and bring to a boil in ovenproof casserole.
2. Add rice to boiling liquid, cover, and place in preheated 350° oven for 45 minutes to 1 hour, or until all liquid is evaporated and rice is tender.* Fluff with fork before serving or storing. (Cool before storing.)

To Serve: Use as an accompaniment to fish or chicken, as a base for steamed vegetable entrées or casseroles, or to add to soups.

Variation: To serve as a hearty hot breakfast cereal, cook rice in water as directed above using only water and 3 tablespoons frozen unsweetened apple juice concentrate and ½ cup raisins. Freeze as suggested above. When serving, add warm nonfat milk and a sprinkle of ground cinnamon or nutmeg.

Per serving: 115 calories; 2.6 gm protein; 0.6 gm fat; 24.9 gm carbohydrate; 2.2 gm fiber; 0 mg cholesterol; 53 mg sodium

---

* You could also cook the rice in a covered saucepan for 25 minutes after the liquid boils. Remove from heat and allow to steam with lid on for 15 minutes.

Chicken Bouillon Cubes ⓠ

Yield: 12 cubes (2 tablespoons = 1 cube)

This basic is a variation of the recipe in *Deliciously Low* using canned salt-free broth instead of homemade chicken soup. These cubes are handy to use in sautéeing instead of oil, and are also good for seasoning vegetables.

2 10½-ounce cans salt-free chicken
   broth, defatted
½ cup dry white wine or vermouth

2 shallots, chopped
1 teaspoon herbes de Provence or
   dried thyme, crushed

1. Combine all ingredients in 1-quart saucepan.
2. Simmer until reduced to 1½ cups.
3. Pour into ice cube tray and freeze.
4. Remove from tray and seal in plastic bags. (Remember not to wet cubes or they will stick together.)

Per cube: 9 calories; 0.2 gm protein; 0 gm fat; 1.7 gm carbohydrate; 0 gm fiber; 0 mg cholesterol; 2 mg sodium

Basic Crêpes
(A Baker's Dozen)

Yield: 13 crêpes (1 crêpe = 1 serving)

In France it's called a crêpe, in Mexico a tortilla, in China a rice doily, in Russia a blini or blintzi, and in Hungary a palascinta. All these versions, the products of different countries, used the available grains. Doesn't it make you realize how very much alike we all are?

Crêpes are really quite simple to make, and they give you the basis of an endless number of dishes, such as cannelloni, vegetable crêpes, blintzes, instead of pasta in lasagna, and so on.

Crêpe Batter:

¼ cup whole-wheat flour
¼ cup buckwheat flour* or cornmeal
½ cup nonfat milk

½ cup Perrier or low-sodium club soda**
2 egg whites

To Make Batter:

1. Place all ingredients in blender or food processor and whirl until batter is smooth—no lumps.
2. Pour batter into jar and store overnight or at least 2 hours before using.

To Prepare Crêpes:

1. Use a 6-inch nonstick skillet coated with nonstick cooking spray before making each crêpe.
2. Mix batter thoroughly and pour into ¼ cup measure. (Approximately ¼ cup minus 1 tablespoon makes 1 crêpe.)
3. Heat skillet and pour batter rapidly into pan, tilting to cover entire bottom of pan.
4. When edges brown slightly, loosen crêpe around edges with metal spatula and turn over to briefly dry opposite side of crêpe.
5. Flip crêpe on waxed paper baggie or 8-inch square of waxed paper.
6. Continue spraying and heating pan before adding batter for each crêpe.

* All the flours are nourishing and tasty; however, I find buckwheat crêpes particularly delicious.
** Using Perrier gives crêpes a light, airy texture.

7. Cover each slightly cooled crêpe with another bag or square of waxed paper and repeat until you have a stack of 13 crêpes.

Helpful Hints: *To freeze*, wrap stacked crêpes in foil and store in tightly sealed plastic bag. In the freezer, they will keep for 6 to 8 weeks, in the refrigerator for 2 to 3 days.

To defrost in the oven, place foil packet of crêpes in a 350° oven and heat for 5 to 7 minutes. To defrost in the microwave, remove foil and defrost on medium for 2 minutes.

Per serving: 22 calories; 1.4 gm protein; 0.1 gm fat; 3.8 gm carbohydrate; 0.2 gm fiber; 0 mg cholesterol; 13 mg sodium

Special Sour Cream Topping Ⓠ

Yield: 2 cups (1 tablespoon = 1 serving)

Regular sour cream, as purchased in your local market, has about 500 calories in one cup. This special sour cream topping contains 160 calories in one cup. Few people can afford the vast differential in calories and none of us can benefit from the large amounts of fat and cholesterol.

1 pint fresh 1% fat cottage cheese*   2 tablespoons nonfat yogurt (optional)

1. Place cheese in blender or food processor and process until smooth. If desired, yogurt may be added at this time for a more piquant flavor.

Variations: Add ¼ cup chopped chives or green onion and blend. This is delicious served over a baked potato or steamed cauliflower. To use as a topping with fruit, add ¼ cup frozen unsweetened apple, pineapple, or orange juice concentrate.

Helpful Hint: This mixture will keep in the refrigerator for several days or may be frozen, then defrosted, and blended well before using.

Per serving: 10 calories; 1.8 gm protein; 0.1 gm fat; 0.4 gm carbohydrate; 0.0 gm fiber; 1 mg cholesterol; 57 mg sodium

* Look at the date on the bottom of the carton to insure freshness. The date listed is the last day that it may be sold in the market. The closer it is to the expiration date, the less fresh it will be.

Speedy Soup Mix

Yield: 2 cups dry mix (⅔ cup prepared soup = 1 serving)

Most commercial soup mixes have monosodium glutamate (MSG), fat, and loads of salt added. Ours has none of those additives. It contains a variety of ingredients that you may vary to suit your taste. For example, lima beans instead of white beans, pinto beans instead of kidney beans, lentils instead of split peas, brown rice instead of barley, and herbes de Provence instead of Italian seasoning. Of course, I suggest saving all vegetable juices and leftover defatted gravies and sauces to use as part of your liquid. You may also add any leftover cooked vegetables (except beets) and cooked grains or pasta. If you have a leftover roast chicken or turkey carcass, toss it in. Every ingredient will add its own enrichment and contribute to a more interesting flavor.

¼ cup small white beans
¼ cup red kidney beans
¼ cup green or yellow split peas
¼ cup barley
3 tablespoons dehydrated onion flakes
3 tablespoons freeze-dried chopped shallot
½ teaspoon garlic flakes
¼ cup freeze-dried mushrooms

3 tablespoons dehydrated vegetable flakes
1 bay leaf
½ teaspoon crushed red pepper flakes
2 teaspoons salt-free vegetable seasoning
1 teaspoon dried Italian herb blend, crushed

To store, combine all ingredients and place in a covered container or plastic bag.

Helpful Hint: If you choose to make several batches of this mix in advance, prepare and package each separately in a plastic bag or jar; otherwise, the seasonings will not be evenly distributed.

To Prepare Soup:

1. Combine 1 recipe dry soup mix with 8 cups water or broth (chicken, turkey, or vegetable) in a 4-quart saucepan.

2. Bring to a boil and simmer for 1 to 1½ hours, or until beans are tender. Taste and adjust seasonings.

3. Remove bay leaf before serving.

Variation: Any or all of the following ingredients may be added to vary the flavor:

16-ounce can salt-reduced stewed
   tomatoes, chopped
10-ounce package frozen chopped
   spinach

½ pound Swiss chard, chopped
10-ounce package frozen mixed
   vegetables
½ cup small macaroni

When served, soup may also be topped with Parmesan cheese.

Per serving: 87 calories; 4.2 gm protein; 0.4 gm fat; 18 gm carbohydrate; 3.7 gm fiber;
0 mg cholesterol; 4.1 mg sodium

Basic Tart Crust ⓠ

Yield: 1 9-inch shell (Serves 10)

Pastry crusts can be overloaded with fat- and sugar-laden calories. This one is not. Its crunchy flavor adds to whatever filling you choose, be it a cheese pie or a strawberry tart.

1 cup fresh whole-wheat bread
   crumbs*
1 cup finely chopped walnuts,
   pecans, or almonds**
2 tablespoons egg whites

1–2 tablespoons frozen
   unsweetened apple juice
   concentrate
½ teaspoon ground cinnamon
½ teaspoon freshly grated nutmeg

1. Combine all ingredients in bowl, stirring with fork to blend.
2. Coat 9-inch tart pan or springform pan with nonstick cooking spray.
3. Place crumb mixture on bottom and sides of pan. Press lightly with back of spoon or hand.
4. Bake in preheated 375° oven for 6 to 8 minutes, or until firm.

Per serving: 56 calories; 2.1 gm protein; 3.7 gm fat; 4.4 gm carbohydrate; 0.4 gm fiber;
0 mg cholesterol; 19 mg sodium

* One cup rolled oats, chopped, may be substituted for the bread crumbs.
** To chop nuts, place in food processor or blender and process until finely chopped.

Onion Magic

Yield: About 4½ cups (1 tablespoon = 1 serving)

I have a friend who likes to play golf, bridge, or anything else that keeps her out of the kitchen. Although she loves to eat, cooking has a very low priority. Over the years, she has come up with a pretty sneaky trick. When she arrives home late and hasn't the faintest idea of what will appear on her dinner table, she quickly slices and sautés onions. The aroma of the simmering onions greets her returning family. In the meantime, she has a chance to come up with some tasty morsel.

I am not suggesting that you take up golf or bridge; I am suggesting, however, that you cook up batches of this magical onion mixture and freeze them for future use. You will find that it is a basis for many dishes, whether it is a frittata or fricassee, soup, or stew. What a pleasure not to have to peel onions before you even *start* to cook!

1 tablespoon extra-virgin olive oil
3 garlic cloves, minced
6 to 8 (4 pounds) yellow or red onions, peeled, quartered, and thinly sliced*
1 tablespoon salt-free vegetable seasoning

Freshly ground black pepper
½ cup salt-free chicken broth, defatted, vegetable broth, or dry white wine

1. Place all ingredients except broth in nonstick sauté pan.
2. Sauté for 4 to 5 minutes, stirring frequently. Add broth, cover and cook gently until wilted and transparent, about 30 minutes. Stir occasionally while cooking. *Do not brown.*

Helpful Hint: To freeze for future use, measure into ½- to 1-cup portions and place in freezer bags or containers. Remove from bag and defrost in microwave oven or in covered sauté pan before using.

Variation: For a more piquant flavor, combine 2 tablespoons of Spicy Barbecue Sauce (page 365) with 1 cup of sautéed onions before using as a topping on your turkey burger.

Per serving: 11 calories; 0.3 gm protein; 0.3 gm fat; 1.9 gm carbohydrate; 0.2 gm fiber; 0 mg cholesterol; 1 mg sodium

* If you have a food processor, the slicing takes only seconds.

Steamed Turkey or Chicken

Yield: 2–3 pounds cooked meat (3 ounces = 1 serving)

Packages of filleted turkey breast or shredded chicken are about as standard in my freezer as ice cubes. I'm always ready for company or a fast meal when this staple is available.

½ raw turkey breast (3–4 pounds)
  or ½ turkey (5–6 pounds),
  fat removed
Juice of ½ lemon
2 teaspoons salt-free vegetable
  seasoning
1½–2 cups salt-free chicken or
  turkey broth, defatted, or water
1 bay leaf

1 teaspoon dried thyme or
  herbes de Provence, crushed
1 celery stalk with leaves, coarsely
  chopped
½ large onion, coarsely chopped
1 carrot, coarsely chopped
4 sprigs parsley
Few black peppercorns

1. Season turkey under the skin with lemon juice and vegetable seasoning and place on steaming rack in Dutch oven or wok.

2. Add remaining ingredients and bring to a simmer.

3. Steam for 1 to 1½ hours, or until juices run clear when turkey is pricked gently with fork (or use thermometer reading of 165°).

4. Let turkey cool for 15 minutes, then remove skin.

To Store: Remove turkey meat from breastbone in one piece; slice and serve or wrap whole cooked piece in plastic wrap, then foil. Place in tightly closed freezer bag and freeze for future use.

Variation: A whole 3½- to 4-pound roasting chicken, cut in half, may be prepared in the same fashion. Cooking time will be about 45 to 60 minutes. Meat may be shredded by hand or cut in chunks and refrigerated or frozen to use in salads or casseroles at a future time. I prefer the flavor of shredded chicken.

Helpful Hint: Place turkey bones and skin in bag; freeze and use in soups at a later date. Strain liquid; chill and remove fat or use gravy strainer or coffee filter. Freeze in ice cube trays. Transfer to freezer bag and save for future gravies or soup stocks.

Per serving: 142 calories; 25.7 gm protein; 2.8 gm fat; 1.7 gm carbohydrate; 0.2 gm fiber; 59 mg cholesterol; 59 mg sodium

Meatball Mania ⓠ

Yield: 90 meatballs (3 meatballs = 1 serving as appetizer)

If you have a really busy life-style, you cannot afford *not* to take the time to make these easy meatballs. There are so many ways to serve them: first, plain as an appetizer; added to minestrone or albondigas soup; with a marinara sauce over spaghetti; with a Stroganoff sauce over rice; or just plain with stir-fried vegetables. Whatever you choose, you can't miss with this easy, convenient aid to speedy, last-minute cooking.

4 slices whole-wheat bread, crumbled
1½ cups nonfat milk
5 egg whites, slightly beaten
3 tablespoons dehydrated onion flakes
½ cup chopped parsley
2 teaspoons dried thyme, crushed

1 teaspoon freshly grated nutmeg
1 teaspoon garlic powder
¼ teaspoon freshly ground black pepper
1 tablespoon Worcestershire sauce
1½ pounds ground veal
1½ pounds ground turkey or chicken

1. Soak bread in milk and add to remaining ingredients except veal and poultry; blend.
2. Add ground meat. Mix well.
3. Shape into 90 1-inch meatballs.
4. Place on 3 15 x 10 x 1-inch nonstick baking sheets. Bake in pre-heated 425° oven for 12–15 minutes.
5. Cool and place 30 meatballs on each of 3 foil baking sheets. Cover with plastic, seal in plastic bag, and freeze for as long as 3 months.

Per serving: 78 calories; 11.1 gm protein; 2.3 gm fat; 2.7 gm carbohydrate; 0.1 gm fiber; 31 mg cholesterol; 62 mg sodium

Marinated Roast Turkey or Chicken Ⓜ

Yield: 3–4 pounds cooked meat (3 ounces = 1 serving)

Whether prepared in the microwave or a conventional oven, this poultry takes on a wonderful flavor from the marinade.

2 cups nonfat yogurt
3 garlic cloves, minced
1 tablespoon peeled, grated fresh ginger
2 tablespoons grated onion
2 tablespoons lemon or lime juice
½ teaspoon each ground coriander and ground cumin

¼ cup frozen unsweetened apple juice concentrate
1 tablespoon Worcestershire sauce
1 teaspoon Hungarian paprika
Few drops hot pepper sauce
4½–5-pound whole turkey breast, with skin and fat removed

1. Combine all ingredients except turkey and mix well.
2. Place turkey breast in large plastic bag. Add marinade, turning bag so that turkey is well covered with the mixture.
3. Refrigerate turkey overnight, turning several times, to absorb flavors.
4. Remove turkey from bag and place on rack in roasting pan.
5. Roast at 325° for 12 to 15 minutes per pound or until thermometer registers 165°.
6. Remove from oven and let stand for 10 to 15 minutes until juices are absorbed. Slice and serve hot, or fillet, cool, and wrap for freezing.

Variation: A whole chicken may be skinned, fat removed, marinated, and prepared in the same fashion. You may also season turkey or chicken with juice of ½ lemon, 1 teaspoon salt-free vegetable seasoning, and garlic and onion powders, and roast it without marinating.

Helpful Hint: Don't forget to save the bones and freeze for future soups.

In Microwave: Place turkey breast directly on bottom of a nonmetal dish. Roast covered with wax paper on medium heat for 8 minutes per pound, or until thermometer registers 165°. (Check manufacturer's directions for your individual microwave oven.) You will find the turkey a bit juicier if done in the microwave.

Per serving: 146 calories; 26.6 gm protein; 2.8 gm fat; 1.8 gm carbohydrate; 0 gm fiber; 60 mg cholesterol; 69 mg sodium

Toast Tartlets ⓠ

Yield: 24 tart shells (1 tart shell = 1 serving)

It is impossible to find shells that are not made of puff pastry or other fat- and cholesterol-laden dough. This easy basic gives you a nutritious headstart for making many appetizers. Whether filled with just plain cottage cheese and vegetables or a more elaborate onion filling, these shells are a crunchy convenience.

2 egg whites, beaten until foamy
1 teaspoon Worcestershire sauce or
   1 tablespoon grated Parmesan
   cheese
½ teaspoon salt-free vegetable
   seasoning

¼ teaspoon onion powder
12 slices *thinly* sliced whole-wheat,
   rye, or pumpernickel bread
   (firm texture)

1. Combine egg whites with seasonings.
2. Cut out 24 rounds of bread with 2-inch cookie cutter.
3. Brush bread rounds on one side with egg white mixture.
4. Press brushed side down into 1¾-inch nonstick muffin tins or tins coated with nonstick cooking spray.
5. Bake in preheated 350° oven for 5 minutes, or until edges are very lightly browned. *Do not overbake.*
6. Remove and cool on wire rack. If not used immediately, place in plastic bags and freeze for future use.

Suggested Fillings: Cold Chicken Salad Spread (page 108), Vegetable-Cheese Stuffing (page 124), Hot Salmon Tartlets (page 67), or Divine Swiss Onion Tarts (page 62).

Per serving: 11 calories; 0.6 gm protein; 0.1 gm fat; 1.9 gm carbohydrate; 0 gm fiber; 0 mg cholesterol; 17 mg sodium

Simply Delicious Tomato Sauce

Yield: 8 cups (½ cup sauce = 1 serving)

My friend Addie's house is always filled with interesting people. Her friend Daniela is from Vicenza, Italy, and shared her mother's favorite light-style Italian tomato sauce with me. I now have the privilege of sharing it with you. It is divine served with pasta or as a topping for chicken or fish.

2 28-ounce cans Italian plum
    tomatoes
3 carrots, peeled and quartered
3 medium onions, peeled and
    quartered
3 stalks celery, quartered

2 large garlic cloves, mashed
1 tablespoon vegetable broth
    powder, 4 Chicken Bouillon
    Cubes (page 31), or ½ cup
    leftover chicken gravy

1. Place all ingredients in 4-quart Dutch oven or saucepan.
2. Bring to boil, reduce heat, cover, and simmer for 1½ hours, or until vegetables are tender. Stir occasionally.
3. Puree mixture in food processor or blender.
4. Taste and adjust seasonings.

To Serve: Alternate layers of sauce with pasta in serving bowl; top with chopped fresh basil or grated Parmesan cheese. Your guests will think they are dining on the Via Veneto.

Helpful Hint: If sauce appears watery, add 1 tablespoon cornstarch mixed with ¼ cup cold water. Heat and stir until liquid is shiny and not watery.

Per serving: 39 calories; 1.5 gm protein; 0.3 gm fat; 8.4 gm carbohydrate; 1.2 gm fiber; 0 mg cholesterol; 25 mg sodium

Appetizers
and Hors d'Oeuvres

IN THE BEGINNING

Asparagus Dip
Hot Bean Dip
Confetti Cottage Cheese Dip
Cucumber–Dill Dip
Spinach Dip
Tuna–Cucumber Dip
Ann's Smoked Tuna Spread
Yogurt–Salsa Dip
Mexicali Bean Spread
Chicken-Stuffed Mushrooms
Harriet's Crispy Cocktail Snacks
Crabmeat-Stuffed Pepper Rings
Tangy Cocktail Sausages
Eggplant Puree
Eggplant Caviar
Spinach Cups

Quick Barbecued Chicken
   Drummettes
Texas-Style Meatballs
Mushroom Pâté
My Favorite Potato Cups with
   Yogurt
Quick Mini-Pizzas
Divine Swiss Onion Tarts
Onion Puffs
Tuna–Green Chili Squares
Fresh Tuna Tartare
Salmon Log
Salmon, Onion, and Tomato Spread
Hot Salmon Tartlets
Julie's Farmer's Pâté

Considering the present obsession with weight control, the term appetizers seems to me to be a misnomer. Most of us hardly need something to stimulate our appetites, although a small serving of something we relish at the beginning of a meal does seem to be in order at times. It could be a simple Asparagus Dip (page 46) attractively served with colorful seasonal vegetables; a Mushroom Pâté (page 60), so tasty yet easy to prepare; or a speedy Fresh Tuna Tartare (page 65) with thinly sliced brown bread. Maybe just a delicious nibble of Harriet's Crispy Cocktail Snacks (page 53) will provide your guests with something to savor while starting to get acquainted. Entertaining guests with delicacies such as My Favorite Potato Cups with Yogurt (page 61) or Hot Salmon Tartlets (page 67) helps to act as an ice-breaker before dinner.

Whatever your choice or life-style, start out simple—simple enough to stimulate the conversation and the palate, yet not so elaborate as to sate your guests with too much food before your dinner starts. Remember—in the beginning keep it light.

Asparagus Dip ⓠ

Yield: 2¼ cups (1 tablespoon = 1 serving)

This beautiful dip looks like guacamole but it has one tenth the calories.

1 pound asparagus (tough ends removed), cut into 1-inch pieces, or 10-ounce package frozen asparagus cuts
¼ red onion
1 garlic clove
1 tablespoon lemon juice

1 teaspoon salt-free vegetable seasoning
2–3 tablespoons nonfat yogurt
1 tablespoon grated Parmesan cheese
1 tomato, peeled, seeded, and chopped

1. Steam asparagus for about 4 to 5 minutes. Drain well and cool.
2. Place asparagus, onion, garlic, lemon juice, and vegetable seasoning in blender or food processor. Process until finely chopped.
3. Add yogurt and cheese. Blend and chill.
To Serve: Place in serving bowl and top with the chopped tomato. Serve with crisp pita bread, wheat crackers, and assorted vegetables.

Per serving: 5 calories; 0.6 gm protein; 0.1 gm fat; 0.9 gm carbohydrate; 0.1 gm fiber; 0.14 mg cholesterol; 4 mg sodium

Hot Bean Dip ⓠ

Yield: 1½ cups (1 tablespoon = 1 serving)

This tasty dip goes well with crudités, fresh warm corn tortillas, or, if diet permits, salt-free corn chips cooked in cold-pressed safflower oil.

14-ounce can vegetarian refried beans
1 tablespoon finely chopped green pepper
1 teaspoon dehydrated onion flakes

¼ teaspoon garlic powder
Few drops hot pepper sauce
1–2 teaspoons taco sauce
½ cup nonfat yogurt

1. Combine all ingredients but the yogurt in 1-quart casserole. Stir to blend, then cover and microwave on high for 5 to 6 minutes. (Stir once during cooking.)

2. Remove from microwave, add yogurt, and stir to blend well.

To Serve: Serve hot in ramekin or small casserole and surround with salt-free tortilla chips, fresh corn tortillas, and crudités such as pencil-thin asparagus, cherry tomatoes, and jicama.

Per serving: 33 calories; 2.1 gm protein; 0.4 gm fat; 5.5 gm carbohydrate; 2.0 gm fiber; 0.08 mg cholesterol; 14 mg sodium

Confetti Cottage Cheese Dip ⓠ

Yield: 2½ cups (1 tablespoon = 1 serving)

Served with fresh vegetables or toasted pita bread, this dip is a delicious light beginning.

1 cup 1% fat cottage cheese, blended until smooth

2 tablespoons chopped green pepper

2 tablespoons chopped pimiento

2 tablespoons chopped green onion

2 tablespoons nonfat yogurt, or as needed

Chopped fresh dill and chopped tomato for garnish

1. Combine first 4 ingredients.
2. Add yogurt only as needed to reach desired consistency.

To Serve: Place in bowl. Sprinkle with dill and chopped tomatoes and surround with crisp vegetables such as radishes, carrots, turnips, sugar snap peas, fresh fennel, and mushrooms.

Per serving: 5 calories; 0.8 gm protein; 0.1 gm fat; 0.3 gm carbohydrate; 0.02 gm fiber; 0.25 mg cholesterol; 24 mg sodium

Cucumber–Dill Dip ⓠ

Yield: 1½ cups (1 tablespoon = 1 serving)

Light in calories, yet quite satisfying in flavor.

1 cup 1% fat cottage cheese
½ cucumber, peeled, seeded, and
  sliced
¼ large white onion, sliced
2 teaspoons lemon juice
1 teaspoon dried dill or
  1 tablespoon fresh dill, chopped

½ teaspoon salt-free vegetable
  seasoning

Fresh dill for garnish

1. Place all ingredients in blender or food processor. Blend until smooth.
To Serve: Place in glass bowl and garnish with sprig of fresh dill. Surround with cauliflowerets, broccoli, cucumber, and carrot sticks, green pepper rings, red radishes, and cherry tomatoes.

Per serving: 9 calories; 1.2 gm protein; 0.1 gm fat; 0.7 gm carbohydrate; 0.1 gm fiber; 0.37 mg cholesterol; 39 mg sodium

Spinach Dip ⓠ

Yield: 2½ cups (1 tablespoon = 1 serving)

The American infatuation with serving quick dips with chips has continued. At least we can make them a bit more nourishing by using yogurt instead of mayonnaise and vegetables instead of chips.

2 10-ounce packages chopped
  spinach, defrosted, drained, and
  cooled
4 canned water chestnuts,
  quartered
½ small onion, sliced

1 cup nonfat yogurt
2 tablespoons light mayonnaise
2 tablespoons dehydrated
  vegetable flakes
¼ teaspoon dried thyme, crushed
Freshly grated nutmeg

1. Place all ingredients in food processor or blender.
2. Process until finely chopped.

3. Chill before serving to let flavors blend.

To Serve: Place dip in seeded acorn or crookneck squash (or bowl). Surround with your choice of raw vegetables, such as rutabaga, radishes, mushrooms, cauliflower, carrots, jicama, broccoli, cucumber, or cherry tomatoes.

Per serving: 9 calories; 0.8 gm protein; 0.1 gm fat; 1.6 gm carbohydrate; 0.3 gm fiber; 0 mg cholesterol; 20 mg sodium

Tuna–Cucumber Dip ⓠ

Yield: 2 cups (1 tablespoon = 1 serving)

¾ cup 1% fat cottage cheese
7½-ounce can salt-reduced tuna in
water, drained
½ cucumber, peeled, seeded, and
quartered
1 tablespoon lemon juice

3 whole green onions, cut into
1-inch pieces
1 tablespoon fresh dill or
1 teaspoon dried dill
1 tablespoon capers, rinsed and
drained

1. Place all ingredients but capers in blender or food processor and blend until smooth.
2. Add capers and process slightly.
3. Taste and adjust seasonings.

To Serve: Pour dip into hollowed-out green or red pepper. Place on serving tray or flat basket and surround with cut-up vegetables, such as cucumber sticks, broccoli, snow peas, cherry tomatoes, carrots, and jicama.

Per serving: 13 calories; 2.4 gm protein; 0.1 gm fat; 0.4 gm carbohydrate; 0.1 gm fiber; 4 mg cholesterol; 24 mg sodium

Ann's Smoked Tuna Spread Ⓠ

Yield: 2⅓ cups (1 tablespoon = 1 serving)

Just a bit of liquid smoke makes a difference in the flavor.

16-ounce can white meat tuna in
  water, drained*
4 tablespoons nonfat yogurt
2 tablespoons light mayonnaise

1 teaspoon liquid smoke
Lettuce leaves
⅔ cup thinly shredded leek
1 teaspoon fines herbes or
  1 tablespoon chopped fresh dill

1. Mash tuna with fork.
2. Add yogurt and mayonnaise and mix thoroughly.
3. Add liquid smoke and stir to blend.
4. Cover and chill in refrigerator for 15 minutes before serving.

To Serve: Mound mixture on lettuce-lined platter. Sprinkle with leek and fines herbes or dill. Surround with squares of thinly sliced dark rye bread.

Per serving: 20 calories; 3.6 gm protein; 0.3 gm fat; 0.4 gm carbohydrate; 0 gm fiber;
8 mg cholesterol; 41 mg sodium

* Leftover fresh tuna or salmon fillets that have been grilled may be substituted for canned tuna. Using fresh fish results in a lower sodium content.

Yogurt–Salsa Dip Ⓠ

Yield: 2 cups (1 tablespoon = 1 serving)

1 large ripe tomato, peeled, seeded,
  and cut into eighths
¼ cup canned mild green chilies,
  seeded

4 whole green onions
1 garlic clove
1 cup nonfat yogurt

1. Add all ingredients but yogurt to blender or food processor. Blend until chopped.

2. Add yogurt and blend slightly, just to mix ingredients.

3. Store in covered container in refrigerator.

To Serve: Place dip in bowl and serve with salt-free chips, warmed pita bread, and assorted vegetables.

Per serving: 6 calories; 0.5 gm protein; 0.0 gm fat; 1.1 gm carbohydrate; 0.1 gm fiber; 0 mg cholesterol; 6 mg sodium

Mexicali Bean Spread Ⓠ

Yield: 4½ cups (3 tablespoons and 1 tortilla = 1 serving)

Your guests will enjoy spooning this piquant mixture of beans, yogurt, and crunchy fresh vegetables into a fresh, warmed corn tortilla.

14-ounce can vegetarian refried
    beans
½ cup red taco sauce
8 ounces nonfat yogurt, mixed until
    smooth
4 whole green onions, finely sliced
½ green pepper, seeded and
    chopped

2 medium tomatoes, seeded and
    chopped
3½-ounce can sliced ripe olives,
    drained (optional)
½ cup green chili salsa (optional)
24 6-inch fresh corn tortillas,
    warmed

1. Combine beans with taco sauce.

2. Spread bean mixture on large platter.

3. Top with yogurt.

4. Sprinkle with onions, pepper, tomatoes, and olives. (If desired, spoon green chili salsa over entire mixture.)

To Serve: Accompany prepared platter with basket of fresh warm tortillas.

Per serving: 154 calories; 5.5 gm protein; 2.4 gm fat; 29.2 gm carbohydrate; 2.5 gm fiber; 0 mg cholesterol; 75 mg sodium

Chicken-Stuffed Mushrooms

Yield: 24 (2 mushrooms = 1 serving)

24 medium mushrooms, cleaned
and stems removed
Juice of ½ lemon
1 teaspoon salt-free vegetable
seasoning
½ cup salt-reduced tomato sauce
2 tablespoons nonfat milk
¼ cup whole-wheat bread crumbs
½ pound ground raw chicken, or
leftover roast chicken, minced
3 tablespoons chopped parsley

1 6-inch zucchini, shredded
1 teaspoon onion powder
1 garlic clove, minced
1 egg white, slightly beaten
2 teaspoons Worcestershire sauce
1 teaspoon Dijon mustard
2 tablespoons grated Parmesan
cheese

Watercress for garnish

1. Sprinkle mushroom caps with lemon juice and vegetable seasoning.
2. Spread tomato sauce on nonstick baking sheet and arrange mushrooms on sheet, tops down.
3. Pour milk over bread crumbs in bowl. Add chicken, parsley, zucchini, onion powder, garlic, egg white, Worcestershire sauce, and mustard. Mix lightly with fork.
4. Roll mixture into 24 1-inch balls.
5. Place meatballs in mushroom caps. Sprinkle lightly with Parmesan cheese.
6. Bake in preheated 350° oven for 15 to 20 minutes.
To Serve: Place hot on platter, garnish with watercress, and pass as hot hors d'oeuvre.

Per serving: 54 calories; 6.1 gm protein; 1.5 gm fat; 4.5 gm carbohydrate; 0.4 gm fat;
13 mg cholesterol; 51 mg sodium

Harriet's Crispy Cocktail Snacks

Yield: 7 cups (1 tablespoon = 1 serving)

You are sure to enjoy this low-fat, low-sodium snack. It is so easy a child can make it and so tasty and crunchy everyone will reach for it. In fact, it is great not only as a cocktail snack but also as a healthy substitute for potato chips or corn chips in a packed lunch.

5 egg whites
Few grains cream of tartar
1 tablespoon Worcestershire sauce
1 teaspoon garlic powder
2 teaspoons onion powder
2 teaspoons salt-free vegetable
  seasoning
3 tablespoons grated Parmesan
  cheese

Few drops hot pepper sauce
5 cups bite-sized shredded
  Wheat 'n Bran or any bite-sized
  shredded wheat
2 cups whole almonds with skins on
Salt-free vegetable seasoning as
  needed
Hungarian paprika
3 tablespoons sesame seeds

1. Beat egg whites with cream of tartar until thick and soft peaks form.
2. Add Worcestershire sauce, garlic and onion powders, vegetable seasoning, Parmesan, and hot pepper sauce.
3. Add bite-sized shredded wheat and almonds and blend well.
4. Place on nonstick baking sheet and spread evenly.
5. Sprinkle with more vegetable seasoning, paprika, and sesame seeds.
6. Bake in preheated 350° oven, stirring every 20 minutes, until golden brown and crisp on all sides, about 45 minutes.

Variation: ½ cup pumpkin seeds or sunflower seeds or 1 cup plumped raisins may be added after toasting.

Helpful Hint: This snack may be frozen in airtight plastic bags for future use and, depending on the humidity, removed from bag and reheated briefly in microwave oven to crisp.

Per serving: 25 calories; 1.0 gm protein; 1.5 gm fat; 2.0 gm carbohydrate; 0.5 gm fiber; 0 mg cholesterol; 6 mg sodium

Crabmeat-Stuffed Pepper Rings ⓠ

Yield: 18 slices (1 slice = 1 serving as appetizer; 4 slices = 1 serving as entrée)

4 ounces fresh or canned crabmeat
8 ounces skim-milk ricotta
3 tablespoons grated onion
3 tablespoons grated carrot
3 tablespoons chopped parsley
2 tablespoons chopped green onion
  or chives
1 tablespoon lemon juice

Freshly ground black pepper
1 small red pepper and 1 small
  green pepper

Watercress, paprika, chopped
  parsley, and cherry tomatoes for
  garnish

1. Combine first 8 ingredients in mixing bowl. Blend thoroughly.
2. Cut off tops of peppers and seed. Stuff peppers with mixture. Wrap with plastic and chill for 30 minutes.
3. Cut crosswise into ⅓-inch thick slices.
To Serve: Arrange slices on bed of watercress and sprinkle with paprika or parsley. Garnish with cherry tomatoes.

Per slice: 28 calories; 2.7 gm protein; 1.2 gm fat; 1.4 gm carbohydrate; 0.1 gm fiber; 11 mg cholesterol; 31 mg sodium

Tangy Cocktail Sausages ⓠ

Serves: 10 (4 halves = 1 serving)

The usual sausages or wieners have too much fat and so many additives, nitrates, and other fillers that I shy away from using them. This jar of chicken sticks for toddlers has more sodium than necessary, but is acceptable as a quick hors d'oeuvre if you are not on a low-sodium diet.

½ cup sugar-free grape jelly
1 tablespoon Dijon mustard
8-ounce can salt-free tomato sauce

3 2½-ounce jars chicken sticks for
  toddlers, drained and halved

1. In a 1-quart saucepan, combine jelly, mustard, and tomato sauce. Heat on high for 5 minutes, stirring occasionally. Continue to cook, and stir, over medium heat for 10 minutes.

2. Add halved chicken sticks and stir until well coated with sauce. Heat for 5 minutes or until meat is hot.

To Serve: Place in chafing dish and serve with toothpicks.

Per serving: 52 calories; 3.5 gm protein; 3.1 gm fat; 2.9 gm carbohydrate; 0.1 gm fiber; 0 mg cholesterol; 108 mg sodium

Eggplant Puree

Yield: 1½ cups (1 tablespoon = 1 serving)

This should be prepared 24 hours before serving.

2 garlic cloves, cut in slivers
½ teaspoon ground allspice
½ teaspoon ground cinnamon
½ teaspoon extra-virgin olive oil

1-pound eggplant
1 tablespoon red wine vinegar
2 teaspoons extra-virgin olive oil

1. In small dish combine garlic slivers, allspice, cinnamon, and ½ teaspoon olive oil.
2. Cut slits into eggplant and insert seasoned garlic.
3. Broil eggplant, turning on all sides, for a total of 20 minutes. Cool.
4. Remove skin and stem. Drain eggplant to remove excess moisture.
5. Place eggplant and vinegar in food processor or blender bowl. Add remaining 2 teaspoons oil with machine running. Puree.
6. Put into bowl. Taste and adjust seasonings.
7. Chill overnight.

To Serve: Surround puree with assorted fresh vegetables and toasted pita bread.

Per serving: 9 calories; 0.2 gm protein; 0.4 gm fat; 1.4 gm carbohydrate; 0.3 gm fiber; 0 mg cholesterol; 1 mg sodium

Eggplant Caviar ⓠ

Yield: 2–3 cups (1 tablespoon = 1 serving as a dip; ¼ cup = 1 serving as first course)

This can be used as a lovely first course in the dining room or served as a dip with fresh vegetables and warm pita bread.

1½-pound eggplant, halved*
2 large garlic cloves, finely chopped
3 tablespoons chopped parsley
½ small red onion, finely chopped
½ green pepper, seeded and finely chopped

2–3 tablespoons red wine vinegar or lemon juice
2 teaspoons extra-virgin olive oil

Lettuce leaves and tomato slices or chopped tomato for garnish

1. Bake eggplant halves on baking sheet in preheated 400° oven for 15 minutes, or until skin is soft and wrinkled.
2. Remove stem and skin. Squeeze out excess liquid from eggplant and chop the flesh of the eggplant.
3. Place chopped eggplant in bowl and add remaining ingredients. Blend well. Taste and adjust seasonings.

To Serve: Place ½-inch slice beefsteak tomato on a lettuce-lined salad plate. Top with mound of eggplant accompanied by toasted pita bread. You may also place eggplant in serving bowl and garnish with chopped tomato if desired.

Per tablespoon: 8 calories; 0.2 gm protein; 0.3 gm fat; 1.4 gm carbohydrate; 0.3 gm fiber; 0 mg cholesterol; 1 mg sodium

* 2 pounds or 2½ cups cooked, chopped, well-drained zucchini may be substituted for the eggplant.

Spinach Cups ⑨

Yield: 12 cups (1 cup = 1 serving)

2 egg whites, slightly beaten
2-ounce jar chopped pimiento, drained
2 whole green onions, thinly sliced
1 teaspoon salt-free vegetable seasoning
Freshly ground black pepper
1 tablespoon grated Parmesan cheese

10½-ounce package frozen chopped spinach, defrosted and squeezed dry
1 tablespoon grated Parmesan cheese

Cherry tomatoes for garnish

1. Spray 1¾-inch muffin tins with butter-flavored nonstick cooking spray.
2. Combine egg whites, pimientos, green onions, vegetable seasoning, pepper, and 1 tablespoon Parmesan cheese. Mix thoroughly with fork.
3. Add chopped spinach and blend.
4. Fill muffin tins ⅔ full with mixture. Sprinkle with 1 tablespoon Parmesan cheese.
5. Bake in preheated 375° oven for 10 to 12 minutes.
To Serve: Remove from muffin tin and arrange on platter lined with doily. Garnish with cherry tomatoes.

Per serving: 15 calories; 1.7 gm protein; 0.4 gm fat; 1.7 gm carbohydrate; 0.6 gm fiber; 1 mg cholesterol; 44 mg sodium

Quick Barbecued
Chicken Drummettes Ⓠ Ⓜ

Yield: About 12 (2 drummettes = 1 serving)

An all-time favorite that takes just minutes to prepare! I use the single-boned portion of the wing only.

1½ pounds chicken drummettes, skinned

1 cup Spicy Barbecue Sauce (page 365), heated

3 tablespoons sesame seeds, lightly toasted in a dry skillet

Watercress for garnish

1. Pour sauce over drummettes in 13 x 9 x 2-inch glass baking dish.
2. Microwave on medium for 12 minutes.
3. Sprinkle with sesame seeds and broil in oven on medium broil until lightly browned and crisped.

To Serve: Arrange chicken drummettes in spokelike design on round serving dish. Fill center with watercress. Don't forget to have plenty of cocktail napkins for sticky fingers.

Note: To prepare in conventional oven, bake in preheated 375° oven for 20 to 25 minutes. Place under broiler and broil until lightly browned and crisp. Sprinkle with toasted sesame seeds.

Per serving: 61 calories; 6.6 gm protein; 2.9 gm fat; 1.9 gm carbohydrate; 0.1 gm fiber; 17 mg cholesterol; 25 mg sodium

Texas-Style Meatballs Ⓠ Ⓜ

Yield: 40 meatballs (2 meatballs = 1 serving as appetizer;
8 meatballs = 1 serving as entrée)

Even though we do limit protein in a prudent life-style, occasionally we all enjoy a good old down-home meatball. These, of course, may also be served over steamed brown rice as an entrée.

1 pound ground raw turkey
2 egg whites
¼ cup nonfat milk
⅓ cup whole-wheat bread crumbs
2 teaspoons dehydrated onion
   flakes
1 teaspoon salt-free vegetable
   seasoning

¼ teaspoon freshly grated nutmeg
¼ teaspoon garlic powder
1 teaspoon Worcestershire sauce
Freshly ground black pepper
1½ cups Spicy Barbecue Sauce
   (page 365)

1. Combine all ingredients except barbecue sauce and shape into 40 1-inch balls.

2. Place meatballs in 2-quart oblong nonmetal baking dish. Bake in microwave on medium for 8 minutes. Turn meatballs over halfway through cooking time.

3. Pour barbecue sauce over meatballs and stir lightly to coat. Cook with microwave on high for 2 minutes, or until sauce is hot.

To Serve: Place in a chafing dish or fondue dish and serve with toothpicks.

Variation: Add a 7½-ounce can unsweetened crushed pineapple with juice to barbecue sauce for a Polynesian flavor.

Note: To prepare in a conventional oven, place meatballs on 15 x 10 nonstick baking sheet. Bake in preheated 450° oven for 12 to 15 minutes. Add meatballs to saucepan with barbecue sauce and heat for 5 to 7 minutes.

For 2 meatballs: 44 calories; 5.8 gm protein; 1.1 gm fat; 2.4 gm carbohydrate; 0 gm fiber; 13 mg cholesterol; 32 mg sodium

Mushroom Pâté Ⓠ

Yield: 1⅓ cups (1 tablespoon = 1 serving)

This low-fat pâté may be served at room temperature or chilled overnight in a small crock and served cold.

1 tablespoon cold-pressed safflower oil
½ red onion, finely chopped
1 pound mushrooms, cleaned and finely chopped in food processor or by hand
¼ teaspoon freshly grated nutmeg
¼ cup lemon juice
¼ cup chopped parsley
2 tablespoons dry sherry

1 teaspoon salt-free vegetable seasoning
½ teaspoon dried thyme, crushed
Freshly ground black pepper
Few drops hot pepper sauce
1 cup slivered almonds, toasted
1 tablespoon nonfat yogurt

2 whole green onions, thinly sliced for garnish

1. Heat oil in 10-inch nonstick skillet. Add onion and cook for 5 to 7 minutes until soft, stirring occasionally.

2. Add mushrooms, nutmeg, and lemon juice. Cook over moderately high heat, stirring until mushroom liquid appears.

3. Add parsley, sherry, vegetable seasoning, thyme, pepper, and hot pepper sauce. Stir over medium heat until liquid has evaporated. Remove from heat.

4. Process almonds in blender or food processor until finely chopped. Add mushroom mixture and puree.

5. Add yogurt, process briefly, and spoon into 8-inch shallow serving dish. Cool to room temperature or store in sealed-top container in refrigerator.

To Serve: Garnish with sliced green onions and surround with quartered, thinly sliced whole-grain rye bread.

Per serving: 52 calories; 1.8 gm protein; 3.9 gm fat; 3.0 gm carbohydrate; 0.5 gm fiber; 0 mg cholesterol; 3 mg sodium

My Favorite
Potato Cups with Yogurt ⓠ

Yield: 24 halves (2 halves = 1 serving)

A hint for you: These small red new potatoes seem to fall to the bottom of the bin, so when you are shopping for these treasures, take the time to search underneath the pile for the little goodies. They also keep for several weeks in the refrigerator (an exception to the storage rules for potatoes)—so by all means, buy them when you see them!

12 small red new potatoes,
  1½ inches in diameter
Freshly ground black pepper
½ cup nonfat yogurt
½ cup chopped chives or whole
  green onions

3 tablespoons Icelandic lumpfish
  caviar, rinsed and drained
  (optional)

Green onion brushes and cherry
  tomatoes for garnish

1. Scrub potatoes with brush thoroughly and place on steamer basket over boiling water. Steam for 15 minutes, or until tender when tested with paring knife.
2. Cool slightly, halve, and remove center with 1-inch melon baller.
3. Sprinkle potato cups with ground pepper.
4. Fill each potato cup with 1 teaspoon yogurt and sprinkle with chives or green onions, or, if used judiciously, the nutritionally questionable caviar.*

To Serve: Arrange on platter garnished with green onion brushes and cherry tomatoes.

Variation: Potato cups may also be filled with salsa, creamed spinach, or cottage cheese with chives.

Per serving: 54 calories; 2.3 gm protein; 0.1 gm fat; 10.6 gm carbohydrate; 0.5 gm fiber; 0.1 mg cholesterol; 12 mg sodium

* 1 tablespoon caviar contains about 70 milligrams of cholesterol, still only 25 percent of that found in chicken egg yolks.

Quick Mini-Pizzas ©

Yield: 24 wedges (1 wedge = 1 serving)

3 Pritikin whole-wheat English
  muffins or whole-wheat bagels,
  halved
⅔ cup salt-free marinara or pizza
  sauce
½ teaspoon Italian herb blend or
  1 tablespoon fresh basil, chopped

Thinly sliced mushrooms, red
  onions, red or green pepper,
  zucchini, or olives as pizza
  topping
3 tablespoons shredded skim-milk
  mozzarella

1. Spoon 1 to 1½ tablespoons sauce on each muffin half.
2. Sprinkle with herbs and add desired vegetable topping.
3. Top each muffin half with shredded mozzarella.
4. Place under preheated broiler or in preheated 475° oven until cheese melts.

To Serve: Cut into quarters for appetizers or serve 2 whole muffin halves as an entrée with a mixed green salad and fruit.

Per serving: 28 calories; 1.5 gm protein; 0.5 gm fat; 4.9 gm carbohydrate; 0.1 gm fiber;
1 mg cholesterol; 26 mg sodium

Divine Swiss Onion Tarts ©

Yield: 24 tarts (2 tarts = 1 serving)

24 Toast Tartlets (page 40),
  unbaked
1 tablespoon Dijon mustard
1 medium onion, sliced and sautéed
  in 1 teaspoon extra-virgin olive
  oil, or ⅔ cup Onion Magic
  (page 36)
2 egg whites

⅓ cup nonfat evaporated milk
¼ cup nonfat yogurt
3 tablespoons shredded salt-free
  Swiss cheese
¼ teaspoon dried thyme, crushed

Hungarian paprika for garnish

1. Spread inside of unbaked tart shells with mustard.
2. Combine all ingredients but paprika thoroughly in mixing bowl.

3. Spoon mixture into unbaked shells. Sprinkle with paprika and bake in preheated 400° oven for 10 to 12 minutes, or until golden brown.

Variation: Substitute 1 cup defrosted frozen peas mixed with thinly sliced green onions for Onion Magic and use 1 tablespoon grated Parmesan instead of shredded Swiss cheese.

Per serving: 48 calories; 2.9 gm protein; 1.2 gm fat; 6.6 gm carbohydrate; 0.2 gm fiber; 2 mg cholesterol; 52 mg sodium

Onion Puffs ⓠ

Yield: 24 (3 slices toast = 1 serving)

This is lovely served as a hot hors d'oeuvre with icy cold salt-free tomato juice.

1 large red onion, minced (about 1 cup)
3 whole green onions, minced
⅓ cup grated Parmesan cheese
2 tablespoons light mayonnaise
2 tablespoons nonfat yogurt
1 teaspoon Worcestershire sauce

1 teaspoon fines herbes, crushed
24 ¼-inch thick slices small French baguette

Green pepper rings and cherry tomatoes for garnish

1. Combine all ingredients except bread and stir thoroughly.
2. Spread about 1½ teaspoons of mixture on each slice of bread.
3. Place on baking sheet and broil in preheated broiler until golden.
4. Serve immediately.
To Serve: Place on serving tray garnished with green pepper rings and cherry tomatoes.

Per serving: 65 calories; 3.3 gm protein; 1.5 gm fat; 10.6 gm carbohydrate; 0.4 gm fiber; 4 mg cholesterol; 153 mg sodium

Tuna–Green Chili Squares

Yield: 48 squares (2 squares = 1 serving)

7-ounce can salt-reduced tuna in
water, drained and flaked
⅔ cup whole-wheat flour
⅔ cup cornmeal
1½ tablespoons low-sodium baking
powder
2 egg whites
1 cup nonfat milk
1 tablespoon cold-pressed safflower
oil

2 tablespoons minced onion
½ cup canned chopped green
chilies or sliced black olives
2-ounce jar chopped pimiento,
drained

Watercress for garnish

1. Mix together all ingredients.
2. Spread mixture into 13 x 9 x 2-inch pan coated with nonstick cooking spray.
3. Bake in preheated 400° oven for 20 to 30 minutes.
4. Cut into 48 squares.

To Serve: Place squares on serving tray with watercress in center. They may be served hot or at room temperature.

Per serving: 46 calories; 3.7 gm protein; 0.9 gm fat; 5.7 gm carbohydrate; 0.7 gm fiber;
5 mg cholesterol; 14 mg sodium

Fresh Tuna Tartare ⓠ

Yield: 8 (2 ounces = 1 serving)

If you prefer a spicier taste, 3 tablespoons green chili salsa may be added to the fish mixture.

1 pound very fresh tuna fillet, finely chopped (fresh flounder or salmon may also be used)
2 teaspoons extra-virgin olive oil
2 Italian plum tomatoes, seeded and finely chopped
2 tablespoons finely chopped red onion

2 tablespoons lemon juice
Freshly ground black pepper
Few drops hot pepper sauce
Red lettuce leaves
2 tablespoons chopped cilantro or parsley

Lemon wedges for garnish

1. Mix first 7 ingredients together. Chill for 15 minutes.

To Serve: Mound mixture on serving plate covered with red lettuce leaves. Sprinkle with chopped cilantro and garnish with lemon wedges. Accompany with toast triangles or thinly sliced whole rye bread.

Variation: Tuna Tartare may be garnished with pencil-thin fresh steamed asparagus.

Per serving: 100 calories; 14.6 gm protein; 3.5 gm fat; 1.8 gm carbohydrate; 0.2 gm fiber; 32 mg cholesterol; 25 mg sodium

Salmon Log ℚ

Yield: 1½ cups (1 tablespoon = 1 serving)

½ small red onion
7½-ounce can red salmon, skinned,
 boned, and drained
4 ounces skim-milk ricotta
2-ounce jar chopped pimiento,
 drained
2 teaspoons lemon juice

½ teaspoon dried thyme, crushed
½ teaspoon dried dill
½ cup chopped parsley or chopped
 fresh spinach

English cucumber slices for garnish

1. Mince onion in food processor or blender.
2. Add salmon, ricotta, pimiento, lemon juice, thyme, and dill to food processor. Process just to blend.
3. Cover and chill in freezer for 20 minutes.
4. Shape into log and roll in parsley or spinach.
To Serve: Place on chilled platter with Melba toast and scored English cucumber slices.

Per serving: 25 calories; 2.4 gm protein; 1.4 gm fat; 0.7 gm carbohydrate; 0.1 gm fiber;
5 mg cholesterol; 11 mg sodium

Salmon, Onion, and Tomato Spread ℚ

Yield: 2½ cups (1 tablespoon = 1 serving)

Years ago I made this spread with smoked salmon. Since it is too high in sodium, I've changed to canned salmon.

5 Italian plum tomatoes, diced
4 whole green onions, thinly sliced
8-ounce can red salmon, skinned,
 boned, drained, and flaked

2 tablespoons red wine vinegar
Freshly ground black pepper

Chopped fresh dill for garnish

1. Place tomatoes, onions, and salmon in mixing bowl.
2. Sprinkle with vinegar and pepper.

3. Stir with fork to blend.

4. Cover and refrigerate for 20 minutes. The spread may be stored in refrigerator for several days.

To Serve: Place in serving bowl, sprinkle with dill, and surround with dark rye bread squares.

Per serving: 15 calories; 1.3 gm protein; 0.7 gm fat; 0.9 gm carbohydrate; 0.2 gm fiber; 2 mg cholesterol; 4 mg sodium

Hot Salmon Tartlets ⓠ

Yield: 24 tartlets (1 tartlet = 1 serving)

If you are clever enough to have stored some tart shells in the freezer, you're halfway there. Just add the salmon filling and your guests will wonder at your culinary creativity.

3½-ounce can red salmon, skinned, boned, and drained
1 egg white
½ cup Special Sour Cream Topping (page 33) or 1% fat cottage cheese
¼ cup peeled and chopped cucumbers

1 teaspoon lemon juice
¼ teaspoon dry mustard
½ teaspoon dried dill
24 Toast Tartlets (page 40), baked
1 tablespoon grated Parmesan cheese

1. Combine first 7 ingredients in bowl; mix thoroughly.

2. Fill tart shells with filling, sprinkle with Parmesan, and place on baking sheet. Broil in preheated broiler until lightly browned and serve immediately.

Per serving: 22 calories; 2.1 gm protein; 0.4 gm fat; 2.4 gm carbohydrate; 0.1 gm fiber; 2 mg cholesterol; 41 mg sodium

Julie's Farmer's Pâté ⓠ

Yield: 3 cups (1 tablespoon = 1 serving)

Julie is a busy health-care professional whose time is limited and palate educated to taste as well as nutrition.

2 carrots, cut into quarters
3 whole green onions, cut into
  quarters
1 3-inch slice cucumber, peeled,
  seeded, and quartered
¼ green pepper, quartered
2 tablespoons lemon juice
¼ cup chopped fresh dill or
  2 teaspoons dried dill

½ teaspoon Italian herb blend,
  crushed
2 teaspoons salt-free vegetable
  seasoning
16 ounces skim-milk ricotta (check
  date for freshness)
Salt-free rye crackers for spreading

1. Place first 4 ingredients in food processor or blender and chop.
2. Add lemon juice, dill, Italian herb blend, and vegetable seasoning, and blend.
3. Add ricotta and blend briefly.

To Serve: Place in serving dish and surround with rye crackers and assorted raw vegetables prepared as you wish—such as green onions, cucumber, green and red pepper, carrots, broccoli, turnip, and rutabaga.

Variation: This also makes a lovely spread for whole-wheat sandwiches or a toasted bagel for brunch.

Per serving: 16 calories; 1.2 gm protein; 0.8 gm fat; 1.1 gm carbohydrate; 0.1 gm fiber; 3 mg cholesterol; 13 mg sodium

Soups

A BOWL OR A CUP,
TO DINE OR TO SUP

Hot Soups

Harriet F's Albondigas Soup
Old-Fashioned Hot Borscht
Almond–Broccoli Bisque
Chicken Sub Gum Soup
Quick Corn Soup
Fish Chowder for Two
French Onion Soup
Goulash Soup (Gulyas)
Lentil–Barley Soup
Hong Kong Baron's Table Fresh
  Pea Soup
Microwaved Minestrone
Speedy Tomato–Rice Soup
Manhattan-Style Tuna Chowder
Superb Vegetable Chowder
Monday's Soup
Quick Vegetable–Barley Soup
Salmon–Leek Bisque
Yummy Yam Soup

Cold Soups

The Best Beet Borscht
Hot or Cold Curried Broccoli
  Bisque
Cold Carrot Soup
Chilled Cantaloupe Soup
Easy Gazpacho
Minted Pea Soup in Minutes
Fresh Tomato Soup

Soup is an all-time favorite in our home. Whether served as a first course or a one-dish meal, it is always thoroughly enjoyed. As the cook, I, of course, enjoy soups because they take so little effort to prepare.

What are the magical powers that soups seem to possess? Is it the medicinal qualities that Mama's chicken soup contains, or the comfort you feel when a friend's soup kettle runneth over and you end up with a jar of her favorite recipe? Is it the satisfaction of a hot and hearty soup on a cold winter's evening, or the refreshing quality of a cold gazpacho or borscht at the end of a scorching summer day?

A few of the soups that follow, such as old-fashioned borscht and albondigas soup, may take longer to simmer, but all of the recipes are easy to prepare.

So, soup lovers of the world, this next chapter is especially for you: a few simple but savory recipes to add to your already overflowing collection.

Hot Soups

Harriet F's Albóndigas Soup

Serves: 10 (1½ cups soup plus 3 meatballs = 1 serving)

A popular Mexican soup served as an entrée. If I have a leftover roast turkey carcass in the freezer, I add it to the broth for 1 hour to enrich the flavor of the broth.

Soup:

1 tablespoon extra-virgin olive oil
1 large onion, thinly sliced, or
  1 cup Onion Magic (page 36)
1 large garlic clove, minced
4 celery stalks, thinly sliced
1 green pepper, diced
3½-ounce can chopped green
  chilies
2 large tomatoes, peeled, seeded,
  and chopped, or 16-ounce can
  salt-free tomatoes, chopped

½ teaspoon each dried thyme,
  marjoram, and oregano, crushed
2 quarts salt-free chicken, turkey,
  or vegetable broth or
  6 10½-ounce cans salt-free
  chicken broth
1 cup frozen peas
2 tablespoons cornstarch dissolved
  in ¼ cup cold water

Meatballs:

1 pound ground raw turkey
½ cup short-grain brown rice
2 egg whites
1 small onion, finely minced
1 garlic clove, minced
¼ cup whole-wheat blend flour

1 teaspoon salt-free vegetable
  seasoning
½ teaspoon chili powder

Chopped cilantro for garnish

1. Place oil in 4-quart saucepan. Add onion, garlic, and celery. Sauté, covered, over medium heat until transparent, about 5 to 10 minutes. Stir occasionally.

2. Add green pepper, chilies, tomatoes, seasonings, and broth. Simmer for 20 minutes.

3. Combine ingredients for meatballs (except garnish) and roll into about 32 balls. (Prepare while soup is simmering.)

4. Add meatballs to soup and simmer for 1 hour.

5. Add peas and cornstarch mixture. Simmer for 5 minutes before serving.

To Serve: Place hot soup in heated tureen, garnish with chopped cilantro and serve with fresh warmed corn tortillas. A halved papaya with lime wedge is a refreshing dessert.

Per serving: 175 calories; 14.1 gm protein; 3.0 gm fat; 20.9 gm carbohydrate; 2.1 gm fiber; 23 mg cholesterol; 73 mg sodium

Old-Fashioned Hot Borscht

Serves: About 12 (1½ cups = 1 serving)

This hearty soup, served as a main dish with country rye or wheat bread, is representative of Middle European country cooking. Like so many soups or stews, it tastes even better the next day.

¾ pound extra-lean ground beef
  (flank steak)
2 garlic cloves, minced
2 onions, thinly sliced
1 small head green cabbage,
  shredded
2 28-ounce cans Italian plum
  tomatoes with juice
4 cups water
¼ cup frozen unsweetened apple
  juice concentrate

½ teaspoon ground ginger
1 teaspoon caraway seeds
Grated rind and juice of 1 lemon
6 carrots, sliced ¼ inch thick
½ cup sun-dried apricots and
  1 cup dark raisins (optional)

Yogurt and fresh dill for garnish

1. Cook meat in nonstick stockpot until no longer pink.

2. Add remaining ingredients, bring to a boil, reduce heat, and simmer for 1½ to 2 hours.* Taste and adjust seasonings.

3. Serve hot in warm bowls with a dollop of yogurt and a sprinkle of fresh dill.

Per serving: 158 calories; 11.3 gm protein; 4.1 gm fat; 21.7 gm carbohydrate; 2.6 gm fiber; 27 mg cholesterol; 76 mg sodium

* May be prepared in morning before work and simmered in crockpot.

Almond–Broccoli Bisque Ⓠ Ⓜ

Serves: 8 (1 cup = 1 serving)

The subtle addition of a few sliced almonds gives this soup a most interesting taste and texture. Serve larger portions when it is used as a main dish.

16-ounce package frozen broccoli, cauliflower, and carrot mix
1 slice onion
⅓ cup nonfat milk
⅔ cup salt-free chicken broth, defatted
2½ cups nonfat milk
2 tablespoons nonfat powdered milk

2 tablespoons whole-wheat flour
1 teaspoon dried thyme, crushed
1 teaspoon salt-free vegetable seasoning
½ teaspoon Worcestershire sauce
½ cup sliced almonds, toasted*

1. Place frozen vegetables, onion, and ⅓ cup milk in nonmetal casserole. Cover and cook on high in microwave for 11 minutes, or for 15 minutes in covered saucepan over medium heat on the stove. (Stir halfway through cooking.)

2. Combine broth, 2½ cups milk, powdered milk, and flour in 2-quart saucepan and cook over medium heat, stirring until sauce coats spoon.

3. Puree cooked vegetables in blender or food processor and add to thickened milk mixture. Add seasonings and ¼ cup almonds and simmer for 10 minutes.

To Serve: Serve in heated cups or soup bowls and garnish with remaining ¼ cup toasted almonds. To complete meal, serve with whole-wheat rolls and a salad of apple and orange slices with 1 percent fat cottage cheese.

Per serving: 105 calories; 6.4 gm protein; 3.5 gm fat; 13.0 gm carbohydrate; 1.3 gm fiber; 2 mg cholesterol; 80 mg sodium

* Place almonds on shallow baking sheet and toast in preheated 325° oven for 8 minutes, or until lightly brown. Mix frequently. To roast in microwave, see directions on page 9.

Chicken Sub Gum Soup ⓠ

Serves: 8 (1 cup = 1 serving)

The Chinese eat their soups at the end of a meal. The soups are generally quite light.

16-ounce package fresh Chinese
   mixed vegetables,* coarsely
   chopped
2 carrots, thinly sliced with
   vegetable peeler
6 cups salt-free chicken broth,
   defatted

1 teaspoon salt-free vegetable
   seasoning
3 egg whites, slightly beaten
1–2 teaspoons mild soy sauce
⅛ teaspoon white pepper

1. Place vegetables, broth, and vegetable seasoning in saucepan. Bring to a boil, cover, and simmer for 8 to 10 minutes.

2. Over low heat, pour egg whites into soup slowly, stirring to form egg drops.

3. Season with soy sauce and pepper to taste.

To Serve: Serve hot in Oriental soup bowls as a first course or as a last course at a Chinese-style dinner.

Per serving: 57 calories; 3.3 gm protein; 0.1 gm fat; 9.4 gm carbohydrate; 0.7 gm fiber; 0 mg cholesterol; 67 mg sodium

* 2 cups sliced bok choy may be substituted for fresh packaged Chinese vegetables.

Quick Corn Soup ℚ

Serves: 4 (⅔ cup = 1 serving)

After years of adding salt, sugar, and sometimes even MSG, the processors of baby food finally stopped using these unnecessary and damaging additives. The result is a pure and tasty product that doesn't predetermine negative acquired tastes in infants—and one that occasionally provides an acceptable, convenient product we can use in our cooking.

2 4½-ounce jars strained creamed corn
⅔ cup nonfat milk
1¼ cups frozen corn*
1 teaspoon salt-free seasoning
½ teaspoon dried chervil, crushed

½ teaspoon dehydrated onion flakes
3 whole green onions, sliced
½ tomato, seeded and diced
Few drops hot pepper sauce (optional)

1. Combine creamed corn, milk, frozen corn, and seasonings.
2. Cover and simmer for 15 minutes, stirring occasionally.
3. Add green onions, tomatoes, and hot pepper sauce, if desired, just before serving and heat for 5 additional minutes.

Per serving: 111 calories; 4.5 gm protein; 0.5 gm fat; 26.1 gm carbohydrate; 1.9 gm fiber; 1 mg cholesterol; 28 mg sodium

* If canned corn used is not salt-free, about 75 mg of sodium per serving will be added.

Fish Chowder for Two ⓠ

Serves: About 2 cups (1 serving)

This recipe is just for two, a one-dish meal that is both simple and satisfying.

½ small onion, chopped
½ stalk celery, chopped
1 small carrot, chopped
1 small potato, chopped
1½ cups nonfat milk
2 tablespoons nonfat powdered milk
¼ cup water
1 bay leaf
¼ teaspoon dried thyme, crushed

½ teaspoon salt-free vegetable seasoning
Few grains white pepper
Few drops Worcestershire sauce
4 ounces white-fleshed fish, cut into ½-inch cubes*

1 tablespoon chopped parsley or dill for garnish

1. Combine all ingredients except fish and garnish in 1-quart saucepan. Bring to a boil, then reduce heat and simmer for 15 minutes.
2. Add fish, bring to a simmer, and cook 5 to 8 minutes more. Remove bay leaf.

To Serve: Serve hot in warm bowl or chowder cup and garnish with parsley or dill. Pritikin whole-wheat dill bread and fresh seasonal fruit complete your meal.

Per serving: 190 calories; 16 gm protein; 4.0 gm fat; 22.3 gm carbohydrate; 1.0 gm fiber; 27 mg cholesterol; 150 mg sodium

* Frozen fish is quite satisfactory for this dish. Choose one of the following fish: haddock, halibut, sole, or orange roughie.

French Onion Soup Ⓠ

Serves: 6 (1 cup = 1 serving)

Once again our Onion Magic comes to the rescue. If you have none in the freezer, however, the total preparation time and cooking time of this recipe is still no more than 30 minutes.

2 teaspoons extra-virgin olive oil
1½ pounds onions, thinly sliced, or
   2 cups Onion Magic (page 36)*
1 teaspoon salt-free vegetable
   seasoning
1 teaspoon Dijon mustard
6 cups salt-free chicken broth,
   defatted

2 tablespoons dry white wine
1 teaspoon Worcestershire sauce
6 ½-inch rounds sourdough
   baguette, toasted
2 tablespoons grated Parmesan
   cheese

1. Heat oil in nonstick sauté pan.
2. Add onions and vegetable seasoning and sauté over medium heat until onions are lightly browned.
3. Add mustard, chicken broth, wine, and Worcestershire sauce. Bring to a boil. Reduce heat, cover, and simmer for 15 minutes.

To Serve: Spoon hot soup into 6 individual heated ramekins, float toast on top, and sprinkle with Parmesan. Serve immediately. To complete your meal, add Kidney Bean Salad (page 116) and Pineapple Parfait (page 326).

Per serving: 82 calories; 2.5 gm protein; 3.1 gm fat; 11.1 gm carbohydrate; 0.9 gm fiber; 1 mg cholesterol; 64 mg sodium

* If you are using Onion Magic, do not use any olive oil.

Goulash Soup
(Gulyas)

Serves: 8 (2 cups = 1 serving as entrée)

Goulash is a popular Hungarian soup often mistakenly regarded as a stew. There are as many versions as there are cooks—this one is my mother's recipe and I love it. It has a hearty quality and may be served as a main course. It also freezes well and, of course, tastes even better the next day.

2 pounds onions, chopped
3 garlic cloves, minced
2 teaspoons cold-pressed safflower oil
2 pounds top round of beef or flank steak (visible fat removed), cut into ½-inch cubes
2 teaspoons salt-free vegetable seasoning
2 tablespoons Hungarian paprika
Freshly ground black pepper
1 bay leaf
1 tablespoon salt-free tomato paste

2 cups light beer or water
8 cups salt-free vegetable broth or water
1 teaspoon caraway seeds
1 pound baking potatoes, diced
1 large green pepper, seeded and diced
2 ripe tomatoes, peeled, seeded, and diced, or 3 canned Italian plum tomatoes

Chopped Italian parsley for garnish

1. Sauté onions and garlic in oil in nonstick sauté pan until transparent.
2. Add beef, vegetable seasoning, paprika, pepper, bay leaf, tomato paste, beer, broth, and caraway seeds. Mix well and bring to a boil.
3. Reduce heat, cover, and simmer for 45 minutes. Stir often.*
4. Add potatoes, green pepper, and tomatoes, and simmer for 30 minutes, or until potatoes are tender.

To Serve: Remove bay leaf. Serve goulash in heated soup bowls and garnish with chopped Italian parsley. Complete your meal with crusty pumpernickel or rye rolls (for dunking), Sweet and Sour Cucumbers (page 114), and a baked pear.

Per serving: 266 calories; 21.7 gm protein; 11.1 gm fat; 18.7 gm carbohydrate; 1.4 gm fiber; 61 mg cholesterol; 62 mg sodium

* This dish may be prepared a day ahead of time up to this point. Or you may complete the cooking process and reheat the following day.

Lentil–Barley Soup

Yield: 16 cups (1 cup = 1 serving)

A hearty, high-fiber soup that is delicious when eaten fresh, the next day, or when reheated after being frozen.

2 cups dried lentils (12 ounces)
½ cup pearl barley
2 teaspoons extra-virgin olive oil
1 large onion, chopped
1 leek (white part only), split, washed, and chopped
4 carrots, chopped
2 celery stalks with leaves, chopped
2 garlic cloves, minced

2 teaspoons salt-free vegetable seasoning
1 teaspoon dried Italian herb blend, crushed
2 bay leaves
Few grains cayenne pepper
28-ounce can crushed Italian plum tomatoes
2½ quarts cold water

1. Rinse and drain lentils and barley.
2. Heat oil in 5-quart stockpot, add onion, and cook until soft, stirring constantly.
3. Add leek, carrots, and celery. Cook 5 minutes.
4. Add garlic, vegetable seasoning, herbs, bay leaves, cayenne pepper, lentils, and barley. Stir well.
5. Add tomatoes and water. Bring to a boil. Cover and simmer slowly for about 1 hour, or until lentils and barley are tender. Remove bay leaves before serving.

Per serving: 133 calories; 7.4 gm protein; 1.0 gm fat; 25.2 gm carbohydrate; 2.2 gm fiber; 0 mg cholesterol; 126 mg sodium

Hong Kong Baron's Table
Fresh Pea Soup ℚ

Serves: 8 (⅔ cup = 1 serving)

Executive Chef Alfred Brugner always has an interesting soup available for those diners who are nutritionally oriented. This is one of my favorites.

3 cups salt-free chicken broth, defatted
1 cup nonfat milk
¼ cup dry white wine or vermouth
1 bay leaf
1 shallot, finely chopped
2 carrots, finely chopped

½ celery stalk, finely chopped
¼ onion, finely chopped
¼ cup leek (white part only), washed and finely chopped
1 shallot, finely chopped
3 cups frozen petit pois

1. Combine broth, milk, wine, bay leaf, and 1 chopped shallot in 2-quart saucepan. Simmer for 10 minutes.

2. While broth mixture is cooking, put carrots, celery, onion, leek, and shallot in a nonstick pan and dry-roast, stirring constantly, until vegetables are lightly browned.

3. Add 2 cups of the peas to simmering broth and cook for 10 minutes more, uncovered. Remove bay leaf and puree this mixture in food processor or blender. Return to saucepan.

4. Add dry roasted vegetables to pureed mixture and cook for 10 minutes.

5. Add remaining 1 cup peas and cook 2 to 3 minutes more.

To Serve: Pour soup into glass cups or bowls to display the lovely green color. Crispy heated pita bread or pumpernickel makes a delicious accompaniment.

Per serving: 92 calories; 4.8 gm protein; 0.3 gm fat; 14.8 gm carbohydrate; 2.7 gm fiber; 1 mg cholesterol; 81 mg sodium

Microwaved Minestrone Ⓜ

Serves: 8 (1 cup = 1 serving)

You don't have to be Italian to love minestrone, but it certainly cuts down on the cooking time of this great soup to use a microwave oven.

1 pound beef bones
5 cups hot water
1 onion, chopped
1 leek (white part only), split, washed, and chopped
½ teaspoon Italian herb blend, crushed
¼ teaspoon freshly ground black pepper
1 teaspoon salt-free vegetable seasoning

3 carrots, diced
16-ounce can Italian plum tomatoes
1 cup shredded green cabbage
2 zucchini, sliced ½ inch thick
16-ounce can salt-reduced kidney beans, drained
½ cup small macaroni or broken spaghetti, cooked and drained

Parmesan cheese as garnish

1. Place first 7 ingredients in 4-quart nonmetal casserole. Cover and cook on high in microwave oven for 25 minutes.
2. Add carrots and tomatoes. Cover and cook on high for 15 minutes. Remove bones.
3. Stir in cabbage, zucchini, and beans. Cover and cook on high for 15 minutes.
4. While soup is cooking, prepare macaroni on stove. Stir cooked pasta into soup; then let soup stand 5 minutes, covered, before serving.

To Serve: Ladle soup into heated bowls, sprinkle with Parmesan, and serve with crusty Italian sesame bread.

Per serving: 111 calories; 5.9 gm protein; 0.6 gm fat; 22.1 gm carbohydrate; 1.6 gm fiber; 0 mg cholesterol; 23 mg sodium

Speedy Tomato–Rice Soup ⓠ

Serves: 4–5 (⅔ cup = 1 serving)

For a zippier flavor, add 1 teaspoon curry powder and a few grains of crushed red pepper to your soup.

2 cups Simply Delicious Tomato
   Sauce (page 41) or canned
   salt-reduced tomato sauce
1 cup water
1 tablespoon frozen unsweetened
   apple juice concentrate
½ teaspoon dried chervil, crushed
1 bay leaf

1 tablespoon cornstarch mixed with
   ¼ cup cold water or salt-free
   chicken broth, defatted
   (optional)
¾ cup cooked brown rice

2 tablespoons chopped parsley for
   garnish

1. Place first 5 ingredients in 1½-quart saucepan. Bring to a boil, reduce heat, cover, and simmer for 15 minutes.

2. Add cornstarch mixture to soup gradually while stirring. Simmer for 5 minutes.

3. Add brown rice and heat for 5 minutes before serving. Remove bay leaf.

To Serve: Serve soup in heated bowls or cups garnished with chopped parsley.

Variation: Both cornstarch and brown rice may be omitted from recipe, resulting in a thinner, lower-calorie soup.

Per serving: 89 calories; 2.7 gm protein; 0.9 gm fat; 17.9 gm carbohydrate; 1.6 gm fiber; 0 mg cholesterol; 25 mg sodium

Manhattan-Style Tuna Chowder ⓠ

Serves: 4 (1½ cups = 1 main-dish serving)

I use kitchen shears to make cuts in canned tomatoes—an easy way of chopping.

1½ teaspoons cold-pressed
   safflower oil
1 small onion, chopped
1 celery stalk with leaves, chopped
1 carrot, chopped
1 small potato, chopped
1 garlic clove, minced
1 zucchini, chopped
28-ounce can Italian plum
   tomatoes with juice, chopped

7½-ounce can salt-reduced tuna in
   water, drained and flaked
1 cup salt-free chicken broth or
   water
2 tablespoons chopped parsley
1 teaspoon Worcestershire sauce
1 cup frozen peas (optional)

1 tablespoon chopped parsley for
   garnish

1. In 4-quart saucepan, heat oil with onion, celery, carrot, potato, and garlic. Cook until tender, about 10 minutes, stirring occasionally.
2. Add zucchini, tomatoes, tuna, chicken broth, parsley, and Worcestershire sauce. Bring to a boil over high heat.
3. Reduce heat and simmer for 20 minutes before serving.

To Serve: Pour hot soup into warm bowls, garnish with parsley, and serve with crisp sourdough rolls.

Per serving: 156 calories; 17.6 gm protein; 2.7 gm fat; 15.3 gm carbohydrate; 1.8 gm fiber; 33 mg cholesterol; 72 mg sodium

Superb Vegetable Chowder Ⓜ

Yield: 16 cups (1 cup = 1 serving)

A flavorful, hearty vegetable chowder is so welcome on cold winter nights. Freeze the unused portions in 1-cup servings for future convenience.

4 cups salt-free chicken or
    vegetable stock or water
½ cup nonfat powdered milk
10-ounce package frozen lima
    beans
10-ounce package frozen corn
1½ celery stalks with leaves,
    chopped
1 medium carrot, chopped
1 medium onion, chopped
1 large baking potato, chopped

16-ounce can salt-reduced stewed
    tomatoes
2 garlic cloves, chopped
1 bay leaf
2 teaspoons salt-free vegetable
    seasoning
1 teaspoon dried basil, crushed, or
    1 tablespoon chopped fresh basil

1 tablespoon finely chopped
    cilantro or parsley for garnish

1. Combine all ingredients except basil and cilantro in large saucepan and bring to a boil. Reduce heat and simmer until vegetables are tender, for about 40 to 45 minutes.

2. Remove bay leaf; place half the mixture in blender and puree. Return to saucepan; add basil and mix thoroughly. Simmer about 10 minutes more.

To Serve: Serve soup in heated bowls with chopped cilantro as garnish; accompany with crisp Wasa bread.

In Microwave: Place lima beans, corn, celery, carrot, onion, and potato in 3-quart casserole. Cook on high for 12 to 15 minutes, stirring once. Add the remaining ingredients, except basil and cilantro. Simmer for 12 minutes and proceed with Step 2.

Per serving: 72 calories; 3.8 gm protein; 0.2 gm fat; 14.0 gm carbohydrate; 1.2 gm fiber; 1 mg cholesterol; 37 mg sodium

Monday's Soup @

Serves: 4 (2 cups = 1 serving)

This low-calorie supper may help make up for some of your gourmandizing over the weekend.

3 10½-ounce cans salt-free chicken broth, defatted
2 teaspoons salt-free vegetable seasoning
1 teaspoon dried dill
1 teaspoon Italian herb blend, crushed
½ teaspoon white pepper
2 medium carrots, chopped
½ onion or 5 whole green onions, chopped
¼ pound mushrooms, cleaned and sliced
2 celery stalks with leaves, chopped
1 medium zucchini, sliced
¼ pound fresh snow peas or frozen peas
3 stalks Swiss chard or ½ 10-ounce package frozen chopped spinach
1 tomato, peeled, seeded, and chopped
Grated Parmesan cheese (optional)

1. Bring broth to a boil in large saucepan with vegetable seasoning, dill, herb blend, and pepper.
2. Spray nonstick skillet with nonstick cooking spray; add carrots and onions and stir-fry over medium heat for 3 minutes, or until barely tender.
3. Add carrots, onions, and mushrooms to broth. Cook for 15 minutes.
4. Add celery, zucchini, snow peas, and Swiss chard or spinach. Cook until barely tender and still crisp.
5. Add tomato and cook for 3 to 5 minutes. Taste and adjust seasonings.
To Serve: Place soup in warm soup bowls and sprinkle each bowl with 1 teaspoon Parmesan cheese if desired. Accompany with crisp brown rice crackers and a fresh apple or orange.

Per serving: 105 calories; 5.5 gm protein; 0.6 gm fat; 19.4 gm carbohydrate; 3.4 gm fiber; 0 mg cholesterol; 95 mg sodium

Quick Vegetable–Barley Soup ⓠ

Serves: 4 (1 cup = 1 serving)

Barley is a much-neglected but nutritious whole grain, usually associated with long, slow cooking. With this quick-cooking variety, you can enjoy a homemade barley soup in minutes.

1 small onion, quartered
½ green pepper, seeded and
  quartered
2 carrots, quartered
4 mushrooms, cleaned and halved
1 celery stalk, quartered
1 garlic clove
1 teaspoon cold-pressed safflower
  oil

3 10½-ounce cans salt-free chicken
  broth, defatted
½ cup quick-cooking barley
2 teaspoons salt-free vegetable
  seasoning
½ teaspoon white pepper
½ teaspoon dried thyme, crushed
½ teaspoon dried marjoram,
  crushed

1. Chop onion, green pepper, carrots, mushrooms, celery, and garlic in food processor or blender.
2. Place oil in 2-quart saucepan. Add vegetables and sauté for 3 minutes over moderate heat, stirring constantly.
3. Add remaining ingredients.
4. Bring to a boil, cover, and simmer for 20 minutes. Stir occasionally.
To Serve: Serve soup in heated bowls with hearty whole-wheat, rye, or pumpernickel bread.

Per serving: 157 calories; 4.0 gm protein; 1.7 gm fat; 30.3 gm carbohydrate; 2.9 gm fiber; 0 mg cholesterol; 29 mg sodium

Salmon–Leek Bisque ⓠ

Serves: 8 (1¼ cups = 1 serving)

A one-dish meal is always a welcome addition to one's recipe collection. This tasty chowder provides an easy answer to a winter evening's supper by the fire. Since it is the main dish, we serve a 10-ounce portion.

15½-ounce can salmon, skinned, boned, drained, and flaked (save ¼ cup of drained liquid)
1 onion, chopped
1 leek (white part only), split, washed, and chopped
2 cups chopped baking potatoes
1 cup chopped celery with leaves or 2 tablespoons dehydrated celery flakes
10-ounce package frozen mixed vegetables

3 cups nonfat milk
½ cup nonfat powdered milk
13-ounce can nonfat evaporated milk
2 teaspoons salt-free vegetable seasoning
¼ teaspoon white pepper
2 tablespoons dry sherry (optional)

3 tablespoons chopped dill for garnish

1. In 4-quart nonstick saucepan, sauté chopped onion and leek in ¼ cup salmon liquid until transparent.
2. Add potatoes and celery. Stir, cover, and cook over low heat for 5 to 10 minutes.
3. Add drained salmon, frozen vegetables, nonfat milk, powdered milk, evaporated milk, and seasonings. Cover and simmer for 15 minutes.
5. Add sherry, if desired, and simmer 5 minutes.
To Serve: Place in warmed tureen, sprinkle with chopped dill, and serve bisque in warm bowls. This main-dish meal can be completed with hearty whole-wheat rolls, a crisp green salad, and Pineapple Ambrosia (page 326) as a dessert.

Per serving: 195 calories; 19.4 gm protein; 2.2 gm fat; 24.1 gm carbohydrate; 0.6 gm fiber; 21 mg cholesterol; 184 mg sodium

Yummy Yam Soup

Serves: 6 (1 cup = 1 serving)

2 leeks (white part only), split and washed

1 tablespoon cold-pressed safflower oil

1 pound yams, peeled and thinly sliced

4 cups water or salt-free vegetable broth

1 tablespoon dehydrated vegetable flakes

½ teaspoon dried thyme, crushed

½ cup nonfat powdered milk

1 tablespoon lemon juice

⅛ teaspoon white pepper

1 tablespoon dry sherry (optional)

Coarsely shredded apple with skin for garnish

1. Sauté leeks in oil in 4-quart saucepan until soft.
2. Add yams, cover, and sauté for 5 minutes.
3. Add water, vegetable flakes, and thyme. Bring to a boil; reduce heat and simmer, covered, for 25 minutes, or until yams are tender. Stir occasionally.
4. Puree vegetables in blender or food processor.
5. Return to saucepan; add milk, lemon juice, pepper, and, if desired, sherry. Heat for 5 minutes more.

To Serve: Place warm soup in cups garnished with shredded apple. Finn Crisp crackers are a tasty accompaniment.

Per serving: 158 calories; 5.1 gm protein; 2.5 gm fat; 29.3 gm carbohydrate; 3.4 gm fiber; 2 mg cholesterol; 64 mg sodium

Cold Soups

The Best Beet Borscht Ⓠ Ⓜ

Serves: 6 (1 cup = 1 serving)

The color is sensational, and so is the taste!

6 small beets, steamed, peeled, and
  chopped (about 3 cups)
3 cups cold buttermilk (strained to
  remove fat globules)
1 cup cold nonfat milk
¼ teaspoon white pepper

1 teaspoon dried dill or
  1 tablespoon chopped fresh dill

Nonfat yogurt and chives for
  garnish

1. Place beets in food processor or blender and process until smooth.
2. Pour into bowl and add buttermilk and milk gradually, stirring until well blended. Add pepper and dill.
3. Chill in freezer for 20 to 30 minutes before serving or chill in refrigerator for several hours or overnight.

To Serve: Pour into tall, chilled glasses, add a dollop of yogurt, and sprinkle with chives.

In Microwave: Cook beets on high with ½ cup water in covered container for 10 minutes.

Per serving: 80 calories; 6.0 gm protein; 1.2 gm fat; 11.1 gm carbohydrate; 0.4 gm fiber;
6 mg cholesterol; 175 mg sodium

Hot or Cold
Curried Broccoli Bisque ⓠ

Serves: 5–6 (1 cup = 1 serving)

To vary this recipe, you may use 2 cups of cooked carrots, squash, or any leftover cooked vegetables except beets.

1 pound broccoli, stems peeled and cut into chunks with flowerets
1 slice onion
3 cups nonfat milk

1½ teaspoons salt-free vegetable seasoning
¼ teaspoon white pepper
1 teaspoon curry powder, or to taste

1. Place broccoli, onion, and milk in saucepan.
2. Bring to a boil, then reduce heat and simmer. Cover and cook for 20 minutes, or until vegetables are tender.
3. Remove broccoli and onion with slotted spoon. Place in food processor or blender and puree.
4. Add milk to pureed mixture while blending.
5. Add vegetable seasoning, white pepper, and curry to taste.
6. Serve hot or chill several hours or overnight before serving.

Per serving: 90 calories; 6.4 gm protein; 3.2 gm fat; 10.3 gm carbohydrate; 1.1 gm fiber; 10 mg cholesterol; 86 mg sodium

Cold Carrot Soup

Serves: 6 (1 cup = 1 serving)

The color is an enticement; the flavor proves it's as good as it looks.

3 tablespoons nonfat milk
4 whole green onions, sliced
3 cups sliced carrots (preferably those with greens attached, not carrots in plastic bags)
½ teaspoon ground ginger
¼ teaspoon ground cinnamon
⅛ teaspoon white pepper
1 teaspoon salt-free vegetable seasoning

1 tablespoon whole-wheat flour
2 cups water
1½ cups orange juice
½ cup nonfat yogurt, mixed until smooth

Freshly grated nutmeg and 4 fresh orange slices for garnish

1. Heat milk in nonstick saucepan; add onions and cook for 2 to 3 minutes.
2. Stir in carrots and seasonings; cook 3 minutes, add flour, mix, and cook for 1 minute. (*Do not brown.*)
3. Add water and orange juice, bring to a boil, then simmer until tender, about 20 minutes.
4. Cool slightly and puree (in batches if necessary) in food processor or blender until smooth.
5. Pour into bowl, add yogurt, and whisk until smooth.
6. Cover and refrigerate overnight or place in freezer for 30 minutes. Taste and adjust seasonings *when thoroughly chilled.*

To Serve: Ladle into chilled glass or white bowls, sprinkle with freshly grated nutmeg, and garnish each bowl with an orange slice. Accompany with whole-wheat Melba toast.

Per serving: 76 calories; 2.9 gm protein; 0.3 gm fat; 16.5 gm carbohydrate; 1.3 gm fiber; 1 mg cholesterol; 39 mg sodium

Chilled Cantaloupe Soup ⓠ

Serves: 8 (⅔ cup = 1 serving)

A refreshing soup to serve in season only. It makes a festive brunch or luncheon dish. Take care that your melons are ripe and sweet; otherwise, the soup will be lacking in taste.

2 very ripe cold large cantaloupes, peeled, seeded, and chopped
1 cup orange juice
½ cup dry sherry
2 tablespoons lime juice

½ teaspoon freshly grated nutmeg
3 tablespoons nonfat milk or yogurt

½ cup blueberries and fresh mint for garnish

1. Puree cantaloupe in blender or food processor.
2. Add orange juice, sherry, lime juice, and nutmeg. Add milk or yogurt. Taste and adjust seasonings.
3. Refrigerate several hours before serving. (Or chill in freezer to shorten time, stirring occasionally.)

To Serve: Make a spectacular presentation by serving soup in small cantaloupe or melon shells. Garnish with a few berries and a sprig of fresh mint.

Per serving: 106 calories; 2.3 gm protein; 0.7 gm fat; 21.2 gm carbohydrate; 0.7 gm fiber; 0 mg cholesterol; 23 mg sodium

Easy Gazpacho ℚ

Serves: 6 (⅔ cup = 1 serving)

No peeled, seeded tomatoes—just a few choice vegetables in a blender or food processor. Salt-free tomato juice or V-8 juice may be used instead of stewed tomatoes.

**2 16-ounce cans salt-reduced
  stewed tomatoes**
½ cucumber, peeled and seeded
½ green pepper, seeded
1 garlic clove
1 teaspoon extra-virgin olive oil
2 tablespoons red wine vinegar
¼ teaspoon dried oregano, crushed

Dash hot pepper sauce
Freshly ground black pepper
4 ice cubes

**Nonfat yogurt and diced cucumber,
  green and red pepper, and green
  onions for garnish (optional)**

1. Place drained tomatoes, cucumber, green pepper, and garlic in food processor or blender. Puree until smooth.
2. Add remaining tomato juice, olive oil, vinegar, oregano, hot pepper sauce, and pepper. Blend.
3. Pour into bowl, add ice cubes, cover, and chill in refrigerator for 20 minutes or more (stir occasionally while chilling).
To Serve: Pour into chilled glasses, coffee mugs, or wine glasses and garnish with a dollop of yogurt and diced vegetables if desired.

Helpful Hint: Taste and adjust seasonings before serving. Chilled soups need heavier seasoning.

Per serving: 43 calories; 1.6 gm protein; 1.2 gm fat; 8.1 gm carbohydrate; 1.5 gm fiber; 0 mg cholesterol; 22 mg sodium

Minted Pea Soup in Minutes ⓠ

Serves: 4 (⅔ cup = 1 serving)

1 teaspoon cold-pressed safflower
  oil
2 tablespoons chopped onion
½ cup salt-free chicken broth,
  defatted
1 cup frozen peas
1 cup romaine or butter lettuce,
  shredded
2 tablespoons chopped parsley

1 sprig mint
½ cup salt-free chicken broth,
  defatted
½ cup nonfat milk or yogurt
Salt-free vegetable seasoning and
  white pepper to taste

Chopped mint or chives for garnish

1. Put oil, onions, and ½ cup broth into saucepan. Cook for 3 minutes, or until onions are soft.

2. Add peas, lettuce, parsley, and mint.

3. Cover and cook for 3 minutes.

4. Add ½ cup broth and bring to a boil.

5. Remove from heat, cool, and blend in food processor or blender until smooth.

6. Add milk or yogurt and blend.

7. Heat for 2 minutes to serve hot, or chill in freezer or refrigerator to serve cold.

To Serve: Whether served hot or cold, with mint or chives, this soup is attractive presented in white or glass coffee mugs.

Per serving: 62 calories; 3.6 gm protein; 1.4 gm fat; 8.7 gm carbohydrate; 1.7 gm fiber; 1 mg cholesterol; 54 mg sodium

Fresh Tomato Soup ⓠ

Serves: 8 (1 cup = 1 serving)

A light summer soup—best prepared in August or September when fresh tomatoes are at their peak and rich with flavor.

6 ripe tomatoes, peeled, seeded, and sliced
1 celery stalk, sliced
½ knob celeriac, peeled and sliced
1 Walla Walla, Vidalia, or white onion, sliced
1 cup water

3 cups salt-free chicken broth, defatted
Few drops hot pepper sauce
1 teaspoon salt-free vegetable seasoning

Chopped dill for garnish

1. Combine vegetables and water in 4-quart saucepan.
2. Bring to a boil, then simmer for 15 to 20 minutes, or until tender.
3. Puree in food processor or blender. Transfer to bowl.
4. Add broth and mix well. Taste and adjust seasonings.

To Serve: The soup may be served the next day either hot or cold.

Variation: Place 1 large sliced orange with skin in food processor or blender. Puree with ½ cup dry white wine. Strain this mixture and add to soup. The result is an interesting combination of flavors.

Per serving: 36 calories; 1.5 gm protein; 0.3 gm fat; 6.9 gm carbohydrate; 0.3 gm fiber; 0 mg cholesterol; 17 mg sodium

Salads

EASY AND ELEGANT

Artichoke and Mushroom Salad
Antipasto Salad
Artichoke, Mushroom, and
  Hearts of Palm Salad
Warm Asparagus Salad
Black-Eyed Pea and Bean Salad
Orangey Beet and Pea Salad
Broccoli, Tomato, and Onion Salad
Greg's Christmas Broccoli Salad
Cauliflower, Crabmeat, and Pea
  Salad
Ever-Ready Red Cabbage Slaw
Chicken Salad Spread
Inscrutable Chinese Chicken Salad
Minced Chicken and Napa
  Cabbage Salad
Chicken–Vegetable Salad
Mandarin Waldorf Salad
Oriental Coleslaw
Harriet's Cobb Salad
Sweet and Sour Cucumbers
Slimmer's Fruit Plate with Fruited
  Yogurt Dressing
Kidney Bean Salad
Two-Pea Salad
Lentil Salad

Hot and Cold Mixed Green Salad
Niçoise Salad in a Sandwich
Red Raspberry and Cottage Cheese
  Salad
Red and Green Slaw
Sea-Fruit Salad
Sweet Potato Salad
Tuna Salad Supreme
Singaporian Waldorf Salad
Tomato Stuffed with Cucumber
  and Fish Salad
"You-Name-It" Salad
Sarah's Hungarian Wilted Salad
Warm Sliced Chicken Salad
Harriet F's Potato Salad Vinaigrette
Sally's Hearts of Palm and Corn
  Salad
Almost Santo Pietro's Salad
Tomato–Rice Salad
Almost Ken's Salad
Red Russian Salad
All-Seasons Freezer Vegetable
  Salad
Mushroom, Snow Pea, and Tomato
  Salad
Julienne Vegetable Salad

A Few Salad Dressings

Cucumber–Dill Dressing
Creamy Garlic Dressing

Pear Vinaigrette Dressing
Fresh Orange Dressing
Fresh Tomato Vinaigrette Dressing

Not so long ago, it was believed that real men didn't eat salads. Today, we realize the importance of the nutritional value of salads in addition to enjoying their taste appeal.

Salads are one of the most versatile courses we prepare. Because of the advances in both agriculture and transportation, they are no longer seasonal. They may be served as an appetizer or first course, entrée, or accompaniment, or dessert. They may be enjoyed hot or cold. Their content includes not only vegetables, fruits, pasta and grains, but fish and poultry as well. In addition to supplying us with vitamins, minerals, and fiber, they also may be especially good sources of inexpensive protein. When served as a first course or appetizer, they excite our appetites or satisfy immediate hunger with a minimum of calories. As an entrée, they may be served hot or cold, and they contain ingredients to fulfill many dietary requirements, including protein.

As an accompaniment, they add endless diversity to our meals. You will find salads of all descriptions in the following pages. Your taste may lean toward a hearty Antipasto Salad (page 101), delicate Sea-Fruit Salad (page 121), a simple Warm Asparagus Salad (page 103), or a more exotic Hot and Cold Mixed Green Salad (page 118). There are over 40 salad recipes from which you may choose. Hopefully, they will stimulate not only your palate but your creativity as well.

Artichoke and Mushroom Salad ⓠ

Serves: 4

Two of my favorite ingredients blend well to make a delicious salad.

10-ounce can quartered artichoke
hearts, rinsed and drained
12 large mushrooms, cleaned and
sliced
1 red pepper, seeded and diced, or
4-ounce jar chopped pimiento,
drained

¼ cup low-calorie vinaigrette
dressing of your choice
8 leaves Boston lettuce, washed,
dried, and chilled

1. Place artichoke hearts, mushrooms, and red pepper or pimiento in bowl with dressing. Combine thoroughly and chill for 20 minutes.

To Serve: Arrange mound of mixture on each of 4 lettuce-lined salad plates.

Per serving: 50 calories; 3.1 gm protein; 0.5 gm fat; 10.6 gm carbohydrate; 1.4 gm fiber; 0 mg cholesterol; 46 mg sodium

Antipasto Salad Ⓠ

Serves: 8 (1 cup = 1 serving)

Most of the time we think of antipasto as a first course. This combination of ingredients makes a delicious salad entrée.

7½-ounce can salt-reduced tuna in water, drained
16-ounce can salt-reduced garbanzo beans, drained
16-ounce can salt-reduced kidney beans, drained
½ cup chopped celery
½ small red onion, finely chopped
½ green pepper, seeded and chopped

1 large carrot, chopped
10-ounce can quartered artichoke hearts, rinsed and drained
8 cherry tomatoes, halved
¾ cup low-calorie Italian dressing plus 1 garlic clove, minced
4 cups shredded romaine lettuce

2 tablespoons chopped parsley for garnish

1. Combine first 9 ingredients in large bowl. Toss lightly.
2. Add salad dressing and chill for 20 to 30 minutes before serving.
To Serve: Place salad on bed of shredded romaine and sprinkle lightly with chopped parsley. Crisp sourdough rolls and fresh fruit complete the meal.

Per serving: 253 calories; 20 gm protein; 2.5 gm fat; 40.5 gm carbohydrate; 3 gm fiber; 17 mg cholesterol; 57 mg sodium

Artichoke, Mushroom, and Hearts of Palm Salad Ⓠ

Serves: 8

How could all of these savory ingredients produce anything but a luscious salad?

10-ounce can quartered artichoke
   hearts, rinsed and drained
¼ pound mushrooms, cleaned and
   sliced
2 cups sliced hearts of palm
4 whole green onions, thinly sliced
¼ cup chopped parsley
2 tablespoons light mayonnaise
½ cup nonfat yogurt
1 teaspoon salt-free vegetable
   seasoning

1 garlic clove, minced
1 tablespoon dry white wine
1 tablespoon chopped fresh basil or
   1 teaspoon Italian herb blend,
   crushed
¼ teaspoon white pepper

Cherry tomatoes and watercress
   for garnish

1. Toss the first 5 ingredients in a bowl.
2. Combine remaining ingredients except garnish in small bowl; blend thoroughly.
3. Add dressing to vegetable mixture and mix gently with fork.

To Serve: Mound on individual salad plates and garnish with sprays of watercress and cherry tomatoes.

Variation: Leftover cooked shredded chicken may be added to the salad so that it may be served as an entrée for lunch or supper.

Per serving: 41 calories; 2.5 gm protein; 0.4 gm fat; 8.0 gm carbohydrate; 0.8 gm fiber; 2 mg cholesterol; 61 mg sodium

Warm Asparagus Salad ⓠ

Serves: 4

I came upon this recipe quite accidentally one evening when I forgot to chill my asparagus after steaming. The resulting salad has proved to be one of my very favorites. Of course, it can be served as a vegetable also.

1–1½ pounds asparagus, washed
  and peeled*
¼ cup low-calorie Italian dressing
1½ tablespoons grated Parmesan
  cheese

4-ounce jar roasted red pepper or
  pimiento, drained and thinly
  sliced, for garnish

1. Lay asparagus on steamer basket or rack and place in skillet with 1 inch boiling water.
2. Cover and steam for 7 to 10 minutes, depending on the thickness of the stalk. *Do not overcook.*
3. Using a slotted spoon, drain and remove asparagus to serving platter. Drizzle salad dressing over asparagus.
4. Sprinkle with Parmesan cheese and garnish with slices of roasted pepper or pimiento.
5. Serve immediately as a first course, salad, or as a vegetable with your entrée.

Per serving: 48 calories; 5.3 gm protein; 0.5 gm fat; 7 gm carbohydrate; 1.7 gm fiber; 1.5 mg cholesterol; 40 mg sodium

* Select asparagus that are firm, straight, and green, with closed tops. Break off tough ends of stalk.

Black-Eyed Pea and Bean Salad ⓠ

Serves: 8 (½ cup = 1 serving)

A hearty, high-protein salad that may be served year round.

16-ounce package frozen
  black-eyed peas, cooked and
  drained
16-ounce package frozen
  French-cut green beans, cooked
  and drained
1 medium red onion, thinly sliced
1 cucumber, peeled, seeded, and
  diced

6 red radishes, thinly sliced
¼ cup chopped parsley
Romaine lettuce leaves
2 tablespoons toasted sesame seeds

6 cherry tomatoes, halved, for
  garnish

Vinaigrette Dressing:
1 tablespoon coarse-grained
  mustard
3 tablespoons white wine vinegar
1 tablespoon Balsamic vinegar
½ cup salt-free chicken broth,
  defatted

1 garlic clove, minced
Few drops hot pepper sauce
1 tablespoon extra-virgin olive oil
  (optional)

1. Combine peas, beans, onion, cucumber, radishes, and parsley in bowl.
2. Combine all dressing ingredients in jar. Shake well.
3. Toss vegetable mixture with Vinaigrette Dressing, cover, and chill.
To Serve: Place salad in romaine-lined bowl, sprinkle with sesame seeds, and garnish with cherry tomato halves.

Per serving: 120 calories; 6.7 gm protein; 1.8 gm fat; 21.2 gm carbohydrate; 2.6 gm fiber;
0 mg cholesterol; 16 mg sodium

Orangey Beet and Pea Salad ⓠ

Serves: 4 (⅔ cup = 1 serving)

Defrost frozen peas by placing them in a colander and running hot water over them for 30 seconds.

2 cups sliced cooked beets
⅓ cup Fresh Orange Dressing
  (page 139)

1 cup defrosted frozen peas
2 cups shredded lettuce

1. Marinate beets in dressing and chill for 20 minutes.
2. Add peas, toss lightly, and serve.
To Serve: Spoon salad mixture on bed of shredded lettuce on individual salad plates.

Per serving: 80 calories; 3.3 gm protein; 2.3 gm fat; 13.2 gm carbohydrate; 2.4 gm fiber; 0 mg cholesterol; 85 mg sodium

Broccoli, Tomato, and Onion Salad ⓠ

Serves: 4

An easy salad that is easy on the eye.

8 leaves romaine lettuce
12 ripe tomato slices
8 broccoli spears, peeled, steamed,
  and chilled in the refrigerator

½ red onion, diced
¼ cup low-calorie vinaigrette or
  Fresh Tomato Vinaigrette
  Dressing (page 139)

1. Place 2 romaine leaves on each salad plate. Arrange 3 tomato slices and 2 broccoli spears on lettuce; sprinkle with diced red onion.
2. Top each serving with 1 tablespoon vinaigrette dressing of your choice.

Per serving: 34 calories; 2.5 gm protein; 0.4 gm fat; 6.9 gm carbohydrate; 1.4 gm fiber; 0 mg cholesterol; 20 mg sodium

Greg's Christmas Broccoli Salad ℚ

Serves: 4

Publicity is not Greg's only forte, as you will soon discover.

1 bunch fresh broccoli, peeled and
  cut into 6-inch lengths and
  steamed until tender-crisp*
1 medium red onion, thinly sliced
1 tablespoon extra-virgin olive oil
Freshly ground black pepper
½ cup Fresh Orange Dressing
  (page 139)

1½ tablespoons finely shredded
  Asiago or Parmesan cheese

Broccoli flowerets and onion rings
  for garnish

1. Coarsely chop broccoli into 1½ to 2-inch pieces.
2. Combine chopped broccoli and sliced onion in salad bowl.
3. Drizzle with olive oil, sprinkle with pepper, and refrigerate.
4. Add salad dressing 15 minutes before serving. Toss lightly with 2 forks to blend.

To Serve: Sprinkle with cheese and garnish with broccoli flowerets and onion rings.

Per serving: 75 calories; 3.7 gm protein; 4.1 gm fat; 8.1 gm carbohydrate; 1.5 gm fiber;
2 mg cholesterol; 62 mg sodium

---

* Save remaining stems to serve as pureed vegetables another day.

Cauliflower, Crabmeat, and Pea Salad ⓠ

Serves: 4

Cauliflower is one of those vegetables that announces itself proudly when it is being cooked. It should be cooked until barely tender or used raw in a salad or with your favorite dip. A member of the cabbage family, it is one of the cruciferous vegetables, recommended by the American Cancer Society.

1 head cauliflower, divided into flowerets and steamed 3 minutes, or until barely tender, then chilled*

1½ cups cooked crabmeat or lobster

4 whole green onions, thinly sliced

3 tablespoons chopped parsley

1 teaspoon chopped fresh tarragon or ½ teaspoon fines herbes, crushed

1 cup defrosted frozen peas

1 cup nonfat yogurt

3 tablespoons light mayonnaise

Butter lettuce or radicchio

Chopped parsley and tomato wedges for garnish (or crab legs for extra-extravagant garnish)

1. Toss first 6 ingredients lightly in bowl.
2. Blend yogurt and mayonnaise and add to mixed ingredients.

To Serve: Arrange lettuce on plate or plates, and mound with salad. Garnish with parsley and tomato wedges.

Helpful Hint: Cauliflower must be served or cooled immediately after cooking. It turns an unappetizing gray color as it stands.

Per serving; 175 calories; 20.7 gm protein; 3.2 gm fat; 16.5 gm carbohydrate; 2.7 gm fiber; 87 mg cholesterol; 305 mg sodium

* Half cauliflowerets and half broccoli flowerets may be substituted for all cauliflower.

Ever-Ready Red Cabbage Slaw ⓠ

Serves: 6

A quick salad that can be prepared from your pantry.

1 small head (1 pound) red
    cabbage, shredded, or 16-ounce
    package shredded red cabbage
7½-ounce can unsweetened
    pineapple tidbits, drained
    (reserve 2 tablespoons juice)

½ cup sliced almonds, toasted in
    oven
½ cup nonfat yogurt
1 tablespoon light mayonnaise

1. Combine cabbage, pineapple, and almonds. Toss lightly.
2. Add blended yogurt, mayonnaise, and pineapple juice. Mix gently
with 2 forks before serving.

Per serving: 99 calories; 3.9 gm protein; 4.7 gm fat; 12.4 gm carbohydrate: 1.6 gm fiber;
2 mg cholesterol; 47 mg sodium

Chicken Salad Spread ⓠ

Yield: 2½ cups spread (½ cup = 1 serving)

A quick sandwich fix for the lunch box or a late supper.

2 cups shredded cooked chicken
    (or turkey)
2 whole green onions, cut into
    pieces
3 tablespoons salt-free chicken
    broth, defatted
2 tablespoons light mayonnaise
3 tablespoons nonfat yogurt

1 teaspoon salt-free vegetable
    seasoning
½ teaspoon Worcestershire sauce
½ teaspoon pure vanilla extract
¼ cup slivered almonds, toasted in
    oven
⅓ cucumber, peeled, seeded, and
    coarsely chopped

1. Process chicken, green onions, and broth in blender or food processor until chunky.
2. Add remaining ingredients and process until minced.

To Serve: Spread on hearty whole-wheat bread, buns, or pita bread. Top with sliced beefsteak tomato, shredded romaine, and, if available, alfalfa sprouts. Accompany with carrot and green pepper sticks, a cold glass of nonfat milk, and a crunchy red apple.

Per serving: 154 calories; 17.9 gm protein; 7.5 gm fat; 3.5 gm carbohydrate; 0.7 gm fiber; 50 mg cholesterol; 65 mg sodium

Inscrutable Chinese Chicken Salad Ⓠ

Serves: 8

I think there are as many recipes around for chicken salad as there are people in China—well, maybe that's a bit of an exaggeration.

8 cups shredded green leaf lettuce
2 cups shredded roast chicken

8-ounce can Mandarin orange segments in water, drained

Salad Dressing:
⅓ cup red wine vinegar
⅓ cup frozen unsweetened apple juice concentrate
3 tablespoons orange juice
1 teaspoon grated orange rind
3 tablespoons salt-free chicken broth, defatted
Few flakes crushed red pepper
¼ teaspoon pure vanilla extract

½ teaspoon ground ginger
1 tablespoon sesame oil
2–3 ounces wonton skins, cut into strips and lightly toasted in a 350° oven
⅓ cup sliced almonds, toasted in oven
2 tablespoons sesame seeds, toasted in dry skillet

1. Toss lettuce, chicken, and Mandarin orange segments in large bowl.
2. Combine dressing ingredients in jar. Shake vigorously.
3. Add dressing to salad ingredients and toss lightly with 2 forks.
4. Sprinkle with toasted wonton strips, almonds, and sesame seeds.

Per serving: 179 calories; 12.7 gm protein; 7.8 gm fat; 14.5 gm carbohydrate; 0.8 gm fiber; 38 mg cholesterol; 95 mg sodium

Minced Chicken
and Napa Cabbage Salad
(From Scratch Restaurant)

Serves: 4

Marinated minced chicken served on a bed of Napa cabbage and garnished with colorful raw vegetables.

Marinade:

1 tablespoon peeled, grated fresh ginger or 1 teaspoon powdered ginger

1 garlic clove, minced

½ cup frozen unsweetened pineapple juice concentrate

2 tablespoons mild soy sauce

½ teaspoon Chinese five-spice seasoning

Few flakes crushed red pepper

4 5-ounce raw chicken thighs, skinned, boned, visible fat removed, and diced

2 teaspoons sesame oil

6 cups shredded Napa (Chinese) cabbage

½ cup dry white wine

2 tablespoons red wine vinegar

8 snow peas, 2 whole green onions, ½ sweet red pepper, seeded, and 1 carrot, all cut into thin strips, for garnish

1. Place ginger, garlic, pineapple juice, soy sauce, five-spice seasoning, red pepper, and diced chicken in a plastic bag or bowl. Marinate for 20 minutes.

2. Add sesame oil to nonstick skillet; heat and add drained chicken. (Save marinade.) Stir-fry chicken for 3 to 5 minutes. Remove chicken and keep warm.

3. Divide shredded cabbage among 4 dinner plates. Top with warm chicken.

4. Add wine, vinegar, and remaining marinade to skillet and simmer for 3 minutes. Drizzle over top of chicken and cabbage.

5. Garnish with assorted julienne vegetables.

To Serve: This is an elegant one-dish meal served with crisp rolls and a Blueberry Blintz for dessert (page 359).

Per serving: 223 calories; 16.6 gm protein; 8.7 gm fat; 15.2 gm carbohydrate; 1.3 gm fiber; 54 mg cholesterol; 216 mg sodium

Chicken–Vegetable Salad ⓠ

Serves: 4 (1 cup = 1 serving)

Any leftover steamed vegetables may be substituted for frozen mixed vegetables.

2 cups skinned and boned, cooked diced chicken or turkey breast
1½ cups mixed frozen vegetables, steamed
½ green pepper, seeded and diced
1 tablespoon chopped parsley
1 teaspoon salt-free vegetable seasoning

1 teaspoon Hungarian paprika
½ cup low-calorie vinaigrette dressing
Red leaf lettuce leaves for serving

8 tomato wedges and 8 steamed asparagus spears for garnish

1. Mix chicken with mixed vegetables and green pepper.
2. Add parsley, vegetable seasoning, paprika, and vinaigrette dressing. Toss lightly.
3. Cover with plastic wrap and chill for 20 to 30 minutes before serving.
To Serve: Arrange on red lettuce leaves and garnish with tomato wedges and asparagus spears.

Per serving: 168 calories; 23.8 gm protein; 3.4 gm fat; 9.8 gm carbohydrate; 1.1 gm fiber; 60 mg cholesterol; 82 mg sodium

Mandarin Waldorf Salad ⓠ

Serves: 6 (1 cup = 1 serving)

Three high-fiber ingredients are blended into a flavorful salad.

4 cups shredded green or red
    cabbage (about 1 pound)*
11-ounce can Mandarin oranges in
    water, drained
1 large red Delicious apple with
    skin, cored and diced

½ cup dark raisins
1 teaspoon celery seeds (optional)
⅔ cup nonfat yogurt mixed with
    1 teaspoon pure vanilla extract

1. Combine cabbage, Mandarin oranges, apple, raisins, and celery seed.
2. Add yogurt, tossing together until all ingredients are well mixed and well coated.
To Serve: Pile lightly on reserved red or green cabbage leaves.

Per serving: 82 calories; 2.2 gm protein; 0.4 gm fat; 19.2 gm carbohydrate; 2.3 gm fiber;
0 mg cholesterol; 24 mg sodium

* Set aside 6 cabbage leaves before shredding.

Oriental Coleslaw ⓠ

Serves: 8 (⅔ cup = 1 serving)

1 pound Napa (Chinese) cabbage,
    shredded
3 large carrots, shredded
5 or 6 whole green onions, sliced
1 cup snow peas
2 tablespoons minced cilantro or
    parsley
¼ cup frozen unsweetened apple
    juice concentrate

3 tablespoons brown rice vinegar
1 teaspoon peeled and minced fresh
    ginger or ½ teaspoon ground
    ginger
1 tablespoon mild soy sauce
2 teaspoons sesame oil
3 tablespoons light mayonnaise

1. Combine cabbage, carrots, green onions, snow peas, and cilantro or parsley.

2. In small bowl, whisk together apple juice, vinegar, ginger, soy sauce, and oil. Gradually combine this mixture with mayonnaise until smoothly blended.

3. Pour dressing over salad mixture, mix gently with fork, cover, and chill for 20 to 30 minutes before serving.

Per serving: 82 calories; 2.1 gm protein; 2.7 gm fat; 14.3 gm carbohydrate; 2.0 gm fiber; 0 mg cholesterol; 105 mg sodium

Harriet's Cobb Salad Q

Serves: 4

Arrange on individual plates and keep chilled until serving time.

6 cups finely chopped assorted
    salad greens (romaine, endive,
    red leaf lettuce, watercress)
2 cups finely chopped cooked
    chicken or turkey
2 ripe tomatoes, seeded and finely
    chopped
1 large green pepper, seeded and
    finely chopped
1 cup peeled, seeded, and finely
    chopped cucumber

3 small cooked beets, chopped
2 tablespoons grated Parmesan
    cheese
½ cup Fresh Tomato Vinaigrette
    Dressing (page 139) or
    low-calorie Italian dressing

4-ounce jar chopped pimiento,
    drained, for garnish

1. For each serving, place one fourth of the chopped greens on a chilled dinner plate. Arrange rows of one fourth turkey, tomato, green pepper, cucumber, and beets on top of greens. Sprinkle each with ½ tablespoon of the Parmesan cheese and drizzle 2 tablespoons of dressing on top. Garnish with pimiento.

Helpful Hint: Chopping the vegetables and turkey in a food processor cuts down on your labor enormously.

Per serving: 190 calories; 26.2 gm protein; 4.8 gm fat; 11.1 gm carbohydrate; 1.4 gm fiber; 55 mg cholesterol; 159 mg sodium

Sweet and Sour Cucumbers ⓠ

Serves: 4 (½ cup = 1 serving)

Served with fish in Scandinavian countries, with chicken in Hungary, and with everything in my house!

½ hothouse cucumber, thinly sliced,* or 1 regular cucumber, peeled, seeded, and sliced
⅓ cup brown rice or cider vinegar
⅓ cup frozen unsweetened apple juice concentrate
1 cup water

Pinch white pepper
3 whole green onions, thinly sliced
½ green pepper, seeded and diced

2 teaspoons dried dill or 2 tablespoons chopped fresh dill for garnish

1. Let sliced cucumber stand for 8 to 10 minutes. Press to remove moisture and pat dry.
2. Combine vinegar, apple juice concentrate, water, and pepper in bowl. Taste and adjust seasonings.
3. Add cucumbers, green onions, and green peppers and mix thoroughly.

To Serve: Place in glass serving bowl and sprinkle with dill. Cover and chill for at least 20 to 30 minutes before serving.

Helpful Hint: This mixture may be stored in a jar in the refrigerator for up to 1 week; its flavor only improves.

Per serving: 56 calories; 0.7 gm protein; 0.2 gm fat; 14.1 gm carbohydrate; 1.3 gm fiber; 0 mg cholesterol; 10 mg sodium

* Hothouse cucumbers have a thin, delicate skin, are unwaxed, and do not have to be seeded. They are generally twice as long as traditional cucumbers, which in most instances are waxed in order to preserve them. If using traditional cucumbers, peel and seed them before shredding.

Slimmer's Fruit Plate
with Fruited Yogurt Dressing ⓠ

Serves: 2 (1 fruit plate and 2 tablespoons dressing = 1 serving)

Of course, a fruit plate is best served in the summer. With modern refrigeration and transportation, however, a wonderful assortment of fresh fruit is made available year round, particularly in larger cities.

Fruited Yogurt Dressing:

¼ cup nonfat yogurt
1 tablespoon orange juice
2 tablespoons crushed pineapple
  or strawberries
Freshly grated nutmeg
Few grains ground cinnamon

8 leaves romaine, shredded
8 1-inch cubes pineapple (fresh or
  canned, unsweetened)
4 1-inch melon cubes
4 1-inch cantaloupe cubes
1 orange, peeled and sliced
8 pear or apple slices
12 green seedless grapes or
  blueberries
12 small strawberries, washed and
  hulled

1. Mix yogurt until smooth. Add fruit juice, crushed fruit, nutmeg, and cinnamon and blend.

2. Place shredded romaine on 2 dinner plates; arrange fruit attractively on romaine and serve with dressing on the side.

Per serving: 174 calories; 6.4 gm protein; 1.2 gm fat; 38 gm carbohydrate; 4.6 gm fiber; 1.5 mg cholesterol; 54 mg sodium

Kidney Bean Salad ⓠ

Serves: 6 (½ cup = 1 serving)

15½-ounce can salt-reduced kidney
  beans, drained
½ cup diced celery
½ cup seeded and diced green
  pepper
2 whites of hard-boiled eggs, sliced

⅓ cup Fresh Tomato Vinaigrette
  Dressing (page 139)
6 red leaf lettuce leaves

2 tablespoons chopped parsley
  for garnish

1. Combine beans, celery, green pepper, and egg whites. Toss lightly to mix.
2. Add Tomato Vinaigrette (or dressing of your choice), stir lightly with fork; cover, and chill for 20 minutes.
3. Line each salad plate with lettuce, spoon mixture on top, and sprinkle with parsley.

Per serving: 80 calories; 5.8 gm protein; 0.4 gm fat; 14.0 gm carbohydrate; 6 gm fiber;
0 mg cholesterol; 29 mg sodium

Two-Pea Salad ⓠ

Serves: 6 (⅔ cup = 1 serving)

If you can't find fresh snow peas, increase the amount of frozen peas to 2½ packages.

½ cup nonfat yogurt
¼ cup chopped fresh dill or
  1 tablespoon dried dill
Freshly ground black pepper
1 teaspoon salt-free vegetable
  seasoning
2 10-ounce packages frozen petit
  pois, defrosted under hot tap
  water for about 30 seconds

1 cup fresh snow peas, stem and
  strings removed
2-ounce jar chopped pimiento,
  drained
4 leaves romaine lettuce, washed
  and dried
¼ cup chopped fresh chives or
  green onions
1 teaspoon chopped mint (optional)

1. Combine yogurt, dill, pepper, and vegetable seasoning in mixing bowl.

2. Add peas, snow peas, and pimiento.

3. Place in glass bowl lined with crisp romaine lettuce leaves.

4. Sprinkle with chives and mint, if desired, cover with plastic wrap, and chill in refrigerator for 15 minutes before serving.

Per serving: 105 calories; 7.3 gm protein; 0.5 gm fat; 18.9 gm carbohydrate; 4.5 gm fiber; 0 mg cholesterol; 104 mg sodium

Lentil Salad

Serves: 8

This seldom-served salad is delicious with cold turkey or chicken.

1 pound lentils, washed and
   drained
5 cups water
1 tablespoon extra-virgin olive oil
Freshly ground black pepper
1 teaspoon salt-free vegetable
   seasoning
1 red onion, finely chopped
1 celery stalk, diced
½ green pepper, seeded and thinly
   sliced

½ sweet red pepper, seeded and
   thinly sliced
½ cup low-calorie Italian dressing
   and 2 tablespoons red wine
   vinegar

2 tablespoons chopped parsley for
   garnish

1. Combine lentils and water in 2-quart saucepan. Bring to a boil, reduce heat, cover, and simmer about 30 minutes, or until just tender.

2. Drain lentils; place in bowl and sprinkle with olive oil, pepper, and vegetable seasoning. Chill.

3. When lentils are cool, add remaining ingredients and marinate in refrigerator for 30 minutes or overnight.

Per serving: 177 calories; 11.5 gm protein; 1.9 gm fat; 29.5 gm carbohydrate; 2.1 gm fiber; 0 mg cholesterol; 19 mg sodium

Hot and Cold
Mixed Green Salad Ⓠ

Serves: 8

A traditional hot spinach salad is wilted with a dressing made of bacon drippings. We substituted hot sautéed mushrooms.

½ pound spinach leaves, washed and dried
1 head Boston lettuce, washed and dried
1 head red leaf lettuce, washed and dried
1 head radicchio, washed and dried
½ small red onion, thinly sliced
2 teaspoons sesame oil
½ pound mushrooms, cleaned and sliced

1 tablespoon lemon juice
2 tablespoons salt-free chicken broth, defatted
¼ cup red wine vinegar
½ teaspoon dried thyme, crushed
1 teaspoon salt-free vegetable seasoning
Freshly ground black pepper
Dash hot pepper sauce (optional)

1. *Tear* spinach and salad greens into bite-sized pieces; add onion slices and place in large salad bowl.

2. Heat oil in nonstick skillet; add mushrooms and lemon juice and cook for 2 to 3 minutes. Stir occasionally.

3. Add broth, vinegar, thyme, vegetable seasoning, pepper, and hot pepper sauce, if desired; heat briefly. Pour hot mushroom mixture over greens. Toss with 2 forks and *serve immediately.*

Per serving: 43 calories; 2.4 gm protein; 2.1 gm fat; 5.3 gm carbohydrate; 1.7 gm fiber; 0 mg cholesterol; 28 mg sodium

Niçoise Salad in a Sandwich ⓠ

Serves: 4 (1 sandwich = 1 serving)

In the Provence region of France, sandwiches are frequently sold in *boulangeries* along with the bread and rolls. When we were traveling there, it was a delight to be able to have a salad sandwich to savor while enjoying the beauty of the countryside. Of course, many times they were dredged with excessive amounts of olive oil, but if we prevailed upon the baker, he was usually only too happy to accommodate our request to limit the oil.

4 round, heavy-crusted French or whole-wheat rolls
2 garlic cloves
2 large ripe tomatoes, sliced ½ inch thick
Freshly ground black pepper
1 small red or white onion, sliced ¼ inch thick
1 small green pepper, seeded and thinly sliced
1 small sweet red pepper, seeded and thinly sliced

3½-ounce can tuna in water, drained
¼ cup low-calorie vinaigrette dressing or Fresh Tomato Vinaigrette Dressing (page 139)
8 leaves Boston lettuce, washed and drained
2 tablespoons thinly sliced fresh basil leaves (optional)

1. Cut rolls in half crosswise and toast bottom halves lightly.
2. While the rolls are still very hot, cut garlic cloves and rub into hot toasted roll (garlic will melt into bread).
3. Layer 2 tomato slices, freshly ground pepper, onion slice, red and green pepper slices, and one quarter of the tuna on bottom halves. Drizzle each with 1 tablespoon salad dressing and top with 2 lettuce leaves and basil.
4. Toast tops of rolls, repeat Step 2, and press down tightly on top of lettuce.
5. Close tightly with rubber band or string and let sit for 5 to 10 minutes before serving.

To Serve: Since the sandwich is rather messy to eat, I like to place it in a waxed paper bag before serving.

Per serving: 165 calories; 12.4 gm protein; 1.4 gm fat; 29.2 gm carbohydrate; 1.9 gm fiber; 16 mg cholesterol; 190 mg sodium

Red Raspberry
and Cottage Cheese Salad ⓠ

Serves: 4 (⅔ cup = 1 serving)

If the raspberries you choose aren't sweet enough, sprinkle them with frozen unsweetened apple juice concentrate before chilling.

½ pint *fresh* red raspberries,
  washed, drained, and chilled
1 pint 1% fat cottage cheese

8 Boston lettuce leaves

1 papaya, peeled and sliced, for
  garnish

Combine chilled raspberries lightly with cottage cheese.
To Serve: Pile lightly on lettuce-lined individual serving plates and garnish with papaya slices.

Per serving: 100 calories; 14.6 gm protein; 1.4 gm fat; 7.3 gm carbohydrate; 1.6 gm fiber; 5 mg cholesterol; 460 mg sodium

Red and Green Slaw ⓠ

Serves: 4 (¾ cup = 1 serving)

A salad that is especially pleasant served with fish.

1 cup shredded red cabbage*
1 cup shredded green cabbage*
½ green pepper, seeded and diced
3 tablespoons nonfat yogurt
1 tablespoon light mayonnaise
1 tablespoon frozen unsweetened
  apple juice concentrate

½ teaspoon Dijon Mustard
½ teaspoon salt-free vegetable
  seasoning
Freshly ground black pepper

1. Place cabbages and pepper in mixing bowl.
2. Blend yogurt, mayonnaise, apple juice concentrate, mustard, vegetable seasoning and pepper.

* Packaged redipac coleslaw may be substituted.

3. Pour over vegetables in bowl and mix lightly with fork.
4. Cover and chill for 20 minutes before serving.

Per serving: 56 calories; 0.8 gm protein; 1.4 gm fat; 11.3 gm carbohydrate; 0.7 gm fiber;
0 mg cholesterol; 39 mg sodium

Sea-Fruit Salad ⓠ

Serves: 2 as an entrée, 4 as an appetizer

Because of the combination of seafood and fruit, no salad dressing is required. Imagine, gastronomic satisfaction without guilt!

1 pink grapefruit, peeled and
  sectioned into segments, or
  16-ounce can unsweetened
  grapefruit segments in juice
2 whole green onions, cut into
  2-inch lengths and slivered
¼ pound fresh bean sprouts,
  washed and drained
1 large tomato, halved, seeded,
  and diced

8 ounces fresh or frozen crabmeat
  or 10-ounce cooked lobster tail,
  cut into chunks
Curly endive or butter lettuce for
  serving

Snow peas and lime wedges for
  garnish

Combine grapefruit, green onions, bean sprouts, tomato, and seafood in bowl. Toss lightly, cover, and chill for 15 minutes.

To Serve as an Entrée: Mound mixture on 2 lettuce-lined salad plates, garnish with 2 or 3 snow peas and a wedge of lime for each.

To Serve as an Appetizer: Divide mixture into 4 portions in glass serving bowls or brandy snifters and garnish with a lime wedge for each.

Per serving: 188 calories; 23.4 gm protein; 2.7 gm fat; 19.7 gm carbohydrate; 2.3 gm fiber;
113 mg cholesterol; 251 mg sodium

Sweet Potato Salad

Serves: 4 (¾ cup = 1 serving)

We rarely think of sweet potatoes when we make potato salad. Try it—new combinations of flavors are always exciting.

3 cups (about 2 pounds) peeled
   and cubed cooked sweet potatoes
1½ cups diced celery
½ cup seeded and diced green
   pepper
1 teaspoon salt-free vegetable
   seasoning

¼–⅓ cup Pear Vinaigrette
   Dressing (page 138)
   (or an acceptable commercial
   vinaigrette dressing)
Romaine leaves for serving

Red-skinned apple slices for garnish

1. Combine sweet potatoes, celery, green pepper, and vegetable seasoning.
2. Add dressing and toss together lightly until all potatoes are coated. Marinate in covered bowl and refrigerate for 30 minutes.

To Serve: Place drained sweet potato mixture into romaine-lined bowl, garnish with thin apple slices, skin side up. This is delicious served with cold sliced turkey.

Per serving: 155 calories; 2.7 gm protein; 1.8 gm fat; 32.8 gm carbohydrate; 1.6 gm fiber; 0 mg cholesterol; 58 mg sodium

Tuna Salad Supreme ⓠ

Serves: 4

3 cups shredded romaine lettuce
½ red onion, finely chopped
2 oranges, peeled (white part
   removed), cut into 1-inch chunks
10-ounce package frozen broccoli
   flowerets, steamed and cut into
   1-inch chunks

7½-ounce can salt-reduced tuna in
   water, drained and flaked
8 cherry tomatoes, halved
½ cup Fresh Orange Dressing
   (page 139)

1. Place all ingredients but the dressing in salad bowl.
2. Mix gently with 2 forks.

3. Drizzle dressing over salad mixture and mix gently. Serve immediately.

Per serving: 167 calories; 18.2 gm protein; 3.3 gm fat; 18.4 gm carbohydrate; 3.6 gm fiber; 31 mg cholesterol; 45 mg sodium

Singaporian Waldorf Salad ⓠ

Serves: 4 (⅔ cup = 1 serving)

If you use your food processor's shredding attachment, this salad is done in minutes.

1 cup shredded carrots
½ cup shredded red apple with skin
½ cup shredded celery
3 tablespoons shredded fresh horseradish
2 tablespoons dark raisins, plumped in hot water and drained

1 tablespoon lemon juice
¼ cup 1% fat cottage cheese
2 tablespoons nonfat milk
1 tablespoon frozen unsweetened apple juice concentrate
Curly endive
1 tablespoon sliced toasted almonds

Seeded red grapes for garnish

1. Combine carrots, apple, celery, horseradish, raisins, and lemon juice in bowl.
2. Process cottage cheese, milk, and apple juice concentrate in blender until smooth. Add salad dressing to shredded ingredients and blend with fork.
To Serve: Arrange salad on bed of endive and sprinkle with toasted almonds; garnish with seeded red grape halves.

Per serving: 60 calories; 2.7 gm protein; 0.3 gm fat; 12.7 gm carbohydrate; 1.2 gm fiber; 1 mg cholesterol; 87 mg sodium

Tomato Stuffed with Cucumber and Fish Salad ⑨

Serves: 4 (1 tomato and ⅔ cup stuffing = 1 serving)

The French slice their tomatoes vertically instead of crosswise. This makes stuffed tomato salad more interesting, easier to eat, and more vitamin-C packed since you use a whole tomato instead of just the shell.

7½-ounce can salt-reduced tuna in water, drained, or 8 ounces poached fish, flaked
½ cup peeled, seeded, diced cucumber
2 red radishes, diced
2 whole green onions, sliced
¼ cup nonfat yogurt

1 tablespoon light mayonnaise
4 small ripe tomatoes
2 cups shredded romaine or green leaf lettuce

2 tablespoons chopped Italian parsley or basil for garnish

1. Place fish, cucumber, radishes, green onions, yogurt, and mayonnaise in a bowl; mix gently with a fork. Chill for 20 to 30 minutes.
2. Core tomatoes and turn cored side down.
3. Slice tomatoes vertically into 5 slices, leaving slices attached at bottom.
4. Spread slices and fill opening with the salad.
To Serve: Place each stuffed tomato on a bed of shredded lettuce and garnish with chopped parsley or basil.

Variations:

Vegetable-Cheese Stuffing: Puree 1 cup hoop cheese or 1 percent fat cottage cheese in blender or food processor and add ½ cup diced cucumber and 2 tablespoons chopped chives. Stuff tomatoes. Top with green pepper rings.

Pineapple-Cheese Stuffing: Combine 1 cup 1 percent fat cottage cheese with ½ cup drained, crushed canned unsweetened pineapple and 1½ tablespoons minced watercress. Stuff tomatoes and garnish with sprig of watercress.

Chicken Salad Spread as stuffing: see page 108.

Cucumber Raita as stuffing: see page 362.

Per serving: 110 calories; 17.3 gm protein; 1.3 gm fat; 7.8 gm carbohydrate; 1.5 gm fiber; 34 mg cholesterol; 48 mg sodium

"You-Name-It" Salad

Serves: 8 (1 cup = 1 serving)

When a group of my friends get together for a potluck supper, you can always depend upon several interesting salads. Here is one for you to try.

⅔ cup low-calorie Italian dressing
2 garlic cloves, minced
1 teaspoon Dijon mustard
1 teaspoon Italian herb blend, crushed
16-ounce package frozen French-cut green beans, briefly cooked and drained
3 new potatoes, steamed and diced

2 stalks broccoli, peeled, steamed, and sliced
1 green pepper, seeded and diced
4-ounce jar sliced pimiento, drained
¼ head red cabbage, shredded
½ hothouse cucumber, diced
12 cherry tomatoes, halved
¼ cup chopped Italian parsley

1. Combine dressing, garlic, mustard, and herbs and stir well.
2. Combine all remaining ingredients except chopped parsley in a salad bowl.
3. Add salad dressing; toss gently with 2 forks.
4. Sprinkle with chopped parsley and chill for 30 minutes before serving.

To Serve: May be served separately in a bowl or on a salad platter surrounded by cold, sliced turkey or chilled, broiled chicken breasts.

Per serving: 86 calories; 3.9 gm protein; 0.6 gm fat; 19.0 gm carbohydrate; 3.0 gm fiber; 0 mg cholesterol; 32 mg sodium

Sarah's Hungarian Wilted Salad Ⓠ

Serves: 4

This is a low-calorie salad frequently served with chicken in Hungary. Be sure to marinate it at least 20 minutes before serving.

1½ cups cold water
¼ cup cider vinegar
⅓ cup frozen unsweetened apple
    juice concentrate
⅛ teaspoon white pepper
1 head Boston lettuce, cored,
    washed, and cut in eighths

2 Italian plum tomatoes, halved
    and cut in 12 slices
½ small red onion, thinly sliced
2 tablespoons chopped fresh dill or
    2 teaspoons dried dill

1. Combine water, vinegar, apple juice concentrate, and pepper in serving bowl.

2. Add lettuce, tomatoes, and onion, and mix thoroughly.

3. Sprinkle with dill, cover with plastic wrap, and chill for 20 minutes before serving.

Per serving: 63 calories; 1.5 gm protein; 0.4 gm fat; 15.2 gm carbohydrate; 1.0 gm fiber; 0 mg cholesterol; 15 mg sodium

Warm Sliced Chicken Salad ⓠ

Serves: 4 (3 ounces cooked chicken = 1 serving)

A neighborhood bistro near my home serves this appealing dish.

4 4-ounce chicken breasts, skinned, boned, all fat removed, and flattened
Juice of ½ lemon
2 teaspoons mild soy sauce
Salt-free vegetable seasoning
Freshly ground black pepper
4 cups shredded green leaf lettuce, chilled

½ cucumber, peeled, seeded, and diced
2 tomatoes, halved, seeded, and diced
¾ cup Fresh Tomato Vinaigrette Dressing (page 139); add 1 tablespoon tarragon vinegar
2 tablespoons sesame seeds, toasted in a dry skillet

1. Season chicken breasts with lemon juice, soy sauce, vegetable seasoning, and pepper.

2. Sear chicken breasts on nonstick griddle sprayed with cooking spray and heated. Cook 3 to 5 minutes on each side. Slice each cooked breast into about 5 1-inch slices cut against the grain. *Keep warm.*

3. Arrange shredded lettuce on 4 individual serving plates. Sprinkle each with one quarter of the cucumber and one quarter of the tomatoes. Drizzle with 3 tablespoons salad dressing.

4. Place 1 sliced chicken breast on top of tomato–cucumber mixture and drizzle with more salad dressing. Sprinkle with sesame seeds and serve warm.

Per serving: 209 calories; 28.9 gm protein; 6.4 gm fat; 9.0 gm carbohydrate; 2.1 gm fiber; 72 mg cholesterol; 84 mg sodium

Harriet F's
Potato Salad Vinaigrette Ⓠ

Serves: 8 (½ cup = 1 serving)

All day long, this lady helps people solve their problems. Her recipe should help you make a quick potato salad.

12–16 (2 pounds) small red new
   potatoes, scrubbed
⅓ cup salt-free chicken broth
   mixed with 1 teaspoon Dijon
   mustard
¼ cup low-calorie Italian dressing
Freshly ground black pepper

1–2 tablespoons white wine vinegar
4 whole green onions, thinly sliced
¼ cup chopped dill or parsley
Lettuce leaves

8 cherry tomatoes, halved, for
   garnish

1. Steam potatoes until they are just tender.
2. Quarter warm potatoes and toss gently with chicken broth, dressing, and pepper. Taste and adjust flavoring with vinegar.
3. Allow to cool. Add green onions and dill or parsley and mix lightly.

To Serve: This salad tastes best served at room temperature. Mound salad on lettuce-lined platter, garnish with cherry tomatoes, and surround with sliced Cold Turkey Breast or cold Diet Watcher's Broiled or Barbecued Chicken (page 187).

Variation: 1½ cups cooked corn may be added to the salad.

Per serving: 103 calories; 2.1 gm protein; 0.2 gm fat; 23.7 gm carbohydrate; 0.7 gm fiber; 0 mg cholesterol; 8 mg sodium

Sally's Hearts of Palm and Corn Salad ⓠ

Serves: 8 (½ cup = 1 serving)

This is a favorite of my daughter Sally, who is a nurse. Her schedule is so busy that this quick, high-fiber recipe right off the pantry shelf is always welcome.

1½ cups canned sliced hearts of palm*
1 cup canned salt-free corn
1 cup canned salt-reduced kidney beans, rinsed and drained
½ green pepper, seeded and cut into ¼-inch squares

½ teaspoon dried tarragon, crushed
3 tablespoons low-calorie Italian dressing
Green leaf lettuce for serving

1. Combine all ingredients except lettuce in mixing bowl. Toss lightly.
2. Cover and chill in refrigerator for 20 to 30 minutes before serving.
To Serve: Mound on salad plates lined with green leaf lettuce.

Per serving: 60 calories; 2.5 gm protein; 0.9 gm fat; 11.2 gm carbohydrate; 2.5 gm fiber; 0 mg cholesterol; 6 mg sodium

* 1½ cups sliced fresh mushrooms may be substituted for the hearts of palm.

Almost Santo Pietro's Salad

Serves: 6 (1 cup = 1 serving)

This salad answers our need for cruciferous vegetables (cabbage family), which are high in fiber and, of course, flavor. It is particularly appealing when served with Italian foods.

3 cups finely chopped green
   cabbage
2 cups finely chopped broccoli
   flowerets* and stems
1 cup green beans, cut into 1-inch
   pieces
¼ cup salt-free chicken broth,
   defatted
1 tablespoon extra-virgin olive oil

½ teaspoon minced garlic
3 tablespoons red wine vinegar
Freshly ground black pepper
1 teaspoon salt-free vegetable
   seasoning
Romaine leaves for serving

1 ripe tomato cut into wedges for
   garnish

1. Place cabbage, broccoli, and beans in a skillet with broth. Cover and steam for 5 to 7 minutes. Remove to a bowl.

2. Combine oil, garlic, vinegar, pepper, and vegetable seasoning. Sprinkle over vegetables and stir lightly.

3. Cover and chill for 20 to 25 minutes before serving.

To Serve: Line chilled platter with romaine, mound salad mixture, and garnish with tomato wedges.

Per serving: 44 calories; 1.7 gm protein; 2.4 gm fat; 5.3 gm carbohydrate; 1.2 gm fiber; 0 mg cholesterol; 16 mg sodium

* Reserve a few for garnish if desired.

Tomato–Rice Salad ⓠ

Serves: 8 (⅔ cup = 1 serving)

What do you do with leftover cooked rice? Make a wonderful cold salad is one answer.

1 tablespoon red wine vinegar
1 tablespoon mild soy sauce
3 cups cooked brown rice, chilled
3 medium tomatoes, seeded and
    diced

1 green pepper, seeded and diced
2 tablespoons chopped basil
½ red onion, diced (optional)
1 tablespoon extra-virgin olive oil
    (optional)

1. Sprinkle vinegar and soy sauce over rice. Mix lightly with fork.
2. Add tomatoes, green pepper, and basil. Add onion and olive oil, if desired, and toss lightly.
3. Chill until serving time.

Variation: 2 cups of any chopped leftover vegetable except beets may be used instead of tomatoes and peppers.

Per serving: 71 calories; 1.9 gm protein; 0.5 gm fat; 15.2 gm carbohydrate; 1.7 gm fiber; 0 mg cholesterol; 79 mg sodium

Almost Ken's Salad ℚ

Serves: 6 as a first course, 3 as an entrée

A small bistro in the San Fernando Valley serves a salad quite similar to this one. Its ingredients combine to make a delicious first course or low-calorie entrée.

1 pound fresh bean sprouts, rinsed
and drained
12 mushrooms, cleaned and thinly
sliced
2 bunches watercress, rinsed and
drained (remove coarse stems)
½ cup Creamy Garlic Dressing
(page 138)

1 tablespoon crumbled bleu cheese
(optional garnish when served
as an entrée)

12 cherry tomatoes, halved, for
garnish

1. Combine bean sprouts, mushrooms, and watercress in salad bowl; cover and chill in refrigerator.
2. Drizzle dressing over salad and toss lightly with 2 forks.

To Serve: Garnish salad in bowl with cheese (if desired) and cherry tomatoes. When served as an entrée, start with Almond–Broccoli Bisque (page 74) and enjoy Harold's Choice: Bread Pudding (page 316) for dessert.

Per serving: 34 calories; 3.0 gm protein; 0.5 gm fat; 6.1 gm carbohydrate; 1.0 gm fiber; 1 mg cholesterol; 30 mg sodium

Red Russian Salad ⓠ

Serves: 6 (⅔ cup = 1 serving)

This is a good choice to serve with fish. Remove 6 red cabbage leaves for serving before shredding cabbage.

3 10-ounce packages frozen mixed vegetables*
1½ cups finely shredded red cabbage or radicchio
Cucumber–Dill Dressing (page 137)

2 tablespoons chopped fresh dill or 1 teaspoon dried dill
6 red cabbage leaves for serving

Fresh dill sprigs for garnish

1. Cook frozen vegetables briefly in saucepan or microwave oven.
2. Drain in colander and refresh under cold running water (or chill in refrigerator if you have time).
3. Place drained vegetables in bowl with shredded cabbage and mix gently.
4. Add dressing and dill, toss; then cover and chill for 20 minutes or longer before serving.
To Serve: Mound salad on red cabbage leaf on individual plate and garnish with dill sprig.

Per serving: 97 calories; 4.9 gm protein; 0.5 gm fat; 20.7 gm carbohydrate; 1.9 gm fiber; 1 mg cholesterol; 69 mg sodium

* 4 cups leftover cooked peas, carrots, lima beans, corn, potatoes, or green beans may be used instead of frozen mixed vegetables.

All-Seasons
Freezer Vegetable Salad ⒬Ⓜ

Serves: 6 (¾ cup = 1 serving)

There's no need to make a trip to the market for this nutritious vegetable salad. All the ingredients can be in your freezer or on your pantry shelf. Of course, fresh vegetables may always be substituted.

16-ounce package frozen mixed cauliflower, broccoli, and carrots
10-ounce package frozen Brussels sprouts
⅔ cup low-calorie Italian dressing

2 tablespoons lemon juice
2 teaspoons poppy seeds or sesame seeds, toasted in a dry skillet
½ teaspoon dry mustard
1 teaspoon fines herbes (optional)

1. Steam or microwave vegetables according to package directions. Drain and place in salad bowl.

2. Combine remaining ingredients in jar and shake well.

3. Pour dressing over vegetables, toss, and let marinate at room temperature for 20 minutes before serving.

Per serving: 50 calories; 3.4 gm protein; 0.8 gm fat; 9.0 gm carbohydrate; 2.1 gm fiber; 0 mg cholesterol; 39 mg sodium

Mushroom, Snow Pea, and Tomato Salad ⓠ

Serves: 6

Defrosted frozen snow peas may be substituted for fresh ones in this salad.

1 pound small mushrooms, cleaned, stems removed, and quartered
½ cup no-oil Russian dressing*
1 garlic clove, minced
1 tablespoon lemon juice
Freshly ground black pepper
¼ pound fresh snow peas, steamed, 30 seconds

2 whole green onions, thinly sliced
12 cherry tomatoes, halved
1½ tablespoons sesame seeds, toasted in a dry skillet
12 leaves curly endive for serving

1. Place mushrooms in bowl. Combine dressing, garlic, lemon juice, and pepper. Pour over mushrooms and toss lightly.

2. Cover with plastic wrap and refrigerate.

3. At serving time, add snow peas, green onions, tomatoes, and sesame seeds. Toss lightly.

To Serve: Line 6 individual plates with 2 endive leaves each and mound salad mixture on top.

Per serving: 52 calories; 3.1 gm protein; 1.6 gm fat; 8.0 gm carbohydrate; 1.6 gm fiber; 0 mg cholesterol; 13 mg sodium

* Pritikin

Julienne Vegetable Salad ℚ

Serves: 6 (1 cup = 1 serving)

Save the broccoli flowerets to serve as a vegetable or in a salad at another time.

1 bunch broccoli, stems only, peeled
2 small rutabagas, peeled
2 turnips, peeled
4 carrots, peeled
½ cup low-calorie Italian dressing or Fresh Tomato Vinaigrette Dressing (page 139)

1 tablespoon lemon juice
Freshly ground black pepper
Freshly grated nutmeg

2 tablespoons chopped parsley for garnish

1. Cut vegetables into julienne slices using food processor or mandoline.
2. Place vegetables in steamer basket and steam over boiling water for 3 to 5 minutes, until tender-crisp.
3. Place vegetables in bowl and chill in refrigerator for 15 to 30 minutes.
4. Sprinkle with dressing, lemon juice, pepper, and nutmeg. Toss lightly, sprinkle with parsley, and serve immediately.

Helpful Hint: If you don't have a food processor or mandoline, try another recipe instead.

Per serving: 45 calories; 1.8 gm protein; 0.3 gm fat; 10.0 gm carbohydrate; 1.8 gm fiber; 0 mg cholesterol; 41 mg sodium

A Few Salad Dressings

Cucumber–Dill Dressing ⓠ

Yield: 3 cups (1 tablespoon = 1 serving)

2 cucumbers, peeled, seeded, and
   coarsely chopped
½ small onion, quartered, or
   6 green onions, cut into pieces
1 large garlic clove
3 tablespoons chopped dill

1½ cups nonfat yogurt or strained
   buttermilk
Freshly ground black pepper
Few drops hot pepper sauce
Salt-free vegetable seasoning to
   taste

Place all ingredients in blender or food processor and puree. Chill for 15 minutes before serving.

To Serve: Delicious served over a salad of sliced cucumbers, red onions, and tomatoes.

Per serving: 6 calories; 0.5 gm protein; 0.0 gm fat; 1.0 gm carbohydrate; 0.2 gm fiber; 0 mg cholesterol; 6 mg sodium

Creamy Garlic Dressing ⓠ

Yield: 1⅓ cups (1 tablespoon = 1 serving)

This is especially tasty served over a salad of tender romaine lettuce leaves.

1 cup lowfat yogurt
2 tablespoons light mayonnaise
¼ cup salt-reduced tomato sauce
4 garlic cloves, minced
1 teaspoon salt-free vegetable
  seasoning

Freshly ground black pepper
1 teaspoon fines herbes, crushed
  (optional)
1 tablespoon lemon juice (optional)

1. Place all ingredients except lemon juice in small bowl. Blend well with whisk. Taste and adjust seasonings. Add lemon juice depending on tartness of yogurt.
2. Cover and store in refrigerator.

Per serving: 11 calories; 0.7 gm protein; 0.4 gm fat; 1.4 gm carbohydrate; 0 gm fiber; 1 mg cholesterol; 9 mg sodium

Pear Vinaigrette Dressing ⓠ

Yield: ⅔ cup (1 tablespoon = 1 serving)

¼ cup pear vinegar
  (or 1 tablespoon pureed ripe pear
  plus 3 tablespoons white wine
  vinegar)
2 teaspoons cold-pressed safflower
  oil
⅓ cup salt-free chicken broth,
  defatted, or orange juice

1 teaspoon lemon juice
1 garlic clove, minced
Freshly ground black pepper
2 tablespoons pureed ripe pear
  (optional)

Place all ingredients in jar, shake well, and let stand at least 15 minutes before using.

Per serving: 11 calories; 0.1 gm protein; 0.8 gm fat; 0.7 gm carbohydrate; 0 gm fiber; 0 mg cholesterol; 0.5 mg sodium

Fresh Orange Dressing ⓠ

Yield: ⅔ cup (1 tablespoon = 1 serving)

This is a delicate dressing that goes beautifully with a fresh fruit salad or mixed greens.

½ cup orange juice or 1 large
   navel orange, peeled, white part
   removed*
1 tablespoon lemon juice
1 teaspoon grated orange rind

1 teaspoon Dijon mustard
2 tablespoons chopped parsley
1 teaspoon extra-virgin olive oil
1 tablespoon red wine vinegar
   (optional)

Place all ingredients in blender or food processor and puree. Chill for 20 minutes before using.

Per serving: 11 calories; 0.2 gm protein; 0.5 gm fat; 1.5 gm carbohydrate; 0 gm fiber; 0 mg cholesterol; 0 mg sodium

* Grate rind before peeling orange.

Fresh Tomato Vinaigrette Dressing ⓠ

Yield: 1¼ cups (1 tablespoon = 1 serving)

1 cup seeded and chopped
   tomatoes or 1 cup canned Italian
   plum tomatoes
1 tablespoon red wine vinegar or
   lemon juice
1 tablespoon finely chopped celery
   leaves or 1 teaspoon dried
   celery leaves

2 tablespoons chopped parsley
2 to 3 garlic cloves, minced
¼ teaspoon dried oregano, crushed
¼ teaspoon Italian herb blend or
   2 leaves fresh basil, chopped
Dash hot pepper sauce

1. Place all ingredients in blender or food processor and puree.
2. Chill for 15 minutes before using.
To Serve: Serve over mixed greens or pasta.

Per serving: 3 calories; 0.1 gm protein; 0 gm fat; 0.7 gm carbohydrate; 0.1 gm fiber; 0 mg cholesterol; 2 mg sodium

Traditional Entrées

Fish
Nutritious and Delicious

Broiled Swordfish Steaks
Broiled Fish Fillets with Tomato
Oven-Fried Fish
California Cioppino
California Sole Rolls
Baked Stuffed Fish
Fish Bundles in Swiss Chard
Executive Chef Bianchi's Fish
 Peri-Peri
Dorothy's Heavenly Halibut
Poached Halibut with Vegetable
 Béchamel
Luscious Lobster Cacciatore
Broiled Orange Roughie
Peruvian Pickled Fish
Barbecued Salmon Steaks
The Most Delicious Broiled Salmon
Paula's Salmon Papillote
My Mother's Salmon Patties

Piquant Broiled Salmon
Poached Salmon
Broiled Salmon Trout
Scallops with Tomato–Garlic Sauce
Poached Sea Bass with Mango
 Sauce
Poached Red Snapper
Gail's Special Swordfish Niçoise
 Salad
Fillet of Sole Rolls, Provençal
Barbecued Fresh Tuna with
 Tomatillo Sauce
Harold's Broiled Whitefish with
 Mushrooms
Swordfish Kebabs
Fish Italiano
Whole Steamed Fish with
 Ginger and Spring Onions
Calorie-Counter's Scrod

Fish has been a food source for man since prehistoric times. In American waters alone, over 200 species of edible fish are available, although problems with pollution and supply and demand have affected the fishing industry. Modern fishermen have been forced to go farther out to sea for big catches. As a result, some fishing vessels have facilities for cleaning and flash-freezing fish on board. This may raise the quality of frozen fish that we have available in our markets; however, frozen fish is still not as desirable as good, fresh fish. Many fish farms have been started to help meet the rising demand for fish as well as to raise fish in a controlled

143

environment. The government has also supported hatcheries to help re-store the fish populations in inland rivers and lakes.

The nutrients found in the edible portion of fish include: protein, potassium, phosphorus, Vitamin A, and fat, in varying amounts, depending upon the variety. Low-calorie diets frequently call for low-fat fish such as cod, haddock, halibut, sole, flounder, pollock, sea bass, and red snapper. Current nutritional research, however, has led to recommendations that fatty fishes such as salmon, carp, tuna, mullet, mackerel, and lake whitefish be consumed. It seems that fish oils contain certain essential fatty acids that may actually help lower blood fats. They also raise levels of high density lipoproteins (HDL), the so-called good cholesterol, which may protect against heart disease, thin the blood, and help prevent the formation of clots.

Dr. William Castelli, director of the Framingham, Massachusetts, heart study, is quoted as saying, "We believe that eating more than 8 ounces of fish per week would cut your risk of death from a heart attack in half." Some researchers believe that it doesn't matter what kind of fish you eat as long as you have 2 or 3 servings per week. If there ever was food for thought, this is it. In the best interest of longevity, it behooves us all not to ignore this current research in lowering cholesterol levels.

Buying and Storing Fresh Fish

When buying fish, it would be beneficial to be able to rely on your local fishmonger. If not—remember, fresh fish's flesh is firm and has *very little odor*. If fish is whole, the eyes should be bright and the gills red. Ask your merchant when he gets fresh fish deliveries; plan meals with fish for these days. To store fish, *wrap loosely* in waxed paper or plastic wrap and refrigerate it no more than 2 days before using it. Avoid buying frozen fish with ice crystals, frost, or freezer burn (white patches). Frozen fish should be thawed in the refrigerator or may be cooked frozen if it is to be poached, broiled, or baked. *Do not refreeze.*

Since we are encouraging the consumption of fish, methods that enhance its full flavor should be used: don't overcook fish or slather it with sauce.

Recommended Cooking Methods

1. Broiling or Barbecuing

Since heat is direct and intense in these methods of cooking, to ensure moistness, the fish optimally should be 1 inch thick, may be marinated beforehand and basted during cooking.

2. Baking

When baked, fish needs the addition of flavoring ingredients and a little liquid. The oven temperature should be about 400°; allow 10 minutes cooking time per inch of thickness.

3. Poaching or Steaming

Prepare a court bouillon (a seasoned liquid) of two thirds water and one third milk, wine, or wine vinegar, and seasonings (onion, carrot, celery, bay leaf, parsley, dill, and thyme). Cook for 10 to 30 minutes and strain before using for poaching. Cook fish briefly in simmering liquid to poach, and over briskly boiling liquid to steam.

Save fish stock for soups, sauces, California Cioppino (page 148), or future poaching. It may be frozen up to 4 months.

Broiled Swordfish Steaks ⓠ

Serves: 4 (4 ounces cooked fish = 1 serving)

1 tablespoon mild soy sauce
¼ cup dry white wine
2 garlic cloves, minced
Juice of 1 lemon (about
  3 tablespoons)

4 5-ounce swordfish steaks, cut
  1 inch thick

2 tablespoons chopped parsley and
  lemon wedges for garnish

1. Combine soy sauce, wine, garlic, and lemon juice.
2. Add swordfish and marinate for 15 minutes at room temperature.
3. Place swordfish on broiling rack and broil in preheated broiler for 5 minutes. Baste with marinade once before turning.
4. Flip fish over, baste, and broil 5 additional minutes, basting several times while broiling. Serve immediately on heated plates and garnish with chopped parsley and lemon wedges.

Per serving: 195 calories; 27.7 gm protein; 5.7 gm fat; 2.1 gm carbohydrate; 0 gm fiber; 78 mg cholesterol; 224 mg sodium

Broiled Fish Fillets with Tomato ⓠ

Serves: 4 (4 ounces cooked fish = 1 serving)

4 5-ounce fish fillets (flounder, sole,
  red snapper, or orange roughie)
1 tablespoon lemon juice
1 teaspoon salt-free vegetable
  seasoning
½ cup finely chopped, peeled
  tomato

½ teaspoon chopped garlic
1 teaspoon extra-virgin olive oil

Lemon wedges for garnish

1. Spray broiler pan with nonstick spray; preheat in broiler for 3 minutes.
2. Arrange fish in preheated pan; sprinkle with lemon juice and vegetable seasoning.
3. Combine remaining ingredients and sprinkle tomato mixture over fish.

4. Broil 3 inches from heat for 6 to 10 minutes, or until fish flakes with a fork.

To Serve: Place fish on warm serving platter. Garnish with lemon wedges, and surround with steamed broccoli, peas, and new potatoes.

Per serving: 129 calories; 24.0 gm protein; 2.3 gm fat; 1.7 gm carbohydrate; 0.2 gm fiber; 71 mg cholesterol; 113 mg sodium

Oven-Fried Fish ⓠ

Serves: 4 (4 ounces cooked fish = 1 serving)

The word "fried" has an undesirable connotation, but not with these fillets. They are breaded without using an egg batter and baked without added fat.

4 5-ounce fillets of flounder, sole, or orange roughie

½ cup buttermilk, strained, or ½ cup nonfat yogurt mixed with 1 tablespoon light mayonnaise

½ cup whole-wheat bread crumbs

2 tablespoons chopped parsley

1 teaspoon Hungarian paprika

4 lemon wedges for garnish

1. Preheat oven to 450°.
2. Dip fillets in buttermilk.
3. Combine bread crumbs, parsley, and paprika. Press mixture onto both sides of fish.
4. Place in shallow, nonstick baking pan.
5. Bake for 10 to 12 minutes, or until fish flakes with a fork.

To Serve: Place fish garnished with lemon on warmed serving platter, surrounded with Twice-Baked Potatoes (page 267) and steamed asparagus spears.

Per serving: 154 calories; 25.9 gm protein; 1.8 gm fat; 7.2 gm carbohydrate; 0.3 gm fiber; 72 mg cholesterol; 176 mg sodium

California Cioppino
(A Truly Fine Fish Stew)

Serves: 10

Cioppino is California's answer to bouillabaisse. It is made with tomatoes and whatever fish or shellfish you desire. Make certain to have plenty of crisp French bread to soak up the succulent juices.

1 tablespoon extra-virgin olive oil
1 medium onion, chopped
1 green pepper, seeded and
    chopped
2 medium carrots, chopped
3 garlic cloves, minced
6-ounce can salt-free tomato paste
28-ounce can chopped Italian plum
    tomatoes
1 cup California red wine
1 cup dry white wine
2 teaspoons Italian herb blend,
    crushed

2 bay leaves
Few grains crushed red pepper
    flakes
2 pounds sea bass or cod fillets
    (cut into bite-sized pieces)
2 pounds raw lobster tails, cut in
    2-inch chunks, shells and all
16 cherrystone clams or mussels,
    scrubbed thoroughly in cold
    water (optional)

1 cup chopped parsley for garnish

1. Heat oil in Dutch oven; add onion, green pepper, carrots, and garlic. Sauté for 3 minutes.
2. Add tomato paste, tomatoes, wines, herb blend, bay leaves, and red pepper flakes.
3. Simmer for 20 minutes, taste and adjust seasonings.
4. Add fish, cook for 5 minutes. Add lobster and clams or mussels, cover, bring to a boil, reduce heat, and simmer for 5 to 8 minutes. Remove bay leaves before serving.

To Serve: Place in heated tureen and serve in soup plates or individual ramekins, garnished with chopped parsley. Have plenty of French bread for dunking. An Artichoke, Mushroom, and Hearts of Palm Salad (page 102) makes a good beginning, and Fresh Strawberry Tart (page 330) a satisfying conclusion.

Per serving: 232 calories; 26.0 gm protein; 4.8 gm fat; 10.6 gm carbohydrate; 1.2 gm fiber; 141 mg cholesterol; 188 mg sodium

California Sole Rolls ⓠ

Serves: 6 (1 roll = 1 serving)

¾ cup fresh whole-wheat bread crumbs
1 teaspoon herbes de Provence, crushed
1 tablespoon chopped parsley
3 tablespoons lemon juice
1 teaspoon grated lemon rind
6 5-ounce fillets sole

1 teaspoon salt-free vegetable seasoning
Freshly ground black pepper
Hungarian paprika
½ cup dry white wine

Watercress for garnish

1. Combine first 5 ingredients.
2. Layer one sixth of mixture onto each fillet.
3. Roll up fillets as jelly rolls.
4. Place seam-side down in small baking dish that has been sprayed with nonstick cooking spray.
5. Sprinkle with vegetable seasoning, pepper, paprika, and wine.
6. Bake in preheated 400° oven for 12 to 15 minutes.

To Serve: Place fish rolls on heated platter garnished with watercress. Accompany with Mexican Red Rice (page 301) and Marinated Vegetable Platter (page 261).

Per serving: 158 calories; 25.0 gm protein; 1.5 gm fat; 7.0 gm carbohydrate; 0.3 gm fiber; 71 mg cholesterol; 145 mg sodium

Baked Stuffed Fish Ⓠ Ⓜ

Serves: 6 (4 ounces cooked fish = 1 serving)

Generally speaking; I shy away from using frozen fish if possible. This, however, is one recipe that does not suffer from using frozen fish because of the method of preparation.

2 teaspoons extra-virgin olive oil
½ cup chopped onion
⅓ cup seeded, chopped green
　pepper
1 garlic clove, minced
1 cup chopped mushrooms
1 cup shredded carrots
1 teaspoon salt-free vegetable
　seasoning
½ teaspoon dried thyme and
　marjoram, crushed
Freshly ground black pepper
2 slices stale whole-wheat bread,
　coarsely chopped

Salt-free chicken or vegetable
　broth, defatted (optional)
2 1-pound frozen fish fillets,
　1-inch thick, defrosted
Juice of ½ lemon
Hungarian paprika
2 tablespoons grated Parmesan
　cheese

Watercress and lemon wedges for
　garnish

1. Sauté oil and onion in nonstick skillet until tender.
2. Add next 7 ingredients and sauté for 3 to 5 minutes. Add bread. (If not sufficiently moist, add a bit of chicken or vegetable broth.) Mix lightly.
3. Split fillets in half lengthwise. Sprinkle one fillet with lemon juice and spread evenly with half the vegetable mixture. Cover with another fillet and cut into thirds crosswise. Sprinkle with paprika and cheese. Repeat with second fillet.
4. Place slices on nonstick baking sheet sprayed with nonstick cooking spray. Bake in preheated 350° oven for 20 to 25 minutes, or until fish flakes with a fork.

To Serve: Place fish portions on warmed platter garnished with watercress and lemon wedges. Accompany with steamed broccoli and cauliflower and corn on the cob.

In Microwave: Cook covered on medium for 9 to 11 minutes, or until fish flakes with a fork.

Per serving: 179 calories; 27.4 gm protein; 3.6 gm fat; 8.2 gm carbohydrate; 0.7 gm fiber; 77 mg cholesterol; 179 mg sodium

Fish Bundles in Swiss Chard ⓠ

Serves: 4 (1 bundle = 1 serving)

1 teaspoon cold-pressed safflower
    oil
1 small leek (white part only),
    split, washed, and chopped
2 carrots, chopped
½ stalk celery, chopped
6 mushrooms, chopped
1 teaspoon salt-free vegetable
    seasoning
½ teaspoon dried thyme, crushed

Freshly ground black pepper
4 5-ounce fish fillets (sea bass,
    monkfish, or red snapper)
4 leaves Swiss chard, romaine, or
    butter lettuce, blanched*
½ cup dry white wine
⅓ cup salt-free fish or chicken
    broth, defatted
1 tablespoon cornstarch mixed with
    3 tablespoons cooking liquid

1. Place oil in nonstick sauté pan. Add leek, carrots, celery, mushrooms, seasonings, and pepper. Sauté for 3 minutes, or until vegetables are limp.

2. Remove half the vegetable mixture and reserve.

3. Roll fillets and wrap each in chard leaf. Place fillets over vegetables in sauté pan and top with reserved vegetables.

4. Pour wine and broth over fish.

5. Bring to a boil, reduce to a simmer, and cover. Cook fish for 12 minutes, or until fish flakes with a fork.

6. Remove fish fillets to heated platter and cover. Add diluted cornstarch to vegetables in pan. Cook and stir until transparent.

To Serve: Pour hot sauce with vegetables over fillets and surround with steamed red potatoes and al dente cooked green beans.

Per serving: 203 calories; 28.8 gm protein; 3.1 gm fat; 9.3 gm carbohydrate; 1.1 gm fiber; 78 mg cholesterol; 156 mg sodium

---

* To blanch, plunge in boiling water for 30 seconds and cool immediately under cold running water.

Executive Chef Bianchi's Fish Peri-Peri ⓠ

Serves: 4 (4 ounces cooked fish = 1 serving)

This dish is an inspiration from the Harbor View Holiday Inn in Hong Kong. In Asia, pomfret is a delicious, popularly used whitefish; however, fillet of sole or flounder may be substituted.

4 5-ounce thick fillets fresh sole or flounder
Juice of ½ lemon
1 teaspoon salt-free vegetable seasoning
Hungarian paprika
1 small green pepper, seeded and chopped
1 small sweet red pepper, seeded and chopped
1 tablespoon chopped, medium-hot canned chili

3 whole green onions, thinly sliced
Few grains crushed red pepper flakes
¼ cup dry white wine or vermouth
⅓ cup salt-free fish stock or chicken broth, defatted

Chopped cilantro and 4 lemon wedges for garnish

1. Sprinkle fish with lemon juice, vegetable seasoning, and paprika.
2. Spray skillet with buttery-flavored nonstick cooking spray and heat.
3. Grill fish in skillet for 2 to 3 minutes on each side.
4. Combine remaining ingredients except cilantro and lemon wedges in small skillet or saucepan. Simmer until liquid is reduced by half.

To Serve: Place hot fish on individual plates and top with hot vegetable mixture garnished with cilantro and lemon wedges. Steamed brown rice, snow peas, and carrot spears complete a colorful and tasty entrée.

Variations: Turkey Peri-Peri may be prepared using a grilled turkey slice. Chicken Peri-Peri may be prepared using a grilled or char-broiled boned chicken breast.

Per serving: 139 calories; 24.3 gm protein; 1.4 gm fat; 3.7 gm carbohydrate; 0.8 gm fiber; 71 mg cholesterol; 114 mg sodium

Dorothy's Heavenly Halibut ⓆⓂ

Serves: 6 (4 ounces cooked fish = 1 serving)

Dorothy is a busy wife, mother, and dietician whose cooking skills are widely recognized and appreciated. This is a microwave recipe.

1 tablespoon cold-pressed safflower oil
1 onion, very thinly sliced
½ cup dry white wine
2 pounds halibut, cut into 2-inch cubes
Nonfat milk as needed
3 tablespoons whole-wheat flour

1 teaspoon salt-free vegetable seasoning
⅛ teaspoon white pepper
10-ounce package frozen peas
2-ounce jar chopped pimiento, drained
2 cups steamed wild rice or cooked linguine

1. Place oil, onion, and wine in 9-inch glass baking dish. Microwave uncovered on high for 3 minutes.

2. Add fish, cover, and microwave for 6 minutes.

3. Drain liquid from fish into 4-cup glass measure. Add milk to measure 1½ cups.

4. Add flour, vegetable seasoning, and pepper to milk and stir vigorously to blend. Microwave on high for 6 minutes, stirring 3 to 4 times during cooking.

5. Add sauce, peas, and pimiento to fish and onions. Mix. Cook uncovered on high for 2 minutes.

To Serve: Spoon fish mixture over rice or pasta and serve with steamed carrots and broccoli.

Per serving: 305 calories; 35.4 gm protein; 4.9 gm fat; 25.1 gm carbohydrate; 2.7 gm fiber; 76 mg cholesterol; 127 mg sodium

Poached Halibut
with Vegetable Béchamel

Serves: 2 (4 ounces cooked fish = 1 serving)

Executive Chef Francis Weihs of the Holiday Inn, Johor Baru, Malaysia, has used his creativity to provide many fish recipes. This is one that is uncomplicated yet seems like haute cuisine.

½ cup salt-free fish stock or chicken broth, defatted
½ cup dry white wine
1 bay leaf
4 slices celery
Fennel bulb, halved (optional)
2 5-ounce halibut fillets
2 shallots, finely chopped
4 mushrooms, cleaned and diced

1 small tomato, peeled, seeded, and diced, or 1 canned Italian plum tomato
2 tablespoons coarsely chopped parsley
½ cup Basic Béchamel (page 28) or ½ cup nonfat milk thickened with 1 tablespoon cornstarch
3 tablespoons nonfat yogurt

1. Bring stock, wine, bay leaf, and celery to a boil in 10-inch skillet.* Add fish and simmer for 8 to 10 minutes, or until fish flakes with a fork. Remove fish to warmed platter. Reserve liquid.

2. In nonstick skillet, dry-roast shallots and mushrooms, stirring constantly until lightly browned. Add tomatoes, parsley, and 3 tablespoons of poaching liquid. Remove bay leaf.

3. Combine warmed béchamel sauce with yogurt. Add sauce to dry-roasted vegetables just before serving.

To Serve: Spoon vegetable sauce over drained fish, garnish with poached fennel, and serve with steamed peas and baked potato.

Per serving: 272 calories; 33.7 gm protein; 2.4 gm fat; 18.3 gm carbohydrate; 0.7 gm fiber; 73 mg cholesterol; 153 mg sodium

* Halved fennel bulbs may be added to stock at this time and poached with fish.

Luscious Lobster Cacciatore ⓠ

Serves: 4

I know that chicken is cheaper and turkey is delicious too, but what a feast it is to have lobster once in a while! Since I don't use a drawn butter sauce, this preparation seems to answer the nutritional as well as gastronomic requirements of my guests.

1 teaspoon extra-virgin olive oil
2 garlic cloves, minced
1 small onion, minced
1 shallot, minced
1 carrot, minced
28-ounce can crushed Italian plum tomatoes in puree
2 tablespoons chopped parsley
1 tablespoon chopped fresh basil or 1 teaspoon Italian herb blend, crushed
1 teaspoon chopped fresh oregano or ½ teaspoon dried oregano, crushed

1 bay leaf
¼ teaspoon crushed red pepper flakes
½ cup dry white or red wine
2 8-ounce raw lobster tails, cut into 1-inch pieces with shell (remove membrane)
1 tablespoon lemon juice
1 teaspoon salt-free vegetable seasoning
6 ounces linguine, cooked al dente
2 tablespoons grated Parmesan cheese (optional)

1. Heat oil in nonstick skillet and sauté garlic, onion, shallot, and carrot until onion is transparent.

2. Add next 7 ingredients and simmer, covered, for 15 minutes.

3. Sprinkle lobster chunks with lemon juice and seasoning. Add to sauce and simmer for 8 to 10 minutes. Remove bay leaf.

To Serve: Place drained linguine on heated platter, spoon sauce over linguine, top with lobster chunks, and sprinkle with Parmesan cheese if desired. Serve with a crisp green salad and Strawberries (or blueberries) with Sabayon Sauce (page 368).

Per serving: 195 calories; 21.8 gm protein; 3.9 gm fat; 14.6 gm carbohydrate; 2.0 gm fiber; 227 mg cholesterol; 274 mg sodium

Broiled Orange Roughie ⓠ

Serves: 4 (4 ounces cooked fish = 1 serving)

A few years ago while visiting Pittsburgh, Pennsylvania, I was interviewed by Woodeen Merriman, then food editor of the *Pittsburgh Press*. She spoke in glowing terms of this relatively new fish available in the market. It is imported "frozen" from New Zealand. I must admit I had never tried it before. Now, I, too, am a fan of this low-calorie, low-cost, wonderfully mild fish. I urge you to discover this new variety.

4 5-ounce portions orange roughie, halibut, or scrod fillets
Juice of ½ lemon
1 tablespoon Worcestershire sauce
1 teaspoon dehydrated onion flakes
1 teaspoon salt-free vegetable seasoning

Hungarian paprika

2 tablespoons chopped parsley and 4 lemon wedges for garnish

1. Rinse fish and pat dry with paper towels.
2. Lay fillets on broiler pan coated with nonstick cooking spray.
3. Sprinkle with lemon juice, Worcestershire, onion flakes, vegetable seasoning, and paprika.
4. Marinate at room temperature for 15 minutes.
5. Place in preheated broiler and broil for 8 to 10 minutes, or until fish flakes with a fork.

To Serve: Garnish with chopped parsley and lemon wedges. Accompany with summer squash and broiled tomato half.

Per serving: 119 calories; 23.9 gm protein; 1.2 gm fat; 1.7 gm carbohydrate; 0.1 gm fiber; 71 mg cholesterol; 148 mg sodium

Peruvian Pickled Fish

Serves: 8 (3 ounces cooked fish = 1 serving)

This recipe was given to me by Carmelita, a dear friend who lived in Lima, Peru, for many years. It is a refreshing summer entrée.

2 pounds filleted and skinned sea
  bass, corbina, or halibut, cubed
Juice of 3 lemons
Juice of 3 limes
Juice of 3 oranges
2 large white onions, thinly sliced
2 small hot peppers, thinly sliced
10-ounce package cooked frozen
  baby corn

2 teaspoons salt-free vegetable
  seasoning
Freshly ground black pepper
Green leaf lettuce

Chopped cilantro and 1 pound
  cooked yams, peeled and sliced,
  for garnish

1. Place fish in colander and pour boiling water over it. Drain well.
2. Combine fish, citrus juices, onions, peppers, and corn, and mix.
3. Season with vegetable seasoning and pepper. Cover tightly and chill for 3 to 4 hours or overnight.

To Serve: Place drained fish mixture on chilled, lettuce-lined platter. Sprinkle with cilantro and garnish with sliced yams.

Per serving: 179 calories; 24.7 gm protein; 1.8 gm fat; 16.9 gm carbohydrate; 1.3 gm fiber; 57 mg cholesterol; 66 mg sodium

Barbecued Salmon Steaks ℚ

Serves: 4 (4 ounces cooked fish = 1 serving)

If the weather is inclement or if no barbecue grill is available, this fish may be broiled indoors.

½ cup low-calorie Italian dressing or Fresh Tomato Vinaigrette Dressing (page 139)
2 tablespoons lemon juice
¼ cup chopped parsley

¼ cup chopped whole green onions
¼ teaspoon dried oregano, crushed
4 6-ounce salmon steaks

4 lemon slices for garnish

1. Combine all ingredients except fish and lemon slices.
2. Pour marinade over fish and let stand at room temperature for 15 minutes (or overnight in refrigerator if you like a stronger flavor).
3. Place fish on oiled grill and broil for 4 minutes on each side. Use remaining marinade for basting as fish cooks.

To Serve: Place steaks on heated platter. Top with lemon slices and accompany with Best-Ever Zucchini–Corn Casserole (page 274) and linguine with cottage cheese.

Per serving: 210 calories; 34.2 gm protein; 6.3 gm fat; 1.5 gm carbohydrate; 0.3 gm fiber; 60 mg cholesterol; 114 mg sodium

The Most Delicious
Broiled Salmon ⦿

Serves: 4 (4 ounces cooked fish = 1 serving)

This dish was inspired while dining at an uncommonly creative restaurant in Los Angeles.

4 5-ounce salmon fillets
Juice of ½ lemon
1 tablespoon soy sauce
1 teaspoon salt-free vegetable
  seasoning
2 teaspoons cold-pressed safflower
  oil
1 leek (white part only), split,
  washed, and thinly sliced

3 tablespoons salt-free chicken
  broth, defatted
⅛ teaspoon white pepper
1 teaspoon dried chervil, crushed
2 cups washed and thinly sliced
  spinach leaves

1. Sprinkle salmon on one side with lemon juice, soy sauce, and vegetable seasoning.

2. Heat oil in nonstick skillet; add leek, chicken broth, pepper, and chervil. Sauté over medium-high heat for 2 minutes; then reduce heat, cover, and simmer for 5 minutes.

3. Place salmon in broiling pan and broil for 8 to 10 minutes in preheated broiler until fish flakes with a fork.

To Serve: Arrange shredded spinach in 4 mounds on heated platter. Place hot salmon fillet on top of each mound and top with spoonful of leek. Accompany with parslied new potatoes and a broiled tomato half. (The tomato may be broiled with the salmon.)

Per serving: 203 calories; 29.4 gm protein; 7.1 gm fat; 3.9 gm carbohydrate; 0.7 gm fiber; 50 mg cholesterol; 251 mg sodium

Paula's Salmon Papillote ⓠ

Serves: 2 (4 ounces cooked fish = 1 serving)

This is another busy person's answer to quick low-calorie, low-sodium cooking. The fish is served sealed in its own juices so that as each person opens the packet, the delicate aroma escapes to stimulate the palate.

2 5-ounce salmon steaks	¼ teaspoon herbes de Provence,
Juice of ¼ lemon	crushed
Freshly ground black pepper	1 whole green onion, sliced

1. Place fish on aluminum foil or parchment paper.
2. Season on one side with lemon juice, pepper, and herbs. Sprinkle with onions.
3. Fold foil over fish and seal.
4. Place on baking sheet in preheated 375° oven and bake for 10 to 12 minutes.

To Serve: Place packet of fish on dinner plate and serve with steamed green beans and Red and Green Slaw (page 120). Fresh melon slices would be excellent as dessert.

Per serving: 174 calories; 28.6 gm protein; 5.3 gm fat; 1.5 gm carbohydrate; 0.3 gm fiber; 50 mg cholesterol; 91 mg sodium

My Mother's Salmon Patties

Yield: 8 patties (2 patties = 1 serving)

When it comes to comfort foods, we all have our favorites. This is one
that my mother served, and now, many years later, I still feel nostalgic
as I prepare and serve it as one of my family's favorites.

1 small carrot, quartered
½ onion, quartered
½ green pepper, seeded and
  quartered
6-ounce baking potato, baked* or
  boiled, peeled and quartered
2 egg whites
1–2 tablespoons lemon juice
2 teaspoons Worcestershire sauce
1 teaspoon salt-free vegetable
  seasoning
15½-ounce can red salmon,
  drained, bones and skin removed

½ cup dried whole-wheat bread
  crumbs
¼ cup nonfat milk
1 cup dried whole-wheat bread
  crumbs mixed with 1 teaspoon
  salt-free vegetable seasoning and
  3 tablespoons grated Parmesan
  cheese

4 lemon wedges dipped in chopped
  parsley for garnish

1. Spray nonstick baking sheet with butter-flavored nonstick cooking
spray.
2. Place carrot, onion, and green pepper in food processor and mince.
3. Add potato and egg whites and process slightly.
4. Add remaining ingredients except bread crumbs–Parmesan mixture
and lemons and process *just to blend.*
5. Shape salmon mixture into 8 patties and coat with bread crumb
mixture.
6. Place on nonstick baking sheet and bake in upper third of preheated
425° oven. After 12 minutes, turn patties over and continue baking for
about 10 minutes.
To Serve: Accompany salmon patties with steamed broccoli, cauliflower,
carrots, and parslied potatoes.

Per serving: 283 calories; 23.9 gm protein; 10.9 gm fat; 21.8 gm carbohydrate; 1.0 gm fiber;
33 mg cholesterol; 210 mg sodium

* It takes about 6 to 7 minutes on high in a microwave oven to bake 1 potato.

Piquant Broiled Salmon Ⓠ

Serves: 4 (4 ounces cooked fish = 1 serving)

4 5-ounce salmon fillets, skinned
Juice of ½ lemon
1 tablespoon light mayonnaise
1 teaspoon Dijon mustard
½ teaspoon dehydrated onion
  flakes

1 teaspoon capers, rinsed and
  drained

1 tablespoon chopped parsley and
  4 lemon wedges for garnish

1. Sprinkle salmon with lemon juice.
2. Place fish in preheated broiler pan and broil for 4 minutes.
3. Combine mayonnaise, mustard, onion flakes, and capers and spread equally over each salmon fillet. Broil for 4 minutes, or until fish flakes with a fork.

To Serve: Garnish with chopped parsley and lemon wedges. A baked potato sprinkled with chopped green onions and Spinach with Corn (page 269) complete an appealing main course.

Per serving: 175 calories; 28.5 gm protein; 5.5 gm fat; 1.1 gm carbohydrate; 0 gm fiber; 51 mg cholesterol; 108 mg sodium

Poached Salmon Ⓠ Ⓜ

Serves: 2 (4 ounces cooked salmon = 1 serving)

2 cups water
1 lemon, quartered and juiced
1 small onion, sliced
4 sprigs parsley or dill
1 celery stalk with leaves, sliced

1 bay leaf
6 peppercorns
2 5-ounce salmon steaks

Fresh dill or watercress for garnish

1. Place all ingredients except salmon in medium-sized skillet. Bring to a boil for 10 minutes.
2. Add salmon and return to a boil. Reduce heat; cover and simmer for 10 minutes, or until fish flakes with a fork.

3. Remove salmon steaks with slotted spoon, drain, and remove skin.
To Serve: Serve hot, drained fish with Cucumber Raita (page 362).
Garnish with fresh dill or watercress. Accompany with baked potato and
Special Succotash (page 271).

Helpful Hint: If cooking for one, serve salmon hot the first night and
chill the remaining portion to serve cold the next day.

In Microwave: Place all ingredients in glass baking dish. Cover with
waxed paper and microwave on high for 4 to 6 minutes, or until fish flakes
with a fork.

Per serving: 264 calories; 29.1 gm protein; 15.5 gm fat; 0 gm carbohydrate; 0 gm fiber;
50 mg cholesterol; 68 mg sodium

Broiled Salmon Trout ⓠ

Serves: 4 (4 ounces cooked fish = 1 serving)

**4 5-ounce salmon trout or rainbow
trout, filleted, head and tail
removed
Juice of ½ lemon
1 tablespoon dry white wine
2 teaspoons Worcestershire sauce
½ teaspoon dried chervil, crushed**

**½ teaspoon dehydrated onion
flakes
1 teaspoon salt-free vegetable
seasoning**

**Cherry tomatoes and lemon wedges
for garnish**

1. Place fish in broiler pan sprayed with nonstick cooking spray.
Sprinkle with lemon juice.
2. Combine remaining ingredients except tomatoes and lemon wedges;
pour over each fillet.
3. Broil for 5 to 7 minutes, or until fish flakes with a fork. Remember,
cooking time for fish is 10 minutes to the inch.
To Serve: Carefully place trout on individual plates. Garnish with
cherry tomatoes and lemon wedges. Accompany with Easy Zucchini with
Peas (page 275) and steamed cracked wheat.

Per serving: 177 calories; 28.6 gm protein; 5.3 gm fat; 1.5 gm carbohydrate; 0.1 gm fiber;
50 mg cholesterol; 116 mg sodium

Scallops with Tomato–Garlic Sauce Ⓠ

Serves: 4

2 teaspoons extra-virgin olive oil
3 garlic cloves, minced
1 pound sea scallops, rinsed and
    quartered
1 tablespoon cornstarch
8 mushrooms, cleaned and sliced
1 large ripe tomato, peeled, seeded,
    and chopped, or 3 canned Italian
    plum tomatoes

6 whole green onions, thinly sliced
1 teaspoon Italian herb blend,
    crushed
⅓ cup dry vermouth
1 tablespoon lemon juice
Freshly ground black pepper

3 tablespoons chopped Italian
    parsley for garnish

1. Place oil and garlic in large, nonstick sauté pan. Sauté for 1 minute and add scallops. Cook until opaque.*
2. Remove scallops from pan to platter, cover, and keep warm.
3. Add cornstarch to sauté pan; mix over medium heat until thickened.
4. Add mushrooms, tomatoes, onions, and herbs and cook for 3 minutes.
5. Add vermouth and lemon juice. Cook for 1 to 2 minutes.
6. Sprinkle scallops with pepper and pour hot sauce over scallops.

To Serve: Sprinkle with chopped parsley and accompany with bulgur wheat with toasted pine nuts and steamed broccoli spears.

Per serving: 162 calories; 20.8 gm protein; 3.6 gm fat; 9.4 gm carbohydrate; 0.8 gm fiber; 45 mg cholesterol; 232 mg sodium

---

* If sauté pan is not large enough, cook in 2 batches.

Poached Sea Bass with Mango Sauce ⓠ

Serves: 4 (4 ounces cooked fish = 1 serving)

A wonderful combination of fish and fruit prepared by Heinz Egley, the executive chef at the Holiday Inn Lido Hotel in Beijing.

⅔ cup salt-free chicken broth, defatted, or fish stock
½ cup port wine
1 teaspoon salt-free vegetable seasoning
1 bay leaf
½ teaspoon herbes de Provence, crushed
1 slice lemon
1 whole green onion, thinly sliced
4 5-ounce fillets sea bass

1 ripe mango, peeled, seeded, and mashed
2 tablespoons nonfat plain yogurt mixed with 2 teaspoons cornstarch
16 assorted melon balls (cantaloupe, honeydew, casaba, or watermelon) and watercress for garnish

1. Place broth, port, vegetable seasoning, bay leaf, herbs, lemon, and onion in nonstick skillet. Bring to a boil and simmer for 6 to 8 minutes.
2. Add fish, bring to boil, reduce heat, cover, and simmer for 10 minutes, or until fish flakes with a fork.
3. Remove fish; cover to keep warm.
4. Strain poaching liquid, return to skillet, and simmer until reduced by half, about 5 minutes. Add mango puree and heat.
5. Remove from heat; slowly add yogurt mixed with cornstarch.
6. Return to very low heat, stirring constantly until shiny, about 3 minutes. Add melon balls to sauce just to coat.
To Serve: Place fish on heated platter, garnish with melon balls and watercress, and spoon sauce over fish. Accompany with steamed snow peas and water chestnuts and brown rice. Serve immediately.

Variations: 1. Curry powder may be added to the mango sauce.
2. If mango is not available, 1 papaya or ⅔ cup nonfat peach yogurt may be substituted.

Per serving: 206 calories; 31.7 gm protein; 1.1 gm fat; 16.6 gm carbohydrate; 1.0 gm fiber; 78 mg cholesterol; 118 mg sodium

Poached Red Snapper Ⓠ Ⓜ

Serves: 4 (4 ounces cooked fish = 1 serving)

This fish may be served hot or may be chilled and served later.

1 cup water
1 cup dry white wine
1 carrot, sliced
1 celery stalk, sliced
¼ onion, sliced
¼ teaspoon dried thyme, crushed
1 bay leaf

4 5-ounce red snapper fillets or
    salmon or halibut fillets
Fresh dill or watercress

Halved lemon shells filled with
    Green Sauce (page 366) for
    garnish

1. Bring first 7 ingredients to a boil in skillet. Simmer for 10 minutes.
2. Place fish on rack and lower into broth.
3. Bring to boil, cover, and simmer for 2 minutes. Let fish cool in liquid. Drain, cover, and chill in refrigerator.

To Serve: Place drained fish on bed of fresh dill or watercress. Garnish with halved lemon shells filled with Green Sauce. Tomato-Rice Salad (page 131) is a flavorful addition.

In Microwave: Place all ingredients except fish in glass baking dish. Cover with wax paper and microwave on high for 3 minutes. Add fish and cook for 4 to 6 minutes.

Per serving: 154 calories; 28.5 gm protein; 1.4 gm fat; 5.4 gm carbohydrate; 0.4 gm fiber; 78 mg cholesterol; 41 mg sodium

Gail's Special Swordfish Niçoise Salad

(From The Scratch Restaurant)

Serves: 4 (4 ounces cooked fish = 1 serving)

When you take away the canned, oily tuna, salty anchovies, high-cholesterol egg yolks, olives, and a calorie-laden salad dressing, what's left? A superb, delicate salad of fresh greens and vegetables with hot, broiled fish is yours to savor.

4 5-ounce swordfish steaks, ¾ inch thick
1 tablespoon mild soy sauce
1 teaspoon garlic powder
Juice of ½ lemon
6 cups shredded romaine and red lettuce combined

1 red onion, sliced ¼ inch thick
2 small ripe tomatoes, halved
10-ounce package frozen whole green beans, defrosted
4 small red potatoes with skins, steamed and halved

Salad Dressing:
1 large shallot, minced
2 tablespoons chopped parsley
1 tablespoon capers, rinsed and drained

2 teaspoons extra-virgin olive oil
3 tablespoons red wine vinegar
½ cup salt-free chicken broth, defatted

1. Combine soy sauce, garlic powder, and lemon juice. Pour over fish and marinate for 15 minutes.
2. Place shredded greens on 4 plates.
3. Remove fish from marinade and barbecue or broil for 6 minutes.
4. Turn fish over; add onions, tomatoes, beans, and potatoes to broiler and finish broiling with fish for 3 to 4 minutes.
5. In a saucepan, combine drained marinade with salad dressing ingredients; bring to a boil.
6. Slice fish into 1-inch strips and arrange with all broiled vegetables on top of greens. Pour hot salad dressing over salad.

Per serving: 327 calories; 32.7 gm protein; 8.6 gm fat; 31.1 gm carbohydrate; 3.0 gm fiber; 78 mg cholesterol; 243 mg sodium

Fillet of Sole Rolls, Provençal ©

Serves: 4 (1 fish roll = 1 serving)

4 5-ounce fillets sole
1 tablespoon lemon juice
1 teaspoon salt-free vegetable
  seasoning
¼ teaspoon dried thyme, crushed
½ teaspoon dried dill
¼ teaspoon white pepper
¼-pound salmon fillet, cut into
  4 cubes
1 cup salt-free stewed tomatoes,
  crushed

½ cup dry white wine
¼ teaspoon herbes de Provence,
  crushed
1 cup sliced mushrooms
½ tablespoon cornstarch
2 tablespoons dry white wine or
  water

2 tablespoons chopped parsley for
  garnish

1. Sprinkle sole fillets with lemon juice, vegetable seasoning, thyme, dill, and pepper.
2. Place salmon cube on each fillet and roll up.
3. In a skillet with a cover, combine tomatoes, ½ cup wine, and herbes de Provence. Simmer for 5 minutes.
4. Place fish rolls seam side down in tomato mixture and sprinkle with mushrooms. Cover and cook over low heat for 10 minutes, or until fish flakes with a fork.
5. Combine cornstarch with 2 tablespoons wine or water, stir into tomato liquid, and cook, stirring gently, until thickened and shiny.

To Serve: Serve fish garnished with parsley and accompany with steamed brown rice and French-cut green beans.

Per serving: 189 calories; 30.5 gm protein; 2.5 gm fat; 5.4 gm carbohydrate; 0.7 gm fiber; 81 mg cholesterol; 139 mg sodium

Barbecued Fresh Tuna
with Tomatillo Sauce ⓠ

Serves: 4 (4 ounces cooked fish plus ¼ cup sauce = 1 serving)

Tomatillos are small green tomatoes with a husk. If fresh ones aren't available, canned tomatillos may be used. They are usually found where Mexican foods are sold.

1 small red onion, coarsely chopped
2 teaspoons extra-virgin olive oil
3 garlic cloves, chopped
1 pound green tomatillos, husked
  and halved
1 bunch cilantro, washed and thick
  stems removed

4 5-ounce fillets fresh tuna
Juice of ½ lemon
1 teaspoon salt-free vegetable
  seasoning

1. Sauté onion in oil in 1-quart saucepan for 3 minutes.
2. Add garlic, tomatillos, and cilantro. Cover and simmer for 15 minutes, or until tomatillos are soft.
3. Puree in blender and keep warm until serving time.
4. Place tuna on broiler rack or barbecue. Sprinkle with lemon juice and vegetable seasoning.
5. Broil for 4 to 5 minutes on each side, or until fish flakes with a fork.

To Serve: Spoon ¼ cup heated sauce on dinner plate for each serving. Place tuna on top. Accompany with Mexican Red Rice (page 301), sliced steamed beets, and steamed broccoli flowerets.

Helpful Hint: Extra sauce may be refrigerated and used as a sauce for making enchiladas or as salsa with warm corn tortillas and crudités.

Per serving: 271 calories; 37.9 gm protein; 8.4 gm fat; 9.9 gm carbohydrate; 1.0 gm fiber; 81 mg cholesterol; 73 mg sodium

Harold's Broiled Whitefish with Mushrooms ⓠ

Serves: 4 (4 ounces cooked fish = 1 serving)

A favorite fatty fish that is now in good favor, since current research indicates that fatty fish lowers cholesterol levels.

4 5-ounce whitefish fillets, skinned
Juice of ½ lemon
1 teaspoon salt-free vegetable seasoning
Hungarian paprika
½ pound mushrooms, cleaned and sliced

1 tablespoon mild soy sauce
1 tablespoon white wine
1 tablespoon lemon juice
1 teaspoon salt-free vegetable seasoning
2 whole green onions, sliced

1. Place fish fillets in broiler pan and season with lemon juice, vegetable seasoning, and paprika. Broil for 7 to 10 minutes, or until fish flakes.

2. While fish is broiling, sauté mushrooms, soy sauce, wine, lemon juice, and vegetable seasoning in nonstick skillet for 3 to 4 minutes.

To Serve: Place fish fillets on heated platter. Spoon hot mushroom mixture over fish and sprinkle with green onions. Serve with baked potato and parslied carrots.

Per serving: 247 calories; 28.6 gm protein; 11.9 gm fat; 5 0 gm carbohydrate; 0.8 gm fiber; 78 mg cholesterol; 223 mg sodium

Swordfish Kebabs ⓠ

Serves: 4 (2 skewers = 1 serving)

A different way of serving fish.

½ cup dry white wine or
vermouth*
1 tablespoon Worcestershire sauce
½ teaspoon garlic powder
½ teaspoon Italian herb blend,
crushed
1 pound swordfish (or shark,
monkfish, or cod), cut into 2-inch
cubes

1 green pepper, seeded and cut into
1-inch cubes
1 small cucumber, peeled, seeded,
and cut into 1-inch cubes
8 mushrooms, cleaned and stems
removed
8 cherry tomatoes

4 lemon wedges for garnish

1. Combine first 4 ingredients. Pour mixture over fish, green pepper, cucumber, and mushrooms in plastic bag.
2. Marinate at room temperature for 10 minutes or overnight.
3. Thread fish, green pepper, fish, cucumber, fish, mushroom, and tomato onto skewer. Alternate ingredients on 8 skewers until all are used.
4. Broil 3 to 4 inches from heat for 10 minutes. Turn frequently. Cook until fish flakes. Brush with marinade while cooking. These kebabs may also be barbecued over hot coals.

To Serve: Place kebabs on bed of steamed barley, garnish with lemon wedges, and serve with No-Crust Broccoli Quiche (page 252). Melon in Strawberry Sauce (page 324) is a suitable dessert.

Per serving: 170 calories; 23.3 gm protein; 4.9 gm fat; 5.7 gm carbohydrate; 1.2 gm fiber; 62 mg cholesterol; 86 mg sodium

* One-half cup of low-calorie Italian dressing may be substituted for the wine.

Fish Italiano Ⓠ Ⓜ

Serves: 6 (4 ounces cooked fish = 1 serving)

⅔ cup chopped onion
2 teaspoons extra-virgin olive oil
2 pounds frozen fish fillets (cod, scrod, or haddock), defrosted
¼ teaspoon white pepper
½ teaspoon garlic powder

1 cup diced tomato (fresh or canned)
1 teaspoon Italian herb blend, crushed
2 tablespoons chopped parsley
¼ cup dry white wine

1. Sauté onion in oil in nonstick skillet until wilted. Place onions in an 8-inch-square glass baking dish.

2. Cut fish fillets into 6 portions and place on top of onions.

3. Season fish with pepper and garlic powder.

4. Place tomatoes on top of fish; sprinkle with herbs, parsley, and wine.

5. Cover and bake in preheated 375° oven for 15 to 20 minutes, or until fish flakes with a fork.

To Serve: Place fish on bed of cooked whole-wheat pasta with peas, spooning pan juices over all. Serve with steamed zucchini and crookneck squash.

In Microwave: In Step 5 cover fish and microwave on medium for 5 to 6 minutes.

Per serving: 100 calories; 13.9 gm protein; 2.6 gm fat; 3.3 gm carbohydrate; 0.5 gm fiber; 38 mg cholesterol; 57 mg sodium

Whole Steamed Fish
with Ginger and Spring Onions ⓠ

Serves: 6 (3 ounces cooked fish = 1 serving)

Have your fishmonger clean the fish, leaving the head and tail on. In China, the head is saved for the most distinguished guest. I would have to pass on this dubious honor.

2½ to 3 pounds cleaned whole carp or red snapper

1 tablespoon mild soy sauce mixed with 1 tablespoon dry sherry

1 tablespoon peeled, grated fresh ginger

4 whole green onions, slivered

1. Wash fish thoroughly in cold water, drain, and pat dry with paper towels.
2. Place fish on heatproof platter and sprinkle with soy sauce mixture inside and out. Let stand for 10 minutes and drain off liquid.
3. Sprinkle with ginger inside and out.
4. Place platter on rack over boiling water in wok or skillet. Cover and steam for 4 minutes.
5. Top with green onions, cover, and steam for 10 to 15 minutes, or until fish flakes with a fork.

To Serve: Serve steamed fish with assorted steamed vegetables such as broccoli, cauliflower, and asparagus, and cooked brown rice. Fresh tangerines or Mandarin oranges complete this lean, Chinese-style meal.

Per serving: 128 calories; 21.8 gm protein; 3.1 gm fat; 1.2 gm carbohydrate; 0.3 gm fiber; 62 mg cholesterol; 175 mg sodium

Calorie-Counter's Scrod ⓠⓜ

Serves: 4 (4 ounces cooked fish = 1 serving)

Sturgeon, sea bass, red snapper, or salmon may be substituted for scrod.

1 small onion, thinly sliced
1¼ pounds scrod fillets, cut in
    4 portions
1 cup small mushrooms, quartered
1 small tomato, chopped
½ green pepper, seeded and
    chopped

2 tablespoons chopped parsley
⅓ cup dry white wine or vermouth
1 tablespoon lemon juice
¼ teaspoon dried dill
1 teaspoon salt-free vegetable
    seasoning
Freshly ground black pepper

1. Arrange onion slices in bottom of 9-inch glass baking dish that has been sprayed with nonstick cooking spray.
2. Place fish on top of onions. Combine remaining vegetables and parsley and spread over fish.
3. Mix wine, lemon juice, and seasonings and pour over vegetables.
4. Bake in preheated 375° oven for 15 minutes, or until fish flakes with a fork. Baste fish once or twice while baking.

To Serve: Remove fish to heated platter, spoon vegetables over fish. Accompany with Oriental Coleslaw (page 112) and fresh strawberries.

In Microwave: Cover fish and vegetables with vented plastic wrap and bake on high for 4 to 6 minutes, or until fish flakes with a fork.

Per serving: 173 calories; 31.5 gm protein; 1.0 gm fat; 5.4 gm carbohydrate; 0.8 gm fiber; 78 mg cholesterol; 111 mg sodium

Game Hens
Fine Fare

Hawaiian Hens with Cabbage
Apricot-Glazed Cornish Game Hens
Cornish Game Hens with
  Brandied Cherry Sauce

Quick Game Hens Fiesta
Tandoori Hens
Cornish Game Hens with
  Fruited Rice Dressing

Your freezer offers the convenience and availability of Cornish game hens. Have your butcher halve them so that they will defrost more readily. They make an uncomplicated and attractive company dish.

Hawaiian Hens with Cabbage

Serves: 4 (½ Cornish game hen = 1 serving)

¼ cup unsweetened pineapple
  juice concentrate
2 tablespoons grated fresh ginger
2 tablespoons mild soy sauce
1 tablespoon lime juice
1 tablespoon dry sherry
2 1-pound Cornish game hens,
  halved, excess skin and fat
  removed

½ head green cabbage, coarsely
  shredded
1 cup salt-free chicken broth,
  defatted

1. Combine first 5 ingredients and pour over hens in plastic bag. Marinate several hours, or overnight for more flavor.
2. Place hens with marinade in baking dish and roast uncovered in upper third of preheated 400° oven for 20 minutes.
3. Add cabbage (placing hens on top). Pour chicken broth over contents, cover, reduce heat to 350°. Bake for 30 minutes, or until tender.

To Serve: Serve hens in cabbage in baking dish if suitable. Accompany with a rice pilaf and Two-Pea Salad (page 116).

Per serving: 302 calories; 35.4 gm protein; 8.9 gm fat; 18.2 gm carbohydrate; 1.1 gm fiber; 101 mg cholesterol; 374 mg sodium

Apricot-Glazed
Cornish Game Hens Ⓠ Ⓜ

Serves: 4 (½ Cornish game hen = 1 serving)

An easy, appealing dish for company.

2 1–1½ pound Cornish game hens, halved, excess skin and fat removed
1 tablespoon Worcestershire sauce
1 tablespoon cornstarch
1 cup unsweetened apricot nectar
2 tablespoons unsweetened apricot jam

1 tablespoon apricot brandy (optional)
¼ cup toasted slivered almonds*
1 navel orange, peeled and cut into slices ¼ inch thick, and watercress for garnish

1. Paint halved hens with Worcestershire sauce. Broil until lightly browned on each side.
2. Combine cornstarch, nectar, jam, and brandy and bring to a boil.
3. Put hens in baking dish, pour sauce over them, and roast in preheated 350° oven for 30 minutes, or until tender.
To Serve: Arrange hens on warm serving platter. Sprinkle with almonds. Garnish with orange slices and watercress. Serve with wild rice with peas and steamed broccoli flowerets.

In Microwave: Cover with wax paper and cook 9 to 10 minutes on high or until tender. Let stand 7 minutes before serving.

Per serving: 234 calories; 25.0 gm protein; 6.4 gm fat; 16.3 gm carbohydrate; 0.2 gm fiber; 76 mg cholesterol; 120 mg sodium

* Toast almonds in a preheated 325° oven for 12 minutes until lightly browned.

Cornish Game Hens
with Brandied Cherry Sauce

Serves: 8 (2 quarters game hen = 1 serving)

Cook the pilaf while preparing the game hens and this meal can be ready for guests in 30 minutes.

4 1-pound Cornish game hens, quartered, excess skin and fat removed
Juice of 1 lemon
2 teaspoons salt-free vegetable seasoning
1 teaspoon onion powder
Hungarian paprika
¼ cup dry red wine
16-ounce can tart, pitted, water-packed cherries
⅓ cup frozen unsweetened apple juice concentrate
2 tablespoons cornstarch

1. Sprinkle hens with lemon juice, vegetable seasoning, onion powder, and paprika.

2. Brown hens on both sides on medium heat in 2-inch nonstick skillet coated with nonstick cooking spray. Pour off any fat. Add wine and cook for several minutes.

3. Drain cherries and save ⅔ cup juice.

4. Combine apple juice concentrate and cornstarch in saucepan. Add cherries and ⅔ cup juice and cook over medium heat, stirring, until thickened and clear.

5. Pour cherry mixture over hens, cover, and cook for 20 minutes, or until tender.

To Serve: Place hens on heated platter and nap with cherry mixture. Surround with steamed ½-inch zucchini spears and Bulgur and Buckwheat Pilaf (page 300).

Per serving: 271 calories; 33.5 gm protein; 9 gm fat; 12.6 gm carbohydrate; 0.1 gm fiber; 101 mg cholesterol; 105 mg sodium

Quick Game Hens Fiesta Ⓠ Ⓜ

Serves: 6 (½ Cornish game hen = 1 serving)

This dish may be prepared in a conventional oven, but for a speedy preparation, use a microwave.

⅔ cup salt-free chicken broth, defatted
1 tablespoon dehydrated vegetable flakes
1 cup salt-free tomato sauce
Few crushed red pepper flakes
½ cup sun-dried apricots, chopped
¼ cup unsweetened crushed pineapple with juice
3 1-pound Cornish game hens, halved, excess skin and fat removed

1 teaspoon salt-free vegetable seasoning
1 large garlic clove, minced
3 cups steamed brown rice mixed with 1 tablespoon soy sauce, ¼ teaspoon each ground ginger and allspice, 2 tablespoons sliced green onions, and 2 tablespoons chopped pecans

Watercress and fresh pineapple spears for garnish

1. Heat broth and dried vegetable flakes in saucepan for 5 minutes. Remove from heat.

2. Stir in tomato sauce, red pepper, apricots, and pineapple.

3. Season hens under skin with vegetable seasoning and garlic. Place on roasting pan and broil lightly on both sides.

4. Spoon sauce over hens and roast in preheated 375° oven for 35 to 40 minutes.

To Serve: Place brown rice mixture on heated serving platter. Arrange glazed hens on top. Spoon remaining sauce over all. Garnish with watercress and fresh pineapple spears.

In Microwave: Place hens skin side down in glass baking dish. Brush with half the sauce, cover with wax paper, and microwave on high for 6 minutes. Turn hens over, baste with remaining sauce, cover with wax paper, and cook on high for 12 minutes, or until juices run clear. (Give pan a half turn every 4 minutes.) Let stand for 5 minutes before serving.

Per serving: 342 calories; 28.4 gm protein; 9.0 gm fat; 36.7 gm carbohydrate; 0.9 gm fiber; 101 mg cholesterol; 186 mg sodium

Tandoori Hens

Serves: 8 (½ Cornish game hen = 1 serving)

The remaining marinade from this recipe may be saved for up to one week to use again with chicken breasts.

2 large garlic cloves
1 small onion, quartered
¼-inch slice peeled fresh ginger
2 cups nonfat yogurt
½ teaspoon each ground coriander
  and cumin
1 tablespoon Worcestershire sauce
¼ cup each lime or lemon juice and
  orange juice

1 teaspoon Hungarian paprika
4 1-pound Cornish game hens,
  halved, excess skin and fat
  removed

Watercress for garnish

1. Place garlic, onion, and ginger in food processor or blender and mince. Add yogurt, spices, Worcestershire sauce, citrus juices, and paprika and blend.
2. Make small slits in each hen with tip of sharp knife.
3. Pour yogurt mixture over hens in bowl, cover, and marinate in refrigerator for several hours or overnight.
4. Remove hens from marinade and broil in the oven or barbecue on a grill until golden brown, about 15 minutes on each side.
To Serve: Place on bed of watercress, serve with Cucumber Raita (page 362) as a condiment, Best-Ever Zucchini–Corn Casserole (page 274), toasted whole-wheat pita bread, and Company Apricot Chiffon Torte (page 320) for dessert.

Per serving: 227 calories; 33.7 gm protein; 8.5 gm fat; 1.8 gm carbohydrate; 0.1 gm fiber; 101 mg cholesterol; 118 mg sodium

Cornish Game Hens
with Fruited Rice Dressing Ⓠ Ⓜ

Serves: 6 (½ hen with stuffing = 1 serving)

This is an attractive presentation for company, and the option of microwave cooking cuts the time involved.

3 tablespoons salt-free chicken
   broth, defatted
2 tablespoons minced onion
1 cup cooked brown rice
¼ cup whole-wheat bread crumbs
1 McIntosh apple with skin,
   coarsely shredded
2 tablespoons dark raisins

2 tablespoons chopped pecans
3 1-pound Cornish game hens,
   halved, excess skin and fat
   removed
Juice of 1 lemon
2 teaspoons salt-free vegetable
   seasoning

Glaze:
2 teaspoons mild soy sauce
⅓ cup frozen unsweetened apple
   juice concentrate

2 tablespoons dry sherry
¼ cup frozen unsweetened orange
   juice concentrate

1. Cook onion in broth for 2 minutes. Add next 5 ingredients and stir.
2. Season hens with lemon juice and vegetable seasoning on both sides.
3. Place ⅓ cup rice dressing in nonstick baking pan. Cover with half a hen. Repeat with remaining dressing and hens.
4. Roast uncovered in preheated 375° oven for 30 minutes, or until tender.
5. Combine ingredients for glaze and simmer for 3 minutes. Baste hens with glaze frequently while cooking.

In Microwave: Arrange hens over stuffing in a nonmetal baking dish; add glaze, cover with wax paper, and microwave on high for 6 minutes. Rotate pan half a turn after 3 minutes. Brush with remaining glaze, cover with wax paper, and cook on high for 8 minutes, or until juices run clear. (Remember to rotate pan during cooking.) Let stand for 5 minutes before serving.

Per serving: 302 calories; 26.7 gm protein; 8.5 gm fat; 27.8 gm carbohydrate; 1.6 gm fiber; 101 mg cholesterol; 156 mg sodium

Poultry
A Chicken for Every Pot

Brazilian Orange Chicken Bravo
Brandied Chicken Breasts
Chicken Breasts in
  Green Peppercorn–Corn Sauce
Fast-Food Chicken Burgers
Chicken Breasts with Orange Sauce
Diet Watcher's Broiled or
  Barbecued Chicken
Speedy Chicken Breasts Pipérade
Grilled Chicken Breasts with
  Tarragon–Garlic Sauce
Springtime Chicken with Asparagus
  Sauce
Perfect Chicken Cacciatore
Nanette's Company Chicken
Oven-Fried Chicken
Chicken Marengo
Chicken Jambalaya
Deviled Drumsticks

Microwaved Chicken Breasts
Harold's Roast Chicken with
  Coleslaw
Quick Chicken Paprikash
Chicken Paprika with Wheat Pilaf
My Favorite Chicken Salad
All-American Chicken Sausage
  Patties
Skinny Scaloppine
Tex-Mex Microwaved Chicken
Chicken Vindaloo
Sherried Chicken with Leek
Teriyaki Chicken Kebabs
Simply Delicious Turkey Burger
Quick Turkey Italiano
Turkey Slices Marinara
Turkey Stroganoff
Pita Pockets with Turkey

A chicken by an other name—that is, poulet, pollo, murgha, torinku, or gai—will still taste as sweet. When Herbert Hoover promised his constituency "two chickens in every pot," he was really ahead of his time. It is only recently that Americans, in their quest for proper nutrition, have dramatically increased their consumption of poultry—a lighter, less fattening, lower cholesterol food that lends itself to a myriad of methods of preparation. Broilers, fryers, and occasionally roasters and turkeys, whole or sectioned, take up large portions of a supermarket meat case.

Broiled or barbecued chicken is always a favorite, but serving it the same way several times a week gets to be tiring. Good cooks are always receptive to new chicken recipes that are not too complicated. Fast Food Chicken Burgers (page 185), Turkey Slices Marinara (page 209), or Teriyaki Chicken Kebabs (page 206) take only minutes to prepare, while

Chicken Marengo (page 194), a one-dish meal, Brazilian Orange Chicken Bravo (page 182), and Turkey Stroganoff (page 210) make interesting additions to serve to guests as well as family.

When purchasing your poultry, make certain that it has no antibiotics, hormones, preservatives, or other chemicals added. Chickens are usually marketed at the age of 7 weeks. They do not need these additional substances if farmed and fed under proper conditions, nor do we as consumers if we are to maintain our pursuit of healthful living.

Brazilian Orange Chicken Bravo

Serves: 6 (4 ounces cooked chicken = 1 serving)

3 whole chicken breasts
   (3 pounds), halved, with skin
   and fat removed
Juice of ½ lemon
2 teaspoons salt-free vegetable
   seasoning
1 teaspoon garlic powder
1 cup orange juice with pulp

1 cup dry white wine
½ cup dark raisins
⅓ cup slivered almonds, ground
   fine
½ teaspoon ground ginger
Freshly ground black pepper

Chopped cilantro for garnish

1. Place chicken breasts in shallow baking pan and season with lemon, vegetable seasoning, and garlic powder. Brown lightly under broiler.
2. Combine remaining ingredients except cilantro in bowl; mix thoroughly and pour over chicken.
3. Bake in preheated 350° oven until tender, about 35 to 45 minutes. *Baste frequently.*

To Serve: Place hot chicken on bed of steamed brown rice with chopped fresh tomatoes. Pour remaining juices over all. Garnish with chopped cilantro.

Per serving: 325 calories; 37.5 gm protein; 9.1 gm fat; 16.8 gm carbohydrate; 1.3 gm fiber; 96 mg cholesterol; 94 mg sodium

Brandied Chicken Breasts

Serves: 4 (4 ounces cooked chicken = 1 serving)

2 whole chicken breasts (about 2
  pounds), halved, skinned, and
  boned
1 teaspoon salt-free vegetable
  seasoning
¼ teaspoon white pepper
2 teaspoons cold-pressed safflower
  oil
2 tablespoons brandy
2 shallots, minced
¼ pound mushrooms, cleaned and
  quartered

1 garlic clove, minced
¼ cup dry red wine
¼ cup dry white wine
¼ cup salt-free chicken broth,
  defatted
½ teaspoon dried thyme, crushed
1 teaspoon cornstarch plus
  2 tablespoons chicken broth
  (optional)

1. Season chicken breasts.
2. Heat oil in nonstick skillet and sauté chicken breasts on both sides.
3. Heat brandy; pour over chicken and flame.
4. When flame burns out, remove chicken from pan.
5. Add shallots and mushrooms to pan and sauté for 2 to 3 minutes.
6. Add garlic, wines, chicken broth, and thyme and bring to a simmer.
7. Return chicken to pan, cover, and simmer for 20 minutes.
8. If desired, thicken sauce with cornstarch mixture and cook until shiny.

To Serve: Place chicken breasts on heated platter and surround with steamed new potatoes, squash, and cauliflower.

Per serving: 278 calories; 36.6 gm protein; 8.7 gm fat; 7.1 gm carbohydrate; 0.5 gm fiber;
96 mg cholesterol; 95 mg sodium

Chicken Breasts in Green Peppercorn–Corn Sauce

Serves: 4 (4 ounces cooked chicken = 1 serving)

The piper nigrum vine is indigenous to Asia. It produces all black, white, and green peppercorns as we know them. Green peppercorns are milder than black or white but still have plenty of zip. They are available preserved in a brine or vinegar, or freeze-dried and vacuum-packed. I recommend you do not use the ones packed in brine because of the sodium content; I prefer using the freeze-dried. Green peppercorns are a wonderful seasoning for both fish and poultry. Since we eliminate salt, the green peppercorns add a special zest to this chicken recipe.

2 whole chicken breasts (about 2 pounds), halved, skin and fat removed
Juice of ½ lemon
1 teaspoon salt-free vegetable seasoning
1 teaspoon Hungarian paprika
1 cup dry red wine
3 tablespoons raspberry wine vinegar
6 shallots, minced
2 garlic cloves, minced

1 bay leaf
½ teaspoon dried thyme, crushed
1 cup canned Italian plum tomatoes in sauce, finely chopped
1 cup salt-free chicken broth, defatted
2 tablespoons tomato paste
1½ cups frozen corn
1 teaspoon ground freeze-dried green peppercorns or
1 tablespoon whole green peppercorns, crushed

1. Sprinkle chicken breasts with lemon juice, vegetable seasoning, and paprika.

2. Place chicken in flameproof baking dish and broil until golden brown on both sides.

3. Remove chicken and deglaze pan over medium heat with red wine and vinegar, scraping up loose particles from pan with a wooden spoon.

4. Add shallots, garlic, bay leaf, and thyme. Simmer uncovered for about 10 minutes to reduce sauce.

5. Add chopped tomatoes, chicken broth, and tomato paste. Stir well, then simmer uncovered for 10 minutes.

6. Add browned chicken breasts to sauce and cook 15 to 20 minutes.

7. Remove chicken to a heated platter and cover.

8. Simmer remaining liquid until reduced to about 2 cups. Add corn and green peppercorns. Simmer for 5 to 10 minutes. Taste and adjust seasonings. Remove bay leaf.

To Serve: Pour sauce over chicken breasts and serve immediately with steamed brown rice and fresh asparagus.

Per serving: 341 calories; 40.0 gm protein; 5.4 gm fat; 34.5 gm carbohydrate; 2.4 gm fiber; 96 mg cholesterol; 113 mg sodium

Fast-Food Chicken Burgers Ⓠ

Serves: 4 (3 ounces cooked chicken = 1 serving)

Served on a toasted whole-wheat bun with sliced beefsteak tomato, mild onion slices, and romaine, this is hardly what you are able to find at your neighborhood hamburger stand.

1 pound coarsely ground raw
   chicken or turkey
1 small onion, chopped
1 green pepper, seeded and
   chopped
1 carrot, chopped
1 garlic clove, minced
¼ cup whole-wheat fresh bread
   crumbs
3 tablespoons salt-free tomato juice
   or salt-free chicken broth,
   defatted

1 teaspoon Dijon mustard
¼ teaspoon dried thyme, crushed
1 teaspoon salt-free vegetable
   seasoning
Freshly ground black pepper
1 tablespoon toasted sesame seeds
   (optional)

1. Combine all ingredients in a mixing bowl and stir lightly with fork until well blended.
2. Shape into 4 patties ¾ inch thick.
3. Heat nonstick skillet or heavy iron skillet; spray with butter-flavored nonstick cooking spray.
4. When hot, add chicken patties and cook until browned on one side. Turn patties over, cover, and cook for 2 minutes. Remove cover and finish browning.
5. Serve immediately on toasted whole-wheat bun.

Per serving: 182 calories; 27.5 gm protein; 4.2 gm fat; 7.2 gm carbohydrate; 0.6 gm fiber; 72 mg cholesterol; 89 mg sodium

Chicken Breasts with Orange Sauce Ⓜ

Serves: 6 (4 ounces cooked chicken = 1 serving)

This chicken dish is lovely as well as delicious.

1 tablespoon grated orange rind
1 teaspoon grated lemon rind
1¼ cups orange juice
½ cup lemon juice
1 tablespoon mild soy sauce
½ teaspoon dried rosemary, crushed
1 teaspoon salt-free vegetable seasoning

3 1-pound whole chicken breasts, halved, with skin and fat removed
3 cups steamed brown and wild rice to serve with chicken
12 orange slices

Watercress for garnish

1. Combine first 7 ingredients.
2. Place marinade in plastic bag with chicken breasts. Marinate for several hours or overnight.
3. Spray 3-quart rectangular baking dish with nonstick cooking spray. Place chicken breasts bone side up and cover with marinade.
4. Cover baking dish with foil and bake in a preheated 350° oven for 50 to 60 minutes, or until tender.
5. Remove chicken and keep warm. Pour marinade into saucepan, bring to a boil, and reduce by half.

To Serve: Place rice on serving platter, top with chicken breasts and orange slices; spoon hot sauce over chicken and oranges. Garnish with sprigs of watercress.

In Microwave: Cook chicken covered with wax paper for 7 minutes on high. Turn breasts over and sprinkle with Micro-Shake. Cover with wax paper and cook for 7 minutes, or until tender. Let stand for 7 minutes before serving.

Per serving: 327 calories; 38.6 gm protein; 6.3 gm fat; 28.2 gm carbohydrate; 0.4 gm fiber; 98 mg cholesterol; 194 mg sodium

Diet Watcher's Broiled or Barbecued Chicken @

Serves: 4 (4 ounces cooked chicken = 1 serving)

Whether broiled or barbecued, this low-calorie chicken is a winner.

1 cup dry white wine
1 large garlic clove, minced
½ teaspoon dried tarragon,
   crushed
1 teaspoon dried Italian herb
   blend, crushed

Freshly ground black pepper
2-pound fryer, quartered, with skin
   and fat removed

1. In small jar, combine first 5 ingredients. Shake well.
2. Place chicken in shallow dish; pour blended marinade over chicken.
3. Marinate for several hours or overnight. Turn several times while marinating.
4. Place chicken on broiler rack and broil 5 to 6 inches from heat for 15 minutes on each side. Brush frequently with marinade while cooking.

To Serve: Start with a crisp green salad. Then serve broiled chicken with Fresh Tomato Relish (page 364), steamed little red new potatoes, lemony Brussels sprouts, and parslied carrots. A good dessert is fresh fruit. From beginning to end, a diet watcher's dream come true.

Per serving: 227 calories; 32.9 gm protein; 8.4 gm fat; 0.5 gm carbohydrate; 0.1 gm fiber; 101 mg cholesterol; 98 mg sodium

Speedy Chicken Breasts Pipérade ⓠ

Serves: 4 (4 ounces cooked chicken = 1 serving)

A pipérade vegetable mixture of peppers, onions, and tomatoes may be served over chicken, fish, veal, or—a baked potato!

2 whole chicken breasts
   (2 pounds), halved, boned, and
   flattened, with skin and fat
   removed
Juice of ½ lemon
½ teaspoon herbes de Provence,
   crushed
1 teaspoon salt-free vegetable
   seasoning
2 teaspoons Worcestershire sauce
1 teaspoon extra-virgin olive oil

1 large garlic clove, minced
1 large red onion, thinly sliced, or
⅔ cup Onion Magic (page 36)
1 small green pepper, seeded and
   thinly sliced
1 small sweet red pepper, seeded
   and thinly sliced
½ teaspoon dried thyme, crushed
Freshly ground black pepper
1 large tomato, halved, seeded, and
   diced

1. Season chicken breasts on both sides with lemon, herbes de Provence, vegetable seasoning, and Worcestershire sauce.

2. Place oil in nonstick skillet; add garlic and onion and sauté for 2 to 3 minutes. Add green and red peppers, thyme, and ground pepper. Cover and cook over medium heat 5 minutes. Add tomato and heat for 2 to 3 minutes. Remove from heat and cover to keep warm.

3. Sauté chicken breasts in nonstick skillet sprayed with butter-flavored nonstick cooking spray for 5 to 6 minutes on each side, or until nicely browned.

To Serve: Place chicken on heated platter and spoon vegetable mixture over each piece. Serve with whole-wheat linguine and steamed summer squash.

Per serving: 250 calories; 36.7 gm protein; 6.7 gm fat; 9.8 gm carbohydrate; 1.4 gm fiber; 96 mg cholesterol; 119 mg sodium

Grilled Chicken Breasts
with Tarragon–Garlic Sauce ℚ

Serves: 4 (4 ounces cooked chicken = 1 serving)

2 1-pound whole chicken breasts, halved, boned, and flattened, with skin and fat removed

1 teaspoon salt-free vegetable seasoning

½ teaspoon white pepper

½ teaspoon dried tarragon, crushed, or 2 tablespoons chopped fresh tarragon

½ cup lowfat milk

½ cup salt-free chicken broth, defatted

1 large garlic clove, minced

1 tablespoon cornstarch diluted in 2 tablespoons cold chicken broth or milk

1. Season flattened chicken breasts with vegetable seasoning, pepper, and tarragon.

2. Coat nonstick skillet with butter-flavored nonstick cooking spray and heat. Sauté chicken in heated skillet about 7 to 8 minutes on each side.

3. Simmer remaining ingredients except cornstarch mixture in uncovered saucepan for 15 minutes.

4. Add cornstarch mixture to sauce; heat and stir until shiny.

To Serve: Place chicken on heated plate, nap with tarragon–garlic sauce, and accompany with Larry's Oven-Fried Potatoes (page 266) and steamed broccoli, cauliflower, and carrots.

Per serving: 225 calories; 36.3 gm protein; 5.7 gm fat; 4.1 gm carbohydrate; 0.1 gm fiber; 99 mg cholesterol; 104 mg sodium

Springtime Chicken
with Asparagus Sauce ⓠ

Serves: 4 (4 ounces cooked chicken = 1 serving)

It's always a treat to use seasonal vegetables. Fresh, tender, green asparagus gives the chicken a different flavor.

1 pound asparagus, thoroughly washed, tough ends removed, and steamed

½ onion, 2 carrots, and ½ stalk celery, finely chopped

10½-ounce can salt-free chicken broth, defatted

1¼ pounds boneless chicken breast, skinned and cut into 1½-inch cubes

4 whole green onions, thinly sliced

1½ teaspoons salt-free vegetable seasoning

½ teaspoon freshly ground black pepper

2 tablespoons whole-wheat flour

2 teaspoons lemon juice

2 ounces sliced pimiento (optional) for garnish

1. Puree steamed asparagus in food processor or blender saving 8 tips for garnish.
2. In an iron skillet sprayed with butter-flavored nonstick cooking spray, dry-roast onion, carrots, and celery for 3 minutes, or until lightly browned, stirring constantly. Add ¼ cup of the chicken broth as needed to keep from scorching.
3. Add chicken and sauté slowly until lightly browned, about 3 minutes.
4. Add green onions, vegetable seasoning, and pepper. Sauté for 2 minutes.
5. Sprinkle with flour, stir, and cook for 2 to 3 minutes.
6. Add remaining chicken broth and lemon juice, cover, and simmer for 15 minutes.
7. Add asparagus puree to cooked chicken and blend. Taste and adjust seasonings.

To Serve: Place bed of brown rice on serving platter. Top with chicken mixture and garnish with asparagus spears and sliced pimiento. Steamed crisp baby carrots add color.

Per serving: 274 calories; 39.6 gm protein; 5.7 gm fat; 15.4 gm carbohydrate; 2.5 gm fiber; 96 mg cholesterol; 112 mg sodium

Perfect Chicken Cacciatore Ⓠ Ⓜ

Serves: 4 (4 ounces cooked chicken = 1 serving)

This dish may be fully prepared the day before. To reheat, place in a preheated 350° oven for 20 minutes. May also be frozen for future use.

16-ounce can Italian plum tomatoes, crushed
⅓ cup dry white wine
1 small onion, chopped
1 small green pepper, seeded and chopped
2 garlic cloves, minced
1 bay leaf
½ teaspoon fennel seeds, crushed with flat side of a knife
1 teaspoon dried oregano, crushed

½ teaspoon ground coriander
¼ teaspoon ground cinnamon
½ teaspoon crushed red pepper
2-pound broiler cut into serving pieces, with skin and fat removed, or 2 whole chicken breasts, halved, with skin and fat removed
Juice of ½ lemon
1 teaspoon salt-free vegetable seasoning

1. Place tomatoes in small saucepan. Add all remaining ingredients except chicken, lemon juice, and vegetable seasoning. Cover and simmer for 5 minutes.

2. Season chicken with lemon juice and vegetable seasoning and broil on both sides until lightly browned.

3. Arrange chicken pieces in baking dish sprayed with nonstick cooking spray. Pour sauce over chicken.

4. Cover and bake in preheated 350° oven for 45 minutes, or until tender. Remove bay leaf.

To Serve: Serve with whole wheat spaghetti and steamed vegetables such as zucchini, green beans, or peas and carrots.

In Microwave: Arrange chicken in glass baking dish, meat-side down, with thick portions toward edge of dish. Cover with wax paper and cook on high for 10 to 13 minutes. Halfway through heating, turn chicken over. Let stand covered for 7 minutes before serving.

Per serving: 253 calories; 36.9 gm protein; 5.7 gm fat; 9.6 gm carbohydrate; 1.4 gm fiber; 96 mg cholesterol; 105 mg sodium

Nanette's Company Chicken

Serves: 8 (4 ounces cooked chicken = 1 serving)

Chicken and rice is a popular combination in many countries: There is Mexican arroz con pollo, Hungarian chicken rice paprikash, and now, for your enjoyment, Nanette's chicken and rice. As an added plus, this dish also freezes beautifully.

1 cup brown rice, washed
2 tablespoons chopped onion
½ cup cleaned and sliced
  mushrooms
4-ounce jar chopped pimiento,
  drained
2 10½-ounce cans salt-free chicken
  broth, defatted
4 1-pound chicken breasts, halved,
  with skin and fat removed
1 teaspoon garlic powder
1 teaspoon salt-free vegetable
  seasoning

Freshly ground black pepper
1½ cups Basic Béchamel (page
  28) or 1 package salt-free dried
  mushroom soup mix
  reconstituted with nonfat milk
3 tablespoons dehydrated onion
  flakes
2 tablespoons grated Parmesan
  cheese

¼ cup sliced whole green onions
  for garnish

1. Place rice in bottom of 3-quart ovenproof casserole (9 x 13 inches).
2. Sprinkle onions, mushrooms, and pimientos over rice. Add chicken broth.
3. Season chicken with garlic powder, vegetable seasoning, and pepper. Place on top of rice mixture.
4. Pour béchamel or soup mix over chicken.
5. Combine onion flakes and cheese and sprinkle on top of chicken.
6. Cover with foil and bake in preheated 325° oven for 40 minutes. Remove foil and bake for 30 minutes, or until tender.

To Serve: Sprinkle with green onions and serve with Ever-Ready Red Cabbage Slaw (page 108). Orange Baked Alaska is an elegant but easy dessert.

Per serving: 276 calories; 38.3 gm protein; 6.3 gm fat; 13.2 gm carbohydrate; 0.3 gm fiber; 98 mg cholesterol; 138 mg sodium

Oven-Fried Chicken

Serves: 4 (4 ounces cooked chicken = 1 serving)

What could be more American than fried chicken? And what could be greasier and higher in fat than most fried chicken served at home or commercially? This oven-cooked chicken tastes crispy and flavorful without all the fat that is presently thought to contribute to heart disease.

2-pound broiler, quartered, with
    skin and fat removed
¼ cup low-calorie Italian dressing
¼ cup salt-free tomato juice
½ teaspoon garlic powder

1 teaspoon onion flakes
½ cup whole-wheat bread crumbs
    or crushed, sugar-free cornflakes
Hungarian paprika

1. Place chicken, Italian dressing, tomato juice, garlic powder, and onion flakes in plastic bag. Let chicken marinate for 30 minutes at room temperature or several hours in refrigerator. Turn frequently.
2. Place crumbs in second plastic bag. Drain chicken and shake 1 piece at a time to coat with crumbs.
3. Arrange crumbed chicken (bone side down) on nonstick baking sheet, sprayed with nonstick cooking spray. Sprinkle with paprika.
4. Bake in upper third of preheated 375° oven for 50 to 60 minutes, or until crisped.

To Serve: Place crisp golden chicken on bed of bulgur wheat pilaf. Surround with broiled tomato halves and steamed green beans and carrots. For dessert, you might serve Strawberry–Banana–Yogurt Pie (page 329).

Per serving: 250 calories; 34.1 gm protein; 8.7 gm fat; 6.4 gm carbohydrate; 0.2 gm fiber; 101 mg cholesterol; 135 mg sodium

Chicken Marengo

Serves: 8 (4 ounces cooked chicken [1 half breast] with vegetables
and ½ cup steamed brown rice = 1 serving)

This makes a spectacular one-dish meal for entertaining!

¾ cup dry whole-wheat bread
crumbs
¼ cup whole-wheat flour
1 teaspoon Hungarian paprika
1 teaspoon onion powder
1 teaspoon garlic powder
1 teaspoon herbes de Provence,
crushed
1 teaspoon salt-free vegetable
seasoning
4 whole chicken breasts, halved,
with skin and fat removed
1 cup buttermilk, strained
3 tablespoons salt-free chicken
broth, defatted, or 1 tablespoon
cold-pressed safflower oil
3 green onions or shallots, minced
¼ cup minced parsley
1 tablespoon mild soy sauce
1 bay leaf

2 tablespoons tomato paste
3 cups salt-free chicken broth,
defatted
¼ cup Madeira or dry sherry
½ pound mushrooms, cleaned and
sliced
10-ounce package frozen peas
¼ pound fresh snow peas
3 tablespoons cornstarch blended
with ½ cup salt-free chicken
broth, defatted
4 ripe tomatoes, peeled, seeded,
and cut into eighths
4 cups steamed brown rice
2 ounces broken whole-wheat
spaghetti, cooked al dente,
drained, and toasted in a
preheated 400° oven until golden
brown

1. Combine first 7 ingredients in shallow dish.
2. Dip chicken in buttermilk, then in seasoned bread crumbs.
3. Place on nonstick baking sheet and bake in upper third of preheated 400° oven for 40 to 45 minutes.
4 While chicken is baking, place chicken broth or oil in large sauté pan, add shallots and parsley. Sauté for 3 to 5 minutes. Add soy sauce, bay leaf, tomato paste, chicken broth, and Madeira or sherry. Stir well and simmer for 20 minutes.
5. Add mushrooms, stir, and simmer for 5 minutes.
6. Add peas and snow peas. Add blended cornstarch to mixture and simmer slowly for 3 minutes, or until shiny.
7. Add tomatoes to sauce and heat for 3 minutes. Remove bay leaf.

To Serve: Arrange brown rice on large, heated platter; place hot chicken breasts over rice and pour sauce with vegetables over chicken. Sprinkle with toasted pasta and serve immediately.

Per serving: 462 calories; 44.8 gm protein; 7.2 gm fat; 52.0 gm carbohydrate; 2.9 gm fiber; 98 mg cholesterol; 262 mg sodium

Chicken Jambalaya

Serves: 4 (4 ounces cooked chicken = 1 serving)

The Cajuns and Creoles of Louisiana have contributed this classic dish to American cuisine. Currently this piquant type of food preparation has become popular throughout the country, mainly because of Paul Prud-homme's great cooking skills.

1 tablespoon cold-pressed safflower oil or 2 chicken bouillon cubes
1 large onion, chopped
1 large green pepper, seeded and chopped
1 large garlic clove, minced
1 celery stalk with leaves, chopped
1 2-pound fryer, quartered with skin and fat removed
3 tablespoons minced parsley

1 teaspoon salt-free vegetable seasoning
1 teaspoon dried thyme, crushed
2 bay leaves
½–1 teaspoon hot pepper sauce
28-ounce can Italian tomatoes in sauce, chopped
2¼ cups water or salt-free chicken broth, defatted
1½ cups brown rice

1 Place oil in sauté pan over medium heat. Add onion, green pepper, garlic and celery and sauté for 2 to 3 minutes, or until lightly browned.

2. Add chicken and brown lightly, about 5 minutes.

3. Add all remaining ingredients except rice and simmer for 5 minutes.

4. Add rice, bring to a simmer, cover, and simmer about 40 to 45 minutes, or until rice is tender. Taste and adjust seasonings. Remove bay leaves. A little more hot pepper sauce may be added, for the stout-hearted.

To Serve: Place jambalaya in heated tureen or casserole and serve with steamed okra and cauliflower.

Per serving: 325 calories; 8.3 gm protein; 2.2 gm fat; 69.5 gm carbohydrate; 7.4 gm fiber; 0 mg cholesterol; 45 mg sodium

Deviled Drumsticks ⓠ
(Served Hot or Cold)

Serves: 8 (2 drumsticks = 1 serving)

⅔ cup dry whole-wheat bread
  crumbs
2 teaspoons onion powder
2 teaspoons curry powder
½ teaspoon dry mustard
¼ teaspoon garlic powder

1 teaspoon Hungarian paprika
1 cup nonfat milk or buttermilk
Few drops hot pepper sauce
2½ pounds drumsticks, skin and fat
  removed

1. Combine first 6 ingredients in plastic or paper bag.
2. Place milk and pepper sauce in shallow dish and soak drumsticks.
3. Shake 2 drumsticks at a time in the crumb mixture.
4. Place drumsticks in nonstick baking dish.
5. Bake in preheated 375° oven for 25 minutes. Turn drumsticks after 15 minutes to brown them evenly.

Per serving: 122 calories; 14.8 gm protein; 3.8 gm fat; 6.4 gm carbohydrate; 0.3 gm fiber; 36 mg cholesterol; 80 mg sodium

Microwaved Chicken Breasts ⓠⓜ

Serves: 4 (1 half breast = 1 serving)

3 tablespoons low-calorie Russian
  dressing
1 garlic clove, minced
1 teaspoon dehydrated onion flakes
¼ teaspoon dry mustard

2 whole chicken breasts (2 pounds),
  halved, with skin and fat
  removed

Watercress and cherry tomatoes
  for garnish

1. Combine first 4 ingredients.
2. Place chicken breasts bone side down in round nonmetal baking dish (thick parts of chicken to outside of dish).

3. Spoon mixture over chicken, cover with plastic wrap, and vent.

4. Microwave on high for 10 to 12 minutes, or until tender. Baste chicken with sauce after 5 minutes of cooking. Let stand 5 minutes before serving.

To Serve: Place chicken breasts on bed of watercress and garnish with cherry tomatoes. Serve with Spinach with Corn (page 269), steamed brown rice, and a Truly Delicious Baked Apple (page 315) for dessert.

Per serving: 148 calories; 27.1 gm protein; 3.1 gm fat; 0.9 gm carbohydrate; 0 gm fiber; 73 mg cholesterol; 65 mg sodium

Harold's Roast Chicken and Coleslaw

Serves: 4 (4 ounces cooked chicken = 1 serving)

A packaged coleslaw mix and seasoned chicken breasts combine to make a delectable dinner. It's even better the next day.

1 small onion, sliced
1 stalk celery, sliced
2 whole chicken breasts (2 pounds), skinned, halved, and fat removed
1 teaspoon each salt-free vegetable seasoning and onion and garlic powders
Freshly ground black pepper
Hungarian paprika

8-ounce package coleslaw mix* or 3 cups finely shredded cabbage
2 cups salt-reduced stewed tomatoes or chicken broth, defatted

1. Place onion and celery in roaster. Top with chicken breasts. Combine seasonings and sprinkle over chicken breasts.

2. Cover and roast for 30 minutes in preheated 375° oven.

3. Add coleslaw or cabbage and tomatoes. Stir mixture to combine.

4. Cover and roast for 15 more minutes.

To Serve: Serve with Near East pilaf mix and steamed green beans.

Per serving: 162 calories; 27.5 gm protein; 3.2 gm fat; 3.7 gm carbohydrate; 0.7 gm fiber; 73 mg cholesterol; 75 mg sodium

* Make certain package of coleslaw mix does not contain sodium bisulfite or other preservatives.

Quick Chicken Paprikash

Serves: 4 (3 ounces cooked chicken = 1 serving)

How could anything that tastes so good be so easy to prepare?

½ onion, finely chopped
2 carrots, finely chopped
½ stalk celery, finely chopped
1¼ pounds chicken breasts, with
  skin and fat removed, cut into
  1½-inch cubes
2 garlic cloves, minced
1 teaspoon salt-free vegetable
  seasoning
Hungarian paprika

½ teaspoon freshly ground black
  pepper
2 cups salt-free chicken broth,
  defatted
2 6-ounce baking potatoes cut in
  1-inch cubes
1 cup quartered mushrooms
2 teaspoons Hungarian paprika
1 cup frozen peas
1 cup frozen cut green beans

1. Dry-roast onions, carrots, and celery in sauté pan sprayed with nonstick cooking spray. Stir constantly until lightly browned. If vegetables stick, add a bit of the chicken broth.

2. Add cubed chicken, garlic, vegetable seasoning, paprika, and pepper. Brown lightly for 3 minutes.

3. Add remaining chicken broth, potatoes, and mushrooms.

4. Mix, sprinkle with additional 2 teaspoons paprika, and bring to a boil.

5. Reduce to a simmer, cover, and cook for 20 minutes. Add peas and beans, cover, and cook 5 more minutes.

To Serve: This one-dish meal is completed with Sarah's Hungarian Wilted Salad (page 126) and a dried fruit compote.

Per serving: 299 calories; 31.7 gm protein; 4.5 gm fat; 32.7 gm carbohydrate; 3.6 gm fiber; 72 mg cholesterol; 129 mg sodium

Chicken Paprika with Wheat Pilaf

Serves: 4 (3 ounces cooked chicken = 1 serving)

The cuisines of Hungary and the Near East are combined in this recipe, resulting in a delicious natural flavor.

½ cup Onion Magic (page 36)
¼ cup salt-free chicken broth, defatted
2-pound frying chicken, cut up, with skin and fat removed
2 teaspoons salt-free vegetable seasoning
½ teaspoon white pepper
1 green pepper, seeded and chopped
1 tomato, seeded and chopped

1 tablespoon Hungarian paprika
½ cup salt-free chicken broth, defatted
8-ounce package Near East wheat pilaf mix

⅔ cup nonfat yogurt mixed with 2 tablespoons chopped fresh dill or green onion for garnish (optional)

1. Heat onion mixture with ¼ cup chicken broth in nonstick sauté pan or Dutch oven for 5 minutes.
2. Add remaining ingredients except pilaf and mix well.
3. Cover and simmer over low heat for 30 minutes.
4. Add wheat pilaf mix and 2 cups boiling water. Cover and simmer for 15 minutes.

To Serve: Place chicken paprika with wheat pilaf on serving platter. Garnish with dollops of yogurt and dill or green onion. Surround with steamed shredded green cabbage. Pineapple Ambrosia (page 326) would be a refreshing dessert.

Per serving: 406 calories; 32.3 gm protein; 7.3 gm fat; 48.3 gm carbohydrate; 1.4 gm fiber; 76 mg cholesterol; 79 mg sodium

My Favorite Chicken Salad Ⓠ

Serves: 6 (⅔ cup = 1 serving)

Speaking of truth in advertising, we have a favorite restaurant in West-wood Village in Los Angeles. When my husband and I eat there, we always chuckle at the listing on the menu for chicken salad—"Chicken Salad: Since 1945, made from turkey."

¼ cup nonfat yogurt
2 tablespoons light mayonnaise
⅛ teaspoon white pepper
½ teaspoon curry powder
1 teaspoon Worcestershire sauce
2 cups shredded, cooked chicken
 mixed with 3 tablespoons
 salt-free chicken broth, defatted
½ cup diced celery
½ cup canned, sliced water
 chestnuts, drained and chopped

7½-ounce can unsweetened,
 crushed pineapple, drained
6 leaves romaine lettuce
3 tablespoons slivered, toasted
 almonds

3 oranges, peeled and sliced, for
 garnish

1. Combine first 5 ingredients in bowl.
2. Add chicken, celery, water chestnuts, and pineapple.
3. Blend with fork.

To Serve: Line platter with crisp romaine leaves. Mound chicken salad, sprinkle with almonds, and garnish with orange slices.

Variation: Seedless grapes may be substituted for pineapple in the chicken salad.

Per serving: 197 calories; 16 gm protein; 6 gm fat; 19 gm carbohydrate; 2.1 gm fiber; 44 mg cholesterol; 100 mg sodium

All-American
Chicken Sausage Patties ⓠ

Yield: 6 patties (1 patty = 1 serving)

Another recipe inspired by my friend Gail de Krassel, the chef-owner of The Scratch Restaurant. This recipe goes faster if your friendly butcher will grind the chicken for you.

2 pounds chicken thighs, boned, with skin and fat removed
½ bulb fresh fennel, cut in 8 pieces
½ large onion, cubed
3 garlic cloves, halved
½ cup parsley without stems

½ teaspoon crushed red pepper flakes
½ teaspoon white pepper
1 teaspoon ground sage
¼ teaspoon salt (optional) *

1. Grind chicken or process in food processor until finely chopped. Remove to mixing bowl.
2. Place fennel, onion, garlic, and parsley in food processor. Process until finely minced.
3. Add to chicken in mixing bowl with red pepper, white pepper, sage, and salt if desired. Blend thoroughly with fork.
4. Shape into 6 patties.
5. Heat nonstick skillet sprayed with nonstick cooking spray and cook sausage patties for 4 to 5 minutes on each side, or until lightly browned.
To Serve: Serve with Onion-Mustard Sauce (page 367), Fresh Tomato Coulis (page 363), a steamed vegetable bouquet of asparagus, broccoli, and string beans, and Pritikin whole-wheat bread.

Per serving: 162 calories; 16.7 gm protein; 7.7 gm fat; 7.3 gm carbohydrate; 1.7 gm fiber; 54 mg cholesterol; 61 mg sodium

* Remember this adds 500 mg. sodium.

Skinny Scaloppine ℚ

Serves: 4 (3 ounces cooked chicken = 1 serving)

If your scaloppine sticks while searing, add a bit of defatted salt-free chicken broth.

2 1-pound whole chicken breasts, halved and boned, with skin and fat removed
Juice of ½ lemon
Hungarian paprika
¼ pound mushrooms, cleaned and sliced

1 garlic clove, minced
1 tablespoon lemon juice
2 teaspoons mild soy sauce
½ cup dry sherry
3 whole green onions, thinly sliced

1. Pound chicken breasts between waxed paper to ½-inch thickness. Season with lemon juice and paprika.

2. Coat nonstick sauté pan with butter-flavored nonstick cooking spray; heat and sear chicken breasts until golden brown on both sides. Remove to serving plate to keep warm.

3. Add mushrooms, garlic, lemon juice, soy sauce, and sherry to sauté pan and cook about 5 minutes. Sprinkle with green onions and heat for 2 to 3 minutes.

4. Pour hot mushroom mixture over chicken scallops and serve immediately.

To Serve: Accompany scaloppine with spinach, Pasta Shells with Herbed Tomato Sauce (page 287), hot crusty Italian bread, and Melon in Strawberry Sauce (page 324).

Per serving: 189 calories; 26.8 gm protein; 3.9 gm fat; 2.1 gm carbohydrate; 0.3 gm fiber; 72 mg cholesterol; 166 mg sodium

Tex-Mex Microwaved Chicken Ⓠ Ⓜ

Serves: 4 (4 ounces cooked chicken = 1 serving)

A quick meal in minutes that tastes as though it took hours!

2-pound broiler, quartered, with skin and fat removed
1 cup Spicy Barbecue Sauce (page 365); add ¼ teaspoon ground cumin

2 tablespoons chopped cilantro or parsley

1. Arrange chicken in round baking dish with meaty portion toward outside of dish and bone side up.
2. Brush chicken with barbecue sauce. Cover with waxed paper.
3. Microwave on high for 7 minutes.
4. Turn chicken pieces meat side up so that less cooked portions are toward the outside. Brush chicken with sauce and cover with wax paper.
5. Microwave on high for 8 to 10 minutes more, or until tender.* Let stand for 7 minutes before serving.

To Serve: Arrange chicken on warm serving platter, brush with remaining sauce, and garnish with chopped cilantro or parsley. Serve with warmed fresh corn tortillas, Mexican Red Rice (page 301), and stir-fried zucchini sticks. Tapioca with Mango (page 332) is a suitable dessert.

Per serving: 221 calories; 33.5 gm protein; 8.6 gm fat; 6.2 gm carbohydrate; 0.2 gm fiber; 101 mg cholesterol; 129 mg sodium

* To prepare in traditional oven, bake at 350° in covered casserole for 20 minutes. Brush with sauce and bake uncovered for 15 minutes, or until tender.

Chicken Vindaloo

Serves: 2 (4 ounces cooked chicken = 1 serving)

While working in Singapore with Executive Chef Arthur Hanie of the Holiday Inn in Kuching, we complemented the mild taste of chicken breasts with a sauce that has the exotic flavors of Malaysia.

2 5-ounce boneless chicken breasts, with skin and fat removed
½ cup nonfat yogurt
1 teaspoon onion powder
1 teaspoon salt-free vegetable seasoning
¾ cup minced onion
2 garlic cloves, minced
½ teaspoon curry powder
¼ teaspoon ground coriander
Dash turmeric
½ cinnamon stick
2 tablespoons chopped green pepper
⅓ cup salt-free chicken broth, defatted
½ ripe mango or papaya, mashed

1. Marinate chicken in yogurt, onion powder, and vegetable seasoning for several hours or overnight.
2. Dry-roast onions in nonstick skillet, stirring constantly, until lightly browned. Add garlic, curry, coriander, turmeric, and cinnamon stick. Stir constantly for 2 minutes.
3. Add green pepper and chicken broth. Simmer for 20 minutes and remove cinnamon stick.
4. Add mango or papaya puree and stir in well.
5. Remove chicken from marinade and broil for 5 to 7 minutes on each side. Add chicken to sauce and cook for 10 minutes.

To Serve: Place chicken, napped with sauce, on platter; surround with wild rice and steamed zucchini spears.

Per serving: 303 calories; 40.0 gm protein; 5.7 gm fat; 21.6 gm carbohydrate; 1.5 gm fiber; 98 mg cholesterol; 136 mg sodium

Sherried Chicken with Leek

Serves: 12 (4 ounces cooked chicken = 1 serving)

Although this wonderful company dish is quickly prepared, the cooking time is a bit longer.

3 2-pound frying chickens, quartered, with skin and fat removed
Juice of 1 lemon
3 teaspoons salt-free vegetable seasoning
Hungarian paprika
1 cup dry sherry
1¼ teaspoons dried thyme, crushed
3 large garlic cloves, minced

3 tablespoons chopped parsley
Few grains crushed red pepper flakes
1 tablespoon Worcestershire sauce
2–3 large leeks (white part only), split, washed, and chopped
Hungarian paprika

Watercress leaves for garnish

1. Season chicken with lemon juice, vegetable seasoning, and paprika. Brown in nonstick skillet sprayed with nonstick cooking spray.
2. Combine sherry, thyme, garlic, parsley, red pepper, and Worcestershire sauce. Stir well.
3. Place half the leeks in baking dish and top with half the chicken pieces. Sprinkle with paprika. Pour some of sherry mixture over chicken. Repeat, layering until all ingredients are used.
4. Cover and bake chicken in preheated 300° oven for 2 to 2½ hours.
To Serve: Serve chicken in baking dish garnished with watercress. Accompany with steamed wild rice, crisp steamed asparagus spears, and an Orangey Beet and Pea Salad (page 105).

Per serving: 226 calories; 33.2 gm protein; 8.5 gm fat; 2.5 gm carbohydrate; 0.2 gm fiber; 101 mg cholesterol; 137 mg sodium

Teriyaki Chicken Kebabs Ⓠⓜ

Serves: 4 (2 kebabs = 1 serving)

In the summer, barbecue these kebabs over hot coals 12 to 15 minutes rather than broiling them in the oven. While they're cooking, enjoy a cold cup of gazpacho!

1 tablespoon mild soy sauce
2 tablespoons frozen unsweetened apple juice concentrate
2 garlic cloves, minced, or
1 teaspoon garlic powder
½ teaspoon ground ginger or
1 teaspoon peeled, grated fresh ginger
¼ cup dry sherry or salt-free chicken broth, defatted
¼ cup drained pineapple juice

4 8-ounce chicken breast halves, boned, with skin and fat removed
16 mushrooms, cleaned and stems removed
1 small red onion cut into 16 1-inch squares
1 green or sweet red pepper, seeded and cut into 16 1-inch squares
8-ounce can unsweetened pineapple chunks, drained

1. Combine first 6 ingredients in bowl.
2. Cut each chicken breast half into 6 squares.
3. Stir chicken, mushrooms, onions, and green pepper into marinade. Marinate at room temperature for 10 minutes.
4. Thread chicken, mushrooms, green pepper, onion, and pineapple onto 8 (9 to 10-inch) wooden skewers. Alternate ingredients until all are used.
5. Broil 3 to 4 inches from heat for 7 to 9 minutes on each side, or until chicken is cooked. Brush several times with remaining marinade while cooking.

To Serve: Serve kebabs on bed of pilaf. A large mixed green salad, and a platter of assorted fresh fruit complete a most pleasing al fresco dinner. For a winter meal serve with Ever-Popular Spinach Casserole (page 270), Kidney Bean Salad (page 116), and a basket of seasonal fruit.

In Microwave: Arrange skewers on 12-inch glass baking dish and cook on high for about 7 minutes.

Per serving: 249 calories; 29.7 gm protein; 3.7 gm fat; 20.4 gm carbohydrate; 1.5 gm fiber; 73 mg cholesterol; 144 mg sodium

Simply Delicious Turkey Burger ⓠ

Serves: 4 (3 ounces cooked turkey = 1 serving)

In most fast-food hamburgers, 50 percent of the calories are derived from *fat*.

4 4-ounce slices raw turkey breast, flattened to ⅓ inch
Juice of ½ lemon
1 teaspoon salt-free vegetable seasoning
½ teaspoon onion powder
½ teaspoon garlic powder

Hungarian paprika
4 whole-wheat buns, sliced and toasted
4 leaves romaine lettuce
4 slices tomato
Dijon mustard (optional)

1. Season turkey slices with all seasonings listed. Let stand for 15 to 30 minutes.
2. Spray nonstick skillet with butter-flavored nonstick cooking spray.
3. Heat pan. (When droplets of water dance on surface of pan, it is hot enough to use.)
4. Lay turkey slices in hot pan and brown lightly, about 3 to 4 minutes on each side.
5. Place hot turkey slice with lettuce and tomato on toasted bun. Serve immediately.

To Serve: Accompany turkey burgers with steamed corn on the cob, Red and Green Slaw (page 120), and refreshing Strawberry–Banana–Yogurt Pie (page 329).

Variation: I love to add sliced grilled red onions to my burger!

Per serving: 253 calories; 30.2 gm protein; 3.9 gm fat; 23.3 gm carbohydrate; 0.8 gm fiber; 59 mg cholesterol; 187 mg sodium

Quick Turkey Italiano ⓠ

Serves: 4 (3 ounces cooked turkey = 1 serving)

This recipe calls for turkey breasts; if you substitute a turkey thigh, you will increase the dish's fat content by about 50 percent.

15½-ounce jar salt-free marinara
    sauce or tomato sauce
1 cup sliced mushrooms
⅓ cup dry red wine
1 green pepper, sliced into 1-inch
    squares
½ onion, thinly sliced

1 pound raw turkey breast slices*
6 ounces soba noodles, cooked
    al dente and drained

Watercress or chopped Italian
    parsley for garnish

1. Combine marinara sauce, mushrooms, wine, green pepper, and onions in nonstick skillet. Bring to a boil, reduce heat, cover, and simmer for 15 minutes.

2. Add turkey strips and cook over medium heat for 10 minutes.

To Serve: Place soba noodles on warmed platter and top with turkey and sauce mixture. Garnish with watercress or chopped Italian parsley. Add a salad of assorted crisp greens and a wedge of melon with lime for dessert.

Per serving: 338 calories; 32.0 gm protein; 3.4 gm fat; 39.9 gm carbohydrate; 1.5 gm fiber; 59 mg cholesterol; 82 mg sodium

* Cut against the grain into strips ½ inch wide.

Turkey Slices Marinara ⓠ

Serves: 8 (3 ounces cooked turkey = 1 serving)

Executive Chef Peter Eckstein of the Holiday Inn Royal Singapore Hotel demonstrated tasty turkey roulades. We simplified the recipe by using turkey slices with his delicious sauce.

2 tablespoons each: chopped carrot, leek, shallot, mushrooms
½ cup salt-free chicken broth, defatted
½ teaspoon dried thyme, crushed
½ teaspoon dried marjoram, crushed
2 cups canned, crushed Italian plum tomatoes in sauce

3-ounce can sliced ripe olives, drained (optional)
1 garlic clove, minced
8 ½-inch thick raw turkey slices,* seasoned with 1 teaspoon each garlic powder, onion powder, and salt-free vegetable seasoning
2 tablespoons grated Parmesan cheese (optional)

1. Dry-roast carrot, leek, shallot, and mushrooms in 10-inch nonstick skillet until lightly browned; stir constantly. Add chicken broth, thyme, and marjoram.
2. Add tomatoes, olives, and garlic.
3. Cook 4 seasoned turkey slices at a time in nonstick skillet sprayed with nonstick cooking spray. Brown lightly for 2 to 3 minutes on each side.
4. Add turkey slices to sauce and simmer over low heat for 15 minutes.
To Serve: Place bed of whole-wheat linguine on heated platter. Arrange turkey slices and spoon sauce over turkey and pasta. Sprinkle lightly with Parmesan cheese before serving.

Per serving: 158 calories; 26.4 gm protein; 2.9 gm fat; 5.2 gm carbohydrate; 0.6 gm fiber; 59 mg cholesterol; 65 mg sodium

* Cut against the grain.

Turkey Stroganoff ⓠ

Serves: 4 (3 ounces cooked turkey = 1 serving)

It wasn't too many years ago that I used beef cooked in butter instead of turkey and sour cream instead of yogurt. My, how my cooking has changed, and all for the better. You will enjoy this tasty low-calorie adaptation.

1 large onion, thinly sliced, or
  ⅔ cup Onion Magic (page 36)
½ green pepper, sliced
1 garlic clove, minced
¼ cup salt-free chicken broth, defatted
2 teaspoons Worcestershire sauce

1 pound raw turkey breast slices*
2 cups mushrooms, cleaned and sliced
¼ cup dry white wine or dry sherry
½ cup salt-free tomato sauce
¼ cup nonfat yogurt mixed with 2 teaspoons cornstarch

1. Place onion, green pepper, garlic, and chicken broth in nonstick sauté pan and simmer for about 5 minutes.
2. Add Worcestershire sauce, turkey strips, and mushrooms. Simmer for about 8 minutes, covered.
3. Stir in wine and tomato sauce and simmer for 10 minutes uncovered.
4. Remove from heat; stir in yogurt mixture. Warm over low heat. Taste and adjust seasonings.

To Serve: Serve mixture over corn pasta noodles. Steamed green beans and Singaporian Waldorf Salad (page 123) complete the meal.

Per serving: 194 calories; 27.4 gm protein; 3.0 gm fat; 10.7 gm carbohydrate; 0.6 gm fiber; 59 mg cholesterol; 99 mg sodium

* Cut against the grain into strips ½-inch wide.

Pita Pockets with Turkey ⓠ

Serves: 8 (½ pita bread plus ⅓ cup filling = 1 serving)

Teenagers will love this recipe: It's a quick supper with few dishes to wash.

½ pound ground raw turkey
1 small onion, chopped
½ green pepper, chopped
1 garlic clove, minced
⅓ cup salt-reduced tomato sauce
1 teaspoon chili powder
½ teaspoon ground cumin

Freshly ground black pepper
1 cup frozen corn
4 whole-wheat pita breads, halved
4 cups shredded lettuce
1 large tomato, chopped
2 whole green onions, thinly sliced

1. Brown turkey, onion, green pepper, and garlic in nonstick skillet sprayed with nonstick cooking spray.
2. Add tomato sauce, chili powder, cumin, pepper, and corn. Simmer for 10 minutes, or until corn is tender.
3. Warm pita bread and spoon ⅓ cup of mixture into each half.
4. Top with ½ cup shredded lettuce, tomato, and green onion.
To Serve: Serve filled pita pockets with a beverage and fresh fruit.

Per serving: 276 calories; 18.2 gm protein; 3.8 gm fat; 41.9 gm carbohydrate; 2.8 gm fiber; 32 mg cholesterol; 66 mg sodium

Red Meat
Served as a Treat

Barbecued Butterflied Lamb
Meat Loaf with Creole Sauce
Fajitas
Lamb Stew
Braised Pork Chops

Penny's Simply Perfect Veal Stew
Veal with Red and Green Peppers
Veal Marengo
Veal-Stuffed Peppers

We know that red meat has more cholesterol in it than fish or chicken does. Veal is lower in fat, but has the same amount of cholesterol as beef. There are those of us who still enjoy an occasional serving of red meat. Needless to say, in buying your meat, avoid marbling and choose leaner cuts of beef (flank steak or top round), of lamb (the leg), or of veal (the leg or shoulder). Try substituting turkey or chicken for veal in some of your favorite recipes and ground turkey for ground beef. Every little change you make helps lower your total fat intake.

Whether you choose beef, lamb, veal, or pork, make it lean, cook it without added fat, and eat it sparingly. A 4-ounce serving no more than once a week is recommended; less frequently is even better.

Barbecued Butterflied Lamb

Serves: 8 (4 ounces cooked meat = 1 serving)

Since I suggest eating red meat rarely, this recipe proves delicious enough to be savored as the exception!

2 red onions, each cut into 8 wedges
1 lemon, cut into 8 wedges
2 shallots, halved
3 garlic cloves
2 teaspoons Dijon mustard
1 teaspoon freshly ground black pepper
1 tablespoon dried rosemary, crushed
2 teaspoons salt-free vegetable seasoning

1 cup unsweetened pomegranate juice
½ cup dry red wine
5-pound leg of lamb, boned* and fat removed

Watercress and cherry tomatoes for garnish

1. In blender or food processor, combine all ingredients except lamb and puree.
2. Rub marinade thoroughly into meat.
3. Place meat in bowl or plastic bag and pour remaining marinade over meat.
4. Marinate in refrigerator overnight or for 24 hours.
5. Wipe off excess marinade and barbecue over medium heat until meat reaches 145° to 160° for medium rare, or roast on rack in preheated 350° oven until desired temperature is reached.

To Serve: Cut into thin slices and serve on platter garnished with watercress and cherry tomatoes. Accompany meat with steamed barley casserole and Green Beans Aubergine (page 256). Amaretto Peach Creme (page 314) provides a light but elegant dessert.

Per serving: 259 calories; 33.0 gm protein; 8.4 gm fat; 10.2 gm carbohydrate; 0.6 gm fiber; 113 mg cholesterol; 84 mg sodium

---

* A leg of lamb with bone in may be substituted. In that case, place lamb on rack and sear it for 15 minutes in preheated 450° oven, then roast in preheated 350° oven, allowing about 15 to 20 minutes per pound.

Meat Loaf with Creole Sauce

Serves: 6 (2 slices with sauce = 1 serving)

After serving 4 people for dinner, you will still have 4 slices left over for a delicious lunch or supper sandwich on Pritikin whole-wheat bread.

1 pound very lean ground beef, veal, turkey, or chicken (or a combination)
1 small onion, chopped
1 garlic clove, minced
2 whole green onions, chopped
1 large carrot, chopped
½ green pepper, seeded and chopped
¼ cup whole-wheat bread crumbs

3 tablespoons oat bran
2 egg whites, lightly beaten
2 teaspoons mild soy sauce
2 teaspoons Dijon mustard
1 teaspoon salt-free vegetable seasoning
1 teaspoon Italian herb blend, crushed
½ teaspoon freshly ground black pepper

Creole Sauce:
15-ounce can salt-reduced stewed tomatoes
1 tablespoon cornstarch or potato starch

1 cup sliced mushrooms

1. Combine all ingredients but those for the sauce in bowl. Mix lightly with fork until blended.
2. Spray a 9 x 9 x 2-inch glass baking pan with nonstick cooking spray.
3. Place meat mixture in pan and shape into 9-inch loaf.
4. Bake in preheated 375° oven for 40 minutes.

To Prepare Creole Sauce:
1. Coarsely chop tomatoes and place in saucepan with cornstarch or potato starch.
2. Heat 2 to 3 minutes, stirring constantly, until shiny and thickened.
3. Sprinkle mushrooms over baked meat loaf. Spoon Creole Sauce mixture over mushrooms and return meat loaf to oven. Bake for 15 additional minutes.
To Serve: Place sliced meat loaf on platter, top with sauce and mushrooms. Serve with a baked potato and steamed broccoli spears.

Per serving: 167 calories; 20.4 gm protein; 3.7 gm fat; 13.0 gm carbohydrate; 2.1 gm fiber; 43 mg cholesterol; 150 mg sodium

Fajitas

Serves: 8 (2 ounces cooked meat = 1 serving)

Whether they originate in Mexico or Texas, fajitas (fah-heát-ahs) are strips of spicy marinated broiled meat served with salsa and wrapped in tortillas. They must be served sizzling hot.

1 cup fresh orange juice
2 tablespoons lime juice
2 tablespoons red wine vinegar
2 large garlic cloves, minced
2 teaspoons chili powder
1 teaspoon ground cumin
½ teaspoon dried oregano, crushed
Freshly ground black pepper

1½ pounds flank steak or pork loin, fat removed, scored lightly
7-ounce can green chili salsa
4 cups shredded lettuce
16 fresh corn tortillas

3 sliced whole green onions for garnish

1. Combine first 8 ingredients and mix well.
2. Place steak in marinade, cover, and refrigerate at least overnight or 24 hours.
3. Drain meat from marinade, then barbecue or broil 7 minutes on each side. Slice meat diagonally into ½-inch slices.
4. Bring marinade to a boil for 2 minutes.

To Serve: Place sliced meat on platter, pour hot marinade over meat, and garnish with sliced green onions. Accompany with salsa, shredded lettuce, and warmed tortillas. Vegetarian refried beans and Mexican rice round out the meal. Papaya Custard (page 324) is just the right light dessert.

Variation: Sliced barbecued or broiled chicken breast may be substituted for flank steak.

Per serving: 349 calories; 24.7 gm protein; 5.7 gm fat; 51.5 gm carbohydrate; 1.4 gm fiber; 37 mg cholesterol; 109 mg sodium

Lamb Stew

Serves: 4 (4 ounces cooked meat = 1 serving)

Whether you call it a stew or a ragout, it's still delicious. As with all stews, it may be prepared a day ahead—the flavors only improve.

1¼ pounds boneless leg of lamb, cut into 1½-inch cubes
⅓ cup salt-free chicken broth, defatted
1 small red onion, chopped
1 small yellow onion, chopped
1 garlic clove, minced
1 cup brown rice
½ cup dry vermouth
Freshly ground black pepper
½ teaspoon dried rosemary, crushed or 1 tablespoon chopped rosemary

2 teaspoons salt-free vegetable seasoning
1 tablespoon lemon juice
3 large carrots, sliced into 2-inch pieces
2 10½-ounce cans salt-free chicken broth, defatted
⅔ cup dark raisins

1. Brown lamb cubes on all sides under broiler.
2. Heat chicken broth in 4-quart nonstick Dutch oven or sauté pan. Add onions, garlic, and rice. Cook 5 minutes, or until transparent, stirring frequently.
3. Add browned lamb, vermouth, and remaining ingredients and bring to a boil.
4. Reduce heat, cover, and simmer until lamb is tender, about 40 minutes. (If necessary, add boiling water or more chicken broth so that rice is kept moist.)
5. Taste and adjust seasonings.

To Serve: Accompany hot stew with steamed green beans and peas and Singaporian Waldorf Salad (page 123) on a bed of greens.

Per serving: 554 calories; 38.1 gm protein; 9.4 gm fat; 71.1 gm carbohydrate; 6.8 gm fiber; 113 mg cholesterol; 129 mg sodium

Braised Pork Chops ℚ

Yield: 4 chops (1 chop = 1 serving)

Because of a conscious effort by breeders, pork's calories and cholesterol content now compare with those of beef. This comparatively inexpensive meat is high in iron, zinc, and vitamin B, particularly thiamine. Trichinosis is so rare today that pork does not have to be overcooked to be safe. Cooked pork should reach an internal temperature of 140° before it is eaten.

4 (1½ pounds) lean rib or loin pork chops or 1 pound pork loin fillets, all fat removed
1 teaspoon salt-free vegetable seasoning
Few flakes crushed red pepper
½ cup unsweetened applesauce
½ teaspoon ground ginger

½ teaspoon crushed garlic
2 tablespoons salt-reduced tomato sauce
1 tablespoon mild soy sauce
1 tablespoon grated orange rind

4 orange slices and 4 green pepper rings for garnish

1. Heat sauté pan coated with nonstick cooking spray over medium-high heat.
2. Add chops and brown both sides, a total of about 7 to 8 minutes.
3. Remove from heat and sprinkle with seasoning and pepper.
4. Combine remaining ingredients and pour over chops.
5. Return to heat, cover and simmer over low heat for about 20 minutes, or until chops are tender.

To Serve: Arrange chops on warm platter and nap with sauce. Garnish with orange slices and green pepper rings. Surround with steamed small turnips, new potatoes, and Brussels sprouts. Lemony Cheese Pie (page 321) sounds good for dessert.

Per serving: 246 calories; 24.4 gm protein; 13.1 gm fat; 6.7 gm carbohydrate; 0.6 gm fiber; 81 mg cholesterol; 213 mg sodium

Penny's Simply Perfect Veal Stew

Serves: 6

With two teenaged sons and a changing career, Penny doesn't make cooking a top priority; however, her discriminating palate still encourages her to turn out uncomplicated, flavorful meals.

2 pounds veal stew meat (leg or
   shoulder), cut into 2-inch pieces
1 onion, chopped
2 stalks celery, sliced ½ inch wide
3 carrots, sliced ½ inch wide
8-ounce can salt-reduced tomato
   sauce
¾ cup dry white wine or vermouth

¾ cup salt-free chicken broth,
   defatted
½ teaspoon garlic powder
1 teaspoon Italian herb blend,
   crushed
1 teaspoon salt-free vegetable
   seasoning
Freshly ground black pepper

1. Place all ingredients in 3-quart flameproof casserole.
2. Bring to boil, reduce heat, cover, and simmer 1 hour, or until tender. (Or cover and put in lower third of preheated 325° oven for 1 hour.) *

To Serve: Serve en casserole with parslied corn pasta noodles and crisply steamed lemony Brussels sprouts.

Variation: Diced potatoes may be added in Step 2, and frozen peas may be added 10 minutes before serving.

Per serving: 308 calories; 32.0 gm protein; 12.8 gm fat; 9.8 gm carbohydrate; 0.9 gm fiber; 115 mg cholesterol; 126 mg sodium

---

* May be prepared ahead to this point and reheated the next day or frozen for future use.

Veal with Red and Green Peppers ⓠ

Serves: 4 (4 ounces cooked veal = 1 serving)

Although veal has the same cholesterol content as lean beef, since it comes from a young animal its fat content is much lower.

2 teaspoons extra-virgin olive oil
2 small red onions, sliced, or
  1 cup Onion Magic (page 36)
3 small sweet red peppers, seeded
  and sliced
3 small green peppers, seeded and
  sliced
2 garlic cloves, minced
2 tablespoons red wine or Balsamic
  vinegar
1 teaspoon Italian herb blend,
  crushed, or 1 tablespoon sliced
  fresh basil

Freshly ground black pepper
1¼ pounds lean veal stew meat
  (shoulder or leg), cut into
  1½-inch cubes
1½ teaspoons salt-free vegetable
  seasoning
⅛ teaspoon white pepper
½ cup salt-free chicken broth,
  defatted

1. Place nonstick sauté pan over medium heat; add oil, onions, peppers, and garlic. Cook 2 minutes, stirring frequently.

2. Add vinegar, Italian herb blend, and pepper. Reduce heat, cover, and cook 5 minutes. Stir frequently. Remove mixture from pan and keep warm.

3. While mixture is cooking, pound veal cubes lightly to ½-inch thickness. Sprinkle with vegetable seasoning and white pepper.

4. Add veal to sauté pan and brown lightly on both sides. Add broth.

5. Return onion mixture to browned meat and heat together for 5 to 10 minutes.

To Serve: Spoon veal mixture over Jan's Microwaved Rice with Vegetables (page 304). Surround with steamed summer squash and carrots. Serve Sarah's Hungarian Wilted Salad (page 126) and fresh pineapple for dessert.

Per serving: 318 calories; 32.6 gm protein; 15.5 gm fat; 11.3 gm carbohydrate; 1.8 gm fiber; 115 mg cholesterol; 97 mg sodium

Veal Marengo

Serves: 6 (4 ounces cooked meat = 1 serving)

A one-dish meal that is nothing more than a fancy stew; however, your guests' raves belie the simplicity of its preparation.

2 teaspoons extra-virgin olive oil
2 pounds lean veal stew meat (shoulder or leg), cut into 1-inch cubes
1 teaspoon salt-free vegetable seasoning
½ teaspoon each dried Italian herb blend and dried thyme, crushed
1 teaspoon each onion powder and garlic powder
Freshly ground black pepper
1 tablespoon whole-wheat flour
1 tablespoon tomato paste
1 bay leaf

1 strip orange peel
½ cup dry white wine or vermouth
1½ cups salt-free chicken broth, defatted
¼ pound mushrooms, cleaned and quartered
12 small whole, peeled frozen onions

1 tablespoon chopped parsley, basil, or tarragon for garnish
12 whole-wheat toast points rubbed with garlic for garnish

1. Combine oil and veal. Place in heavy flameproof casserole and brown lightly on all sides under broiler.
2. Add seasonings and flour. Mix well and continue to brown a few minutes longer.
3. Add tomato paste, bay leaf, orange peel, wine, and chicken broth. Bring to a boil, reduce heat, cover, and simmer about 45 minutes, or until tender.*
4. Add mushrooms and onions and simmer 20 minutes more. Remove bay leaf.

To Serve: Serve veal from heated tureen or casserole. Garnish with chopped parsley and toast points. Accompany with a Pilaf of Wild Rice (page 305) and steamed broccoli. Lemony Cheese Pie with Strawberry Sauce (page 321) is a suitable dessert.

Per serving: 308 calories; 32.3 gm protein; 14.4 gm fat; 7.4 gm carbohydrate; 0.7 gm fiber; 115 mg cholesterol; 97 mg sodium

* This dish may be prepared a day ahead to this point.

Veal-Stuffed Peppers Ⓠ Ⓜ

Serves: 4 (1 pepper = 1 serving)

Using a microwave oven saves time and flavor.

4 medium green or sweet red peppers
½ cup minced onion
⅔ pound lean ground veal (or turkey)
2 cups cooked brown rice
1 teaspoon salt-free vegetable seasoning

½ teaspoon dried oregano, crushed
½ teaspoon garlic powder
½ teaspoon white pepper
16-ounce can salt-reduced tomato sauce (save ¼ cup)
1½ tablespoons grated Parmesan cheese

1. Cut stem ends of peppers 1 inch from top. Remove seeds and membranes from inside peppers; chop remaining top of pepper to measure ½ cup.
2. Place peppers in round glass dish, cover loosely with plastic wrap, and microwave on high for 5 minutes. Invert peppers on paper towels to drain.
3. Combine onions, chopped green pepper, and veal in 2-quart non-metal casserole. Cook on high 5 minutes, or until meat is no longer pink. Stir twice during cooking.
4. Add rice, vegetable seasoning, oregano, garlic powder, pepper, and all but ¼ cup tomato sauce to meat mixture. Mix lightly with fork.
5. Stuff peppers with meat–rice mixture. Return to glass dish and top with remaining tomato sauce. Sprinkle with Parmesan cheese, cover and bake in microwave oven on high for 15 minutes.

Per serving: 320 calories; 22 gm protein; 8.8 gm fat; 39.7 gm carbohydrate; 1.6 gm fiber; 60 mg cholesterol; 108 mg sodium

Casseroles

A MEAL IN ONE
THAT SUITS EVERYONE

Baked Beans Bravo
On Again, Off Again Cassoulet
False Alarm Chili
Chili and Beans
Secondhand Crêpes
Eggplant Parmesan
Enchilada Casserole
Leftover Chicken Casserole
Low and Behold Macaroni
Main Dish Hi-Fiber Casserole
No-Noodles Lasagna

Perfect Party Paella
Eight-Vegetable Pastitsio
Dilled Salmon Crêpes
Seafood Tetrazzini
Tuna, Mushroom, and Artichoke
  Casserole
All-American Turkey Hash
Turkey Shepherd's Pie
Laini's Layered Vegetable
  Casserole

Our lives are often so busy today that one of the few times many people take to relax is mealtime. Whether you are alone or sharing these moments with friends or family, it's important to take the time to recharge your battery or just exchange information about one another. Home must be more than a depot. It must be a place where you can give and receive encouragement, warmth, and understanding, a place where people care. Without this, who cares whether you are eating, or what you are eating?

So much for philosophy, and back to casseroles—a meal in one for everyone.

Baked Beans Bravo Ⓠ Ⓜ

Serves: 4

What could be easier? This dish may be served as an entrée or as an accompaniment at a barbecue.

2 16-ounce cans chili beans without meat
2 tablespoons frozen unsweetened apple juice concentrate
2 tablespoons salt-free tomato sauce

2 teaspoons dehydrated onion flakes
2 teaspoons Dijon mustard
7½-ounce can crushed, unsweetened pineapple

1. Combine all ingredients in shallow 2-quart nonmetal casserole with lid.
2. Cover and bake in preheated 350° oven for 15 minutes.
3. Remove lid, stir, and bake uncovered for 15 minutes.
To Serve: Serve baked beans in casserole with Oriental Coleslaw (page 112) and Special Strawberry Ice Cream (page 331) for dessert.

In Microwave: Cover with wax paper and bake on high for 3 minutes. Stir and bake uncovered on medium for 12 minutes.

Per serving: 256 calories; 13.4 gm protein; 1.1 gm fat; 50.1 gm carbohydrate; 2.5 gm fiber; 0 mg cholesterol; 11 mg sodium

On Again, Off Again Cassoulet

Serves: 8 to 10

A traditional cassoulet is made of beans and whatever meats the regional cook can provide for flavor. Any leftover meat, gravies, or soups can be added as enrichment. The preparation time is minimal, but the cooking time is longer; in fact, if you have a crockpot, this recipe lends itself to long, slow cooking.*

1¼ cups small white beans,**
  rinsed
1 cup barley, rinsed
¾ pound flank steak or first-cut
  brisket, fat removed and cut
  against the grain into
  ¾-inch-wide strips
4 chicken thighs, skin removed and
  halved lengthwise
½ pound veal or beef bones, fat
  removed
2 teaspoons salt-free vegetable
  seasoning

1 tablespoon Hungarian paprika
½ teaspoon dried thyme, crushed
Freshly ground black pepper
1 bay leaf
1 large onion, sliced, or
  1 cup Onion Magic (page 36)
3 garlic cloves, minced
16-ounce can salt-reduced tomatoes
2 tablespoons salt-free tomato paste
1 cup dry white wine
4 cups salt-free chicken broth,
  defatted, vegetable broth, or
  water

1. Place all ingredients in ovenproof casserole or Dutch oven. Bring to a boil, cover, reduce heat, and simmer on top of stove or in preheated 325° oven for 1 to 1½ hours.

2. Uncover, remove bones, raise heat to 400°, and bake until browned and bubbly, about 30 minutes. (Remove bay leaf before serving.)

Helpful Hint: This dish may be prepared with on-and-off cooking, stopping or starting at any point to suit your schedule.

Per serving: 248 calories; 19.7 gm protein; 3.2 gm fat; 36.2 gm carbohydrate; 7.8 gm fiber; 26 mg cholesterol; 38 mg sodium

* For crockpot cooking, place all ingredients in pot and follow manufacturer's directions.
** Soak beans in water to cover overnight or bring to a boil for 5 minutes and drain off water.

False Alarm Chili ©

Serves: 12 (1 cup = 1 serving)

All chili aficionados are familiar with One-, Two-, and Three-Alarm Chili. This is my version, called False Alarm Chili because it uses ground turkey instead of beef!

1 large onion, quartered
6 garlic cloves
3 stalks celery, coarsely chopped
1 cup parsley, without stems
6 mushrooms, cleaned and halved
2 teaspoons cold-pressed safflower oil
1 pound ground raw turkey
1 teaspoon each dried thyme, rosemary, chili powder, and cumin

2 teaspoons dried oregano, crushed
1 tablespoon salt-free vegetable seasoning
¼ cup dry white wine
2 28-ounce cans crushed Italian plum tomatoes in puree
15½-ounce can salt-reduced red kidney beans, drained
1 tablespoon cornstarch mixed with ¼ cup tomato puree

1. Chop onion, garlic, celery, parsley, and mushrooms in food processor or blender or mince by hand.
2. Sauté for 5 minutes in oil in 4-quart nonstick pan, stirring often.
3. Add turkey and all seasonings, and sauté for 5 minutes while stirring constantly.
4. Add wine and tomatoes. Cook for 3 minutes and adjust seasonings.
5. Add kidney beans and cornstarch mixture. Stir, cover, and simmer for 20 to 30 minutes, stirring occasionally to prevent food from sticking.
To Serve: Serve in warm bowls with diced red onion or shredded low-fat cheese if desired; it is delicious, however, served just as is. To complete the meal, add large, crisp green salad with Italian dressing, hot sourdough rolls, and a seasonal fresh fruit.

Per serving: 138 calories; 12.5 gm protein; 2.9 gm fat; 15.9 gm carbohydrate; 1.8 gm fiber; 22 mg cholesterol; 53 mg sodium

Chili and Beans Ⓠ Ⓜ
(In the Microwave)

Serves: 4

½ pound ground turkey or very
    lean beef
1 tablespoon dehydrated onion
    flakes
16-ounce can salt-free tomatoes
8-ounce can salt-free tomato sauce

7-ounce can green chili salsa
14-ounce can chili beans or
    drained kidney beans
½ teaspoon dried oregano, crushed
½ teaspoon chili powder

1. Crumble ground turkey and onion into 2½-quart nonmetal casserole. Cook on high in microwave oven for 4 minutes until meat loses its pink color, stirring once during cooking.

2. Add remaining ingredients and mix thoroughly.

3. Cover and cook on medium for 10 to 12 minutes, or until thoroughly heated.

To Serve: A large, crisp green salad, a bowl of chili, hearty Pritikin whole-wheat bread, and fresh fruit provide a meal in minutes.

Per serving: 220 calories; 20.4 gm protein; 3.0 gm fat; 29.4 gm carbohydrate; 2.5 gm fiber; 32 mg cholesterol; 65 mg sodium

Secondhand Crêpes ⓠ

Serves: 4 (2 crêpes = 1 serving)

Béchamel sauce and crêpes from the freezer, turkey and vegetables from the refrigerator: The ingredients may be old, but the wonderful flavor is new!

2 cups Basic Béchamel (page 28)
1 cup leftover cooked turkey or
  chicken, chopped
1 cup leftover cooked vegetables,
  chopped
8 Basic Crêpes (page 32)
1 cup chopped tomatoes in puree or
  canned salt-free stewed tomatoes

1 teaspoon Worcestershire sauce
Few drops hot pepper sauce
2 tablespoons shredded salt-free
  Swiss cheese or skim-milk
  mozzarella

1. Combine 1 cup of the béchamel with turkey and vegetables.
2. Spoon one eighth of mixture into center of crêpe and roll.
3. Place stuffed crêpes seam side down in shallow 2-quart baking dish sprayed with nonstick cooking spray.
4. Combine remaining 1 cup béchamel with chopped tomatoes, Worcestershire sauce, and hot pepper sauce. Mix thoroughly.
5. Pour sauce over crêpes and sprinkle with shredded cheese.
6. Bake in preheated 350° oven for 20 minutes, or until bubbly.

Variation: 1½ cups lowfat yogurt may be substituted for béchamel sauce. Combine 1 cup yogurt with turkey and vegetables. Mix ½ cup yogurt with tomato mixture and pour over each crêpe.

Per serving: 239 calories; 21.8 gm protein; 3.9 gm fat; 29.4 gm carbohydrate; 1.8 gm fiber; 37 mg cholesterol; 192 mg sodium

Eggplant Parmesan Ⓠ

Serves: 6

An uncomplicated vegetarian main dish.

1 large eggplant with skin, sliced
  into rounds ½ inch thick
2 teaspoons extra-virgin olive oil
16-ounce jar salt-free tomato sauce
  or salt-free marinara sauce
¼ cup chopped parsley

2 tablespoons grated Parmesan
  cheese
2 tablespoons shredded skim-milk
  mozzarella cheese

1. Brush eggplant slices lightly with oil. Place on nonstick baking sheet and broil until lightly browned on both sides.
2. Moisten bottom of 9-inch glass baking dish with sauce.
3. Add a layer of eggplant slices, top with some sauce, chopped parsley, and 1 tablespoon Parmesan cheese. Repeat, making a second layer.
4. Sprinkle with shredded mozzarella cheese.
5. Bake in preheated 375° oven for 20 minutes.

To Serve: Serve hot with crunchy whole-wheat rolls and "You-Name-It" Salad (page 125). Complete the meal with Pantry-Fresh Fruit Cup (page 322).

Per serving: 93 calories; 3.7 gm protein; 2.5 gm fat; 16.0 gm carbohydrate; 2.3 gm fiber; 3 mg cholesterol; 66 mg sodium

Enchilada Casserole Ⓠ Ⓜ

Serves: 4

½ pound ground raw turkey, crumbled
1 medium onion, chopped
1 garlic clove, minced
16-ounce can chili beans
1 teaspoon dried oregano, crushed
1 tablespoon chili powder

2 tablespoons seeded diced green chilies (fresh or canned, drained)
8-ounce can salt-free tomato sauce
½ cup water
4 fresh corn tortillas
½ cup shredded skim-milk mozzarella cheese

1. Sauté turkey, onion, and garlic in nonstick pan until no longer pink, stirring often.

2. While turkey is cooking, combine beans, oregano, chili powder, chilies, tomato sauce, and water in saucepan. Bring to a boil and simmer for 5 minutes.

3. Pour small amount of tomato sauce in bottom of 6-inch casserole. Combine the rest of the sauce with cooked turkey.

4. Alternate layers of tortilla, turkey mixture, and cheese.

5. Bake in preheated 375° oven for 25 to 30 minutes.

In Microwave: Proceed as in Steps 1, 2, 3, and 4 in directions, using a nonmetal dish. Bake on medium for 15 minutes, or until hot and bubbly.

Per serving: 359 calories; 26.6 gm protein; 6.5 gm fat; 50.2 gm carbohydrate; 2.1 gm fiber; 41 mg cholesterol; 165 mg sodium

Leftover Chicken Casserole
(For Company)
Serves: 8

As a young girl, I loved eating at the home of one of my friends whose mother was a creative cook. This was one of her favorite recipes, as I remember it.

1-pound loaf stale whole-wheat bread, crumbled
2 stalks celery, chopped
1 medium onion, chopped
1 small green pepper, seeded and chopped
¼ cup chopped parsley
1 cup cleaned, sliced mushrooms
¼ teaspoon white pepper
3 egg whites, slightly beaten
1 teaspoon salt-free vegetable seasoning

1 teaspoon poultry seasoning
2 teaspoons low-sodium baking powder
6 cups salt-free chicken broth, defatted, mixed with 2 teaspoons Worcestershire sauce
1½ pounds leftover cooked chicken, coarsely shredded—the chicken from 3-pound Steamed Chicken (page 37) or leftover cooked turkey
Hungarian paprika

1. Place crumbled bread in bowl. Add the rest of the ingredients except chicken and paprika; mix well.
2. Coat 3-quart rectangular casserole with nonstick cooking spray.
3. Alternate layers of dressing and chicken, ending with dressing. Sprinkle with paprika.
4. Bake in preheated 350° oven for 1 hour, or until lightly browned and bubbly.

To Serve: Start with an All-Seasons Freezer Vegetable Salad (page 134); accompany casserole with steamed spinach and steamed carrots. A baked pear may be served for dessert.

Per serving: 328 calories; 31.8 gm protein; 7.8 gm fat; 29.9 gm carbohydrate; 1.0 gm fiber; 76 mg cholesterol; 272 mg sodium

Low and Behold Macaroni Ⓠ

Serves: 10

Only one pot to clean, but many flavorful nutrients to consume.

1 pound macaroni shells
1 tablespoon extra-virgin olive oil
1 pound ground raw turkey
1 teaspoon salt-free vegetable
  seasoning
1 teaspoon Italian herb blend,
  crushed
Freshly ground black pepper

1 large onion, chopped
1 large green pepper, seeded and
  chopped
1 stalk celery, chopped
¼ pound mushrooms, cleaned and
  chopped
1 tablespoon Worcestershire sauce
48-ounce can salt-free tomato juice

1. Brown uncooked macaroni shells in oil in nonstick sauté pan or iron skillet.

2. Add ground turkey and cook until no longer pink. Mix in vegetable seasoning, herb blend, pepper, onion, green pepper, celery, mushrooms, and Worcestershire sauce.

3. Add 5 cups tomato juice, bring to a boil, and reduce heat to a simmer. Cover and cook for 12 to 15 minutes, or until macaroni is tender and juice absorbed. *Do not overcook.* If it is too dry, add more juice.

Per serving: 277 calories; 17.4 gm protein; 3.9 gm fat; 43.4 gm carbohydrate; 2.2 gm fiber; 26 mg cholesterol; 58 mg sodium

Main Dish Hi-Fiber Casserole

Serves: 4

2 carrots (1 cup), thinly sliced
1 small onion, chopped
½ teaspoon chopped garlic
¼ cup chopped parsley
1 cup frozen black-eyed peas or
   1 cup salt-reduced kidney beans
1 cup frozen corn
½ cup quick-cooking barley
3 tablespoons bulgur

Freshly ground black pepper
1 teaspoon salt-free vegetable
   seasoning
1 teaspoon Worcestershire sauce
   (optional)
1½ cups salt-free chicken broth,
   defatted
¼ cup shredded skim-milk
   mozzarella cheese

1. Place all ingredients except cheese in 1½-quart casserole. Mix until blended.

2. Cover casserole and place in preheated 350° oven. Bake for 25 minutes.

3. Sprinkle with cheese and bake, uncovered, for 3 minutes, or until cheese is melted.

To Serve: Serve as main dish with steamed cauliflower, broccoli and zucchini, and a baked sweet potato.

Per serving: 259 calories; 10.6 gm protein; 2.0 gm fat; 51.5 gm carbohydrate; 6.2 gm fiber; 4 mg cholesterol; 55 mg sodium

No-Noodles Lasagna ⓠ

Serves: 6 (1½ cups = 1 serving)

No noodles, but it's still lasagna!

6 medium zucchini (about
  2 pounds)
32-ounce jar salt-free marinara
  sauce
2 garlic cloves, minced
1 teaspoon dried Italian herb
  blend, crushed

16 ounces skim-milk ricotta cheese,
  mixed with ¼ cup chopped
  parsley
4 ounces skim-milk mozzarella
  cheese, shredded
1 tablespoon grated Parmesan
  cheese

1. Steam whole zucchini for 5 minutes. Cool and cut lengthwise into
⅓-inch-thick slices.
2. Combine marinara sauce with garlic and herb blend.
3. Coat 2-quart shallow casserole with nonstick cooking spray. Make
a layer of sauce, zucchini slices, ricotta cheese, and mozzarella; then
repeat layers, ending with mozzarella.
4. Sprinkle with Parmesan cheese and bake in preheated 400° oven
for 20 minutes.

To Serve: Accompany with a mixed green salad with garbanzo beans,
crisp sourdough rolls, and Sherried Orange Gelatin with Fruit (page
312).

Per serving: 183 calories; 17.7 gm protein; 4.3 gm fat; 19.7 gm carbohydrate; 0.8 gm fiber;
15 mg cholesterol; 244 mg sodium

Perfect Party Paella

Serves: 8

A festive one-dish meal that has a Spanish origin. Like gazpacho, it depends on the locale as to the variety of ingredients used. Rice, of course, is always the basic ingredient. I prefer using chicken thighs because they are a little moister; however, you may substitute chicken breasts.

1 tablespoon extra-virgin olive oil
1 onion, chopped
1 stalk celery, chopped
3 garlic cloves, minced
8 small chicken thighs, skinned and halved lengthwise
2 cups brown rice
½ cup dry white wine or vermouth
2 cups canned Italian plum tomatoes, chopped

3 cups hot, salt-free chicken broth, defatted, with ½ teaspoon each dried thyme and powdered saffron
10-ounce package frozen artichoke hearts, defrosted
1 cup frozen snow peas
1 pound frozen crab claws, defrosted
1 sweet red pepper, seeded and thinly sliced crosswise

1. Heat oil in nonstick sauté pan; add onion, celery, and garlic, and sauté for 3 minutes. Add chicken and sauté for 5 minutes.
2. Add rice and stir briefly.
3. Add wine and stir in; then add tomatoes.
4. Add hot broth with thyme and saffron. Bring to a boil, reduce heat, cover, and simmer for 30 minutes, or until rice is tender.
5. Stir in artichokes, peas, and crab claws and lay pepper strips on top. If rice is dry, add more broth. Simmer covered for 10 minutes, or until mixture is heated through.

Per serving: 353 calories; 19.8 gm protein; 7.5 gm fat; 48.4 gm carbohydrate; 5.2 gm fiber; 56 mg cholesterol; 134 mg sodium

Eight-Vegetable Pastitsio Ⓜ

Serves: 8

To cut down on the cooking time, I sometimes prepare this in two 8-inch-square baking dishes instead of one large one, and freeze one for future use.

1 small onion, quartered
2 shallots or 2 garlic cloves
1 stalk celery, quartered
2 carrots, quartered
½ green pepper, seeded and quartered
½ sweet red pepper, seeded and quartered
1 large zucchini, quartered
1 tablespoon extra-virgin olive oil
1½ teaspoons Italian herb blend, crushed

2 tablespoons grated Parmesan cheese
½ cup dry red wine
8-ounce can Italian plum tomatoes, crushed
12 ounces penne or ziti
1 pound unpeeled eggplant, sliced into rounds ½ inch thick
1 pound skim-milk ricotta, pureed until smooth
2 ounces shredded skim-milk mozzarella cheese

1. Place first 7 vegetables in food processor or blender and chop coarsely.
2. Sauté vegetables in oil in nonstick sauté pan for 5 minutes.
3. Add herbs and Parmesan cheese; sauté for 3 to 5 minutes.
4. Add red wine and tomatoes, bring to a boil, reduce heat, and simmer for 10 minutes.
5. While sauce is simmering, cook pasta. Place sliced eggplant on nonstick baking sheet and broil lightly on both sides.
6. To assemble, in a shallow 3-quart casserole sprayed with nonstick cooking spray, layer one fourth of the sauce, all of the pasta, one fourth of the sauce, all of the ricotta cheese, one fourth of the sauce, the eggplant, and remaining sauce. Top with shredded mozzarella.
7. Bake in preheated 375° oven for 40 minutes, or until bubbly.

Helpful Hint: Let casserole stand for 10 minutes before serving.

In Microwave: Cook casserole, covered, on medium for 20 minutes. Let stand for 15 minutes before serving.

Per serving: 325 calories; 15.7 gm protein; 8.5 gm fat; 44.7 gm carbohydrate; 2.9 gm fiber; 23 mg cholesterol; 148 mg sodium

Dilled Salmon Crêpes ℚ

Yield: 8 crêpes (1 crêpe = 1 serving as appetizer; 2 crêpes = 1 serving as entrée)

The recipe for these dilled salmon crêpes originated in the kitchens of Executive Chef Alfred Brugner at the Holiday Inn's Golden Mile Hotel in Hong Kong. It was served as one of the courses at a press luncheon to introduce the new gourmet health menu, which provides diners with a healthful alternative.

½ cup water
½ cup dry white wine
1 shallot, chopped
1 whole green onion, chopped
½ carrot, chopped
½ stalk celery, chopped
12 ounces fresh salmon, cut into
  ½-inch cubes
1 cucumber, peeled, seeded, and
  cut into ½-inch cubes

6 small mushrooms, cleaned and
  cut into ½-inch cubes
⅔ cup nonfat milk
1 tablespoon cornstarch, dissolved
  in 3 tablespoons milk
1 tablespoon nonfat yogurt
3 tablespoons chopped fresh dill
8 Basic Crêpes (page 32)

1. Bring first 6 ingredients to a boil; reduce heat and simmer for 10 minutes.
2. Add salmon and simmer 3 minutes longer.
3. Add cucumbers and mushrooms; poach for 2 minutes.
4. Remove salmon, cucumbers, and mushrooms with slotted spoon.
5. Combine ⅓ cup strained poaching liquid and milk with dissolved cornstarch and bring to a simmer. Stir until sauce is shiny and coats the spoon.
6. Remove from heat, add yogurt, dill, salmon, cucumbers, and mushrooms. Blend.
7. Divide mixture among 8 warm crêpes, roll, place on plate, and nap with sauce.
To Serve: Serve hot stuffed crêpes with grilled tomato halves and steamed snow peas.

Per crêpe: 115 calories; 12.3 gm protein; 1.8 gm fat; 9.8 gm carbohydrate; 1.0 gm fiber; 16 mg cholesterol; 74 mg sodium

Seafood Tetrazzini

Serves: 8 (1¼ cups = 1 serving)

If cholesterol is not an ongoing problem, you may substitute crabmeat and scallops for the fish in this recipe.

1 small onion, chopped
1 green pepper, chopped
2 stalks celery, chopped
2 teaspoons cold-pressed safflower oil
⅔ cup nonfat powdered milk
3 tablespoons whole-wheat flour
1 teaspoon salt-free vegetable seasoning
½ teaspoon white pepper
1 cup water
1 cup salt-free chicken broth, defatted
1½ pounds orange roughie (sea bass, halibut, haddock, or any other firm-fleshed whitefish), cubed

½ pound mushrooms, cleaned and sliced
½ cup shredded salt-free Swiss cheese
2 tablespoons grated Parmesan cheese
10 ounces whole-wheat linguine or spaghetti, cooked al dente and drained
1 tablespoon grated Parmesan cheese mixed with 3 tablespoons bread crumbs

1. Sauté first 3 ingredients in oil in Dutch oven for 3 minutes.
2. Remove from heat and add powdered milk, flour, and seasonings. Gradually stir in water and chicken broth.
3. Add fish and mushrooms. Heat to boiling, stirring occasionally. Reduce to a simmer and cook for 5 minutes.
4. Remove from heat, add cheeses, and stir until melted.
5. Stir in cooked pasta. Pour into shallow 3-quart casserole. Sprinkle with bread crumb mixture.
6. Bake in preheated 375° oven for 20 to 25 minutes, or until bubbly.

To Serve: To complete the meal, serve Marinated Vegetable Platter (page 261), crisp sourdough rolls, and Tapioca with Mango (page 332).

Variation: One and one quarter pounds tuna, chicken, turkey, or cooked vegetables may be used to vary this basic recipe.

Per serving: 282 calories; 24.0 gm protein; 8.3 gm fat; 36.5 gm carbohydrate; 2.8 gm fiber; 40 mg cholesterol; 141 mg sodium

Tuna, Mushroom, and Artichoke Casserole

Serves: 6

Many familiar ingredients from your pantry shelf combine to make this fast, flavorful casserole.

½ pound mushrooms, cleaned and sliced
3 tablespoons salt-free chicken broth, defatted
3 tablespoons whole-wheat flour
3 tablespoons nonfat powdered milk
2 cups nonfat milk
1 teaspoon Worcestershire sauce
⅛ teaspoon white pepper
2 tablespoons dry sherry

10½-ounce can quartered artichokes, drained, or 9-ounce package frozen artichoke hearts, defrosted
13½-ounce can white salt-reduced tuna in water, drained and flaked
1 cup frozen peas
2 tablespoons dried whole-wheat bread crumbs or crushed sugar-free cereal flakes
½ cup slivered almonds

Watercress for garnish

1. Sauté mushrooms in broth in large nonstick saucepan for about 5 minutes.
2. Stir in flour and powdered milk over medium heat for 3 minutes. Remove from heat.
3. Add milk, stirring constantly. Return to heat and stir until mixture comes to a boil. Remove from heat.
4. Add remaining ingredients except bread crumbs and almonds. Stir lightly to blend.
5. Pour into shallow 2-quart casserole sprayed with nonstick cooking spray.
6. Sprinkle with bread crumbs and almonds and bake in preheated 375° oven for 15 minutes, or until bubbly.
To Serve: Garnish with watercress and serve hot in casserole at table. Accompany with Black-Eyed Pea and Bean Salad (page 104) and Pineapple Ambrosia (page 326) for dessert.

Per serving: 256 calories; 26.9 gm protein; 6.9 gm fat; 21.6 gm carbohydrate; 2.4 gm fiber; 41 mg cholesterol; 150 mg sodium

All-American Turkey Hash ⓠ

Serves: 4

My family often looks forward to dishes I concoct from leftovers. In this instance, leftover baked potatoes and roast turkey make an elegant hash.

1 small onion, finely chopped
1 small green pepper, seeded and chopped
1 small sweet red pepper, chopped, or 2 ounces canned chopped pimiento, drained
1 tablespoon cold-pressed safflower oil
2 cups chopped cooked turkey
2 cups chopped cooked potato
1 teaspoon salt-free vegetable seasoning

1 cup Basic Béchamel (page 28), optional
½ cup salt-free chicken broth, defatted, or leftover defatted turkey drippings
1½ tablespoons grated Parmesan cheese mixed with ½ cup whole-wheat bread crumbs

Chopped parsley for garnish

1. Sauté onion and peppers in oil in nonstick skillet until limp.
2. Add turkey, potatoes, and vegetable seasoning. Heat briefly.
3. Stir béchamel with broth and add to turkey mixture. Mix lightly.
4. Spoon into heated shallow casserole or pie plate sprayed with non-stick cooking spray.
5. Sprinkle with cheese mixture and bake in upper third of preheated 400° oven for 20 minutes, or until browned and bubbly.*

To Serve: Sprinkle with chopped parsley and serve with steamed broccoli, Orangey Beet and Pea Salad (page 105), and Banana-Nut Muffins (page 339) for dessert.

Per serving: 278 calories; 27.0 gm protein; 5.8 gm fat; 28.6 gm carbohydrate; 1.1 gm fiber; 56 mg cholesterol; 148 mg sodium

* Browning can be completed under broiler. Place under broiler until lightly browned.

Turkey Shepherd's Pie

Serves: 4

Prepared, baked, and served in one dish, preferably an iron skillet.

1 medium onion, finely chopped
2 carrots, finely chopped
½ stalk celery, finely chopped
½ green pepper, seeded and finely chopped
1 pound ground raw turkey or 2 cups diced cooked turkey
1 tablespoon whole-wheat flour

1 tablespoon salt-free tomato paste
1 cup salt-free chicken broth, defatted
1 tablespoon Worcestershire sauce
2 tablespoons chopped parsley
¼ teaspoon each dried thyme, oregano, rosemary, and freshly ground black pepper

Potato Topping:
1½ pounds baking potatoes, peeled, boiled, and mashed
2 egg whites
¼ cup nonfat milk
2–3 tablespoons nonfat yogurt

⅛ teaspoon white pepper
1 teaspoon onion powder
1 tablespoon each grated Parmesan cheese and dehydrated onion flakes

1. In 8-inch iron skillet sprayed with nonstick cooking spray, dry-roast onion, carrots, celery, and green pepper until lightly browned. Stir constantly.
2. Add turkey and stir for 3 minutes.
3. Stir in flour.
4. Add remaining ingredients, bring to a simmer, and remove from heat.
5. To make the potato topping, beat egg whites, milk, yogurt, pepper, and onion powder into hot mashed potatoes.
6. Spread potato topping over meat mixture and sprinkle with Parmesan cheese.
7. To finish the pie, bake for 20 minutes in preheated 400° oven, or until lightly browned (or complete browning under broiler for 2 minutes).

To Serve: Serve from skillet with steamed zucchini spears and carrots.

Per serving: 274 calories; 22.6 gm protein; 3.5 gm fat; 37.6 gm carbohydrate; 1.5 gm fiber; 44 mg cholesterol; 144 mg sodium

Laini's Layered
Vegetable Casserole ⓆⓂ

Serves: 6

For a change, try a vegetarian one-dish meal.

1 cup nonfat milk
2 tablespoons whole-wheat flour
¼ teaspoon each dry mustard,
    garlic powder, and white pepper
1 teaspoon salt-free vegetable
    seasoning
1 cup skim-milk ricotta cheese
20-ounce package frozen broccoli
    flowerets, defrosted
1 medium green or sweet red
    pepper, seeded and cut into
    slivers

2 medium zucchini cut into ¼-inch
    slices (2 cups)
½ onion, chopped
3 carrots, thinly sliced
¼ cup dried whole-wheat bread
    crumbs
2 tablespoons grated Parmesan
    cheese
¼ cup raw cashews, chopped

1. In small saucepan, blend milk with flour until smooth. Add mustard, garlic powder, pepper, and vegetable seasoning. Place over medium heat and stir until mixture coats spoon.

2. Add ricotta cheese to sauce and whisk until smooth.

3. Combine broccoli, green or red pepper, zucchini, onion, and carrots. Place half the vegetables in 1½-quart casserole and top with half the sauce. Repeat.

4. Mix bread crumbs, cheese, and cashews together. Sprinkle over casserole.

5. Bake in preheated 375° oven for 25 minutes.

In Microwave: Bake on high for 8 to 10 minutes.

Per serving: 187 calories; 12.4 gm protein; 7.0 gm fat; 21.6 gm carbohydrate; 3.3 gm fiber; 15 mg cholesterol; 153 mg sodium

Vegetables

HIGH FIBER
BUT LOW CALORIE

Fresh Artichoke
Baked Artichoke Hearts
No-Crust Broccoli Quiche
Broccoli-Stuffed Tomatoes
Mexican-Style Cabbage
Pretty Easy Cauliflower
Helen's Celery Amandine
Deviled Green Beans
Green Beans Aubergine
Praised Fennel (Finocchio)
Easy Stuffed Green Peppers
Lima Bean Puree
Swiss Onion Pie
Curried Okra
Marinated Vegetable Platter
Peas à la Française

Ratatouille
Santa Barbara Potatoes
Scalloped Potatoes and Corn
Stuffed Sweet Potatoes
Larry's Oven-Fried Potatoes
Twice-Baked Potatoes
Simply Stuffed Onions
Spinach with Corn
Ever-Popular Spinach Casserole
Sweet Potato Pie
Special Succotash
Tomato–Lima Bean Mélange
Vegetable–Potato Pancakes
Best-Ever Zucchini–Corn Casserole
Easy Zucchini with Peas
Skillet Zucchini Parmesan

The nutritional importance of vegetables in our diet has long been recognized, whether by what we consider the primitive suggestions of medicine men in Africa or the practice of herbal medicine in China. We all remember our mothers cajoling us into eating our vegetables or we got no dessert. (But that's another story—see page 309.)

What was this innate attraction to the qualities of vegetables? We know, of course, that many vegetables are high in energy-giving carbohydrates (potatoes, corn, peas, lima beans). They are high in dietary fiber (we used to call it roughage). Vegetables are also rich in Vitamin A—especially carrots, sweet potatoes, red peppers, yellow squash, and green, leafy vegetables. Vitamin C is found in potatoes—baked potatoes particularly. Broccoli, Brussels sprouts, spinach, kale, green peppers, cabbage, and turnips are all high in Vitamin C as well as being excellent sources of calcium. In fact, the only vitamin not found in vegetables is B_{12}. We must obtain this vitamin from animal foods, such as meat, fish, and dairy products. Dried peas, beans, and lentils are important sources of protein. The American Cancer Society in a special report entitled "Nutrition and Cancer: Cause and Prevention" recommends including cruciferous vegetables* in your diet. They suggest that consumption of these vegetables may reduce the risk of cancer, particularly of the gastro-intestinal and respiratory tracts.

To get the optimum nutrients from your vegetables, you should remember a few guidelines:

1. Don't cook it if you can eat it raw.
2. Don't peel it if you can eat the skin.
3. Don't overcook or over-sauce.
4. If you do cook, cook by steaming, pressure cooking, microwaving, or in as little water as possible.

There are times, of course, when we would like to interrupt the boredom of "plain" vegetables. To help you with this, the following chapter will provide you with some interesting yet easy vegetable recipes.

In shopping for vegetables, I cannot overemphasize the importance of freshness. Vegetables are tenderer, juicier, and more flavorful just before they are full grown. Since food costs are constantly rising, it helps to be a savvy shopper and choose vegetables for your menus that are in season. They will be cheaper and certainly more flavorful.

The Look of Good Fresh Vegetables

Artichokes
Heavy, compact, and tightly closed green petals. Surface blemishes are sometimes caused by frost.

Asparagus
Straight, green stalk with tightly closed buds.

Beets (and Turnips)
Small, 2 to 3 inches in diameter, with fresh green leaves attached. Ones without green leaves are more mature and lack flavor. Larger ones may be fibrous and tough.

Beans (green or yellow)
Young, smooth, bright-colored, slender pods that snap when bent. Thick, wrinkled pods are old.

Bok Choy (and Swiss Chard)
White stalks and shiny green leaves.

Broccoli
Firm, dark-green buds, sometimes tinged with blue or purple, but not yellow—that indicates age.

Brussels Sprouts
Green, tightly closed, hard, heavy for size. Yellowing indicates age.

* These include red, green, and white cabbages, Brussels sprouts, radishes, horseradish, watercress, collard and mustard greens, rutabaga, turnips, broccoli, bok choy, and Chinese cabbage.

Cabbage

Intense red or green color, heavy, crisp, shiny, tightly closed leaves. Yellowing indicates age.

Carrots

Bright orange color, smooth, firm, and well formed. Those with green tops are fresher. Avoid packages.

Cauliflower

Heavy, firm, compact, unblemished, creamy-white head with fresh green leaves.

Corn

The best, of course, is picked daily and smells sweet. Husks are green and moist. Kernels are firm, plump, and spurt a milky liquid when pierced with fingernail. Color varies from white to yellow according to variety.

Cucumbers

Dark-green color, slender and firm. Avoid ones with soft or yellow spots. Peel before using, since most are waxed for storage. The exception is hothouse or European cucumbers. They are long green ones wrapped in plastic. They are sweeter and do not require peeling or seeding.

Eggplants

Glossy, dark-purple color, with no soft or brown spots. Choose lighter weight ones; they have fewer seeds.

Lettuces

Choose brightly colored, heavy heads with crisp green leaves, not too compact. Avoid bruised, very dirty, or wilted heads.

Mushrooms

Smooth, unblemished skin with tightly closed caps. It is best to have no gills showing around stems.

Okra

Young, firm, crisp pods, 2 to 4 inches long, that snap when bent. The large ones are woody.

Onions (red, yellow, white, shallots, or garlic)

Firm and dry, with no greens sprouting. Do not store in refrigerator; it encourages rot.

Peas and Snow Peas

Pods are large, bright green, and well filled. Snow peas are small, bright green, and flat.

Peppers

Shiny skin, with no soft or bruised spots. They change from green to red when ripened, increasing sweetness and Vitamin A content.

Potatoes

Firm, smooth skin, with no sprouting eyes, black spots, or green areas. Store outside refrigerator in dark place.

Radishes (red or white)
Firm, medium size with greens attached. Packaged ones are not as fresh.
Spinach
Loose, fresh, crisp, dark-green leaves. In bags, check for yellow and bruised leaves.
Sweet Potatoes or Yams
Firm, medium size; tapered at both ends. Smooth skins without cracks or signs of decay. Store outside refrigerator in cool, dry place.
Tomatoes
Plump, heavy, and free from bruises or cracks. Particularly delicious in season. Will ripen at room temperature.
Zucchini (green or yellow squash)
Firm, dark green or yellow, glossy and small in size, 3 to 6 inches long. Large ones are seedy.

———————————————

Fresh Artichoke Ⓠⓜ
(In the Microwave)

Serves: 1

Artichokes come from a thistlelike plant. The flowerlike head is eaten as a vegetable. Remember to remove the choke carefully before serving. Graceful eating takes time and is quite satisfying to calorie counters.

1 fresh artichoke	2 tablespoons dry white wine
Water	1 garlic clove, mashed
1 tablespoon lemon juice	1 bay leaf

1. Cut 1 inch off top and trim stem. Remove tough outer leaves and, with scissors, snip thorny tips. Rinse well.

2. Place upside down in 1 inch of water in a shallow nonmetal dish. Add remaining ingredients.

3. Cover with plastic wrap and cook on high in microwave for 7 to 10 minutes, or until leaf is easily pulled from stalk and stem can be pierced easily with fork.

4. Turn right side up and let stand for 5 minutes before serving.

5. Drain and *remove choke with grapefruit spoon.*

To Serve: Fill cavity of artichoke with additional lemon juice and serve hot.

Variation: You may also pour low-calorie vinaigrette dressing over artichoke and serve hot or chilled.

Per serving: 81 calories; 3.0 gm protein; 0.2 gm fat; 14.9 gm carbohydrate; 1.1 gm fiber; 0 mg cholesterol; 81 mg sodium

Baked Artichoke Hearts Ⓠ Ⓜ

Serves: 4 (½ cup = 1 serving)

A fancy vegetable that's simple to prepare.

10-ounce package frozen artichoke
hearts, cooked and drained*
10-ounce can salt-free stewed
tomatoes, chopped

1 garlic clove, minced
1 teaspoon dried oregano, crushed
2 teaspoons grated Parmesan
cheese

1. Combine artichoke hearts, tomatoes, garlic, and oregano.
2. Place in 8-inch glass baking dish sprayed with nonstick cooking spray.
3. Sprinkle with Parmesan cheese.
4. Bake in preheated 325° oven for 20 to 25 minutes. Let stand for 3 minutes before serving.

In Microwave: Bake covered on high for 5 minutes.

Per serving: 51 calories; 2.7 gm protein; 0.6 gm fat; 10.9 gm carbohydrate; 1.2 gm fiber;
1 mg cholesterol; 72 mg sodium

* A 10½-ounce can drained, quartered artichoke hearts may be substituted for frozen.

No-Crust Broccoli Quiche Ⓠ Ⓜ

Serves: 8 (⅛ quiche = 1 serving)

¼ cup chopped onion
4 egg whites
¾ cup nonfat milk
¼ teaspoon dry mustard
1 teaspoon salt-free vegetable
seasoning
¼ teaspoon freshly grated nutmeg

1 cup 1% fat cottage cheese
2 10-ounce packages chopped
frozen broccoli, defrosted and
drained
1 tablespoon grated Parmesan
cheese

1. Combine onion, egg whites, milk, mustard, and seasonings.
2. Add cottage cheese and broccoli.

3. Place mixture in 9-inch pie pan or quiche dish sprayed with non-stick cooking spray. Sprinkle with Parmesan cheese.

4. Bake in preheated 350° oven for 45 minutes, or until just soft in center.

5. Allow to set for 10 minutes before serving.

To Serve: Place wedge of quiche on plate with steamed carrots and Special Succotash (page 271).

In Microwave: Bake uncovered on medium for 7 to 11 minutes, or until center is just soft. Rotate a half turn every 3 minutes.

Per serving: 62 calories; 8.5 gm protein; 0.7 gm fat; 6.5 gm carbohydrate; 1.6 gm fiber; 2 mg cholesterol; 181 mg sodium

Broccoli-Stuffed Tomatoes ⓠⓜ

Serves: 6 (½ tomato = 1 serving)

3 large ripe tomatoes, halved and seeded
1 teaspoon salt-free vegetable seasoning
10-ounce package frozen chopped broccoli, defrosted and drained
½ red onion, minced
½ cup whole-wheat bread crumbs

3 tablespoons chopped parsley
1 teaspoon dried basil, crushed, or 1 tablespoon chopped fresh basil
2 tablespoons nonfat yogurt or light mayonnaise
2 tablespoons grated Parmesan cheese

1. Season tomatoes with vegetable seasoning.

2. Place broccoli, onion, bread crumbs, parsley, basil, and yogurt or mayonnaise in bowl. Mix lightly with a fork.

3. Stuff tomato halves with broccoli mixture and sprinkle with Parmesan.

4. Place in shallow ovenproof baking dish and bake in preheated 350° oven for 20 to 25 minutes. Let stand 2 minutes before serving.

To Serve: Tomatoes may be served from baking pan or placed on platter with broiled fish or chicken.

In Microwave: Bake covered on high for 2 minutes.

Per serving: 68 calories; 4.3 gm protein; 1.0 gm fat; 12.4 gm carbohydrate; 2.2 gm fiber; 1 mg cholesterol; 77 mg sodium

Mexican-Style Cabbage ⓠ

Serves: 4

A very easy way to make an otherwise ordinary vegetable taste delicious.

1 small head (1 pound) green
    cabbage, cut into 1½-inch pieces
1 cup frozen or canned corn
½ green pepper, seeded and diced
2 teaspoons cold-pressed safflower
    oil
1 teaspoon salt-free vegetable
    seasoning

Freshly ground black pepper
8-ounce can salt-free tomato sauce
    or 4 fresh plum tomatoes cut in
    eighths plus ½ cup water

2 tablespoons chopped cilantro or
    parsley for garnish

1. Sauté cabbage, corn, and pepper in oil in nonstick saucepan or skillet for 5 minutes.
2. Add seasonings and tomato sauce. Mix lightly to combine.
3. Cover and simmer for 15 minutes.

To Serve: Spoon over steamed brown rice or serve as a vegetable accompanying Diet Watcher's Barbecued Chicken (page 187). Garnish with chopped cilantro or parsley.

Per serving: 121 calories; 4.8 gm protein; 3.0 gm fat; 24.7 gm carbohydrate; 4.2 gm fiber; 0 mg cholesterol; 46 mg sodium

Pretty Easy Cauliflower ⓠ Ⓜ

Serves: 6

1 head cauliflower, steamed or
    cooked in microwave
1 cup nonfat milk plus
    2 tablespoons whole-wheat flour
    or 1 cup Basic Béchamel
    (page 28)

⅛ teaspoon white pepper
1 teaspoon salt-free vegetable
    seasoning
2-ounce jar roasted sweet red
    peppers, drained

1. In saucepan over low heat, blend flour with milk and heat, stirring, until sauce coats the spoon. Add pepper and vegetable seasoning.

2. Puree pimientos in blender or food processor, add to sauce, and blend.

To Serve: Place hot cauliflower on platter and top with sauce. Surround with steamed peas, snow peas, and carrots.

Per serving: 49 calories; 3.4 gm protein; 0.4 gm fat; 8.9 gm carbohydrate; 1.5 gm fiber; 1 mg cholesterol; 31 mg sodium

Helen's Celery Amandine ⓠ

Serves: 6 to 8 (½ cup = 1 serving)

A plain yet fancy vegetable whose natural sodium content is a bit higher than most vegetables.

1 tablespoon cold-pressed safflower oil (optional)
4 cups diagonally sliced celery
1 shallot, minced
1 small garlic clove, minced
¼ cup salt-free chicken broth, defatted

2 tablespoons dry white wine
½ cup slivered almonds, toasted in oven

2 tablespoons chopped parsley for garnish

1. Heat oil in nonstick skillet.* Add celery, shallot, and garlic and sauté over medium heat for 2 minutes.
2. Add chicken broth, cover, and cook for 10 minutes.
3. Add wine and almonds. Cook uncovered for 2 to 3 minutes.

To Serve: Serve hot, garnished with chopped parsley. This celery is a wonderful accompaniment to chicken, turkey, or Cornish game hens.

Per serving: 75 calories; 2.5 gm protein; 5.1 gm fat; 5.4 gm carbohydrate; 1.1 gm fiber; 0 mg cholesterol; 62 mg sodium

* If you wish, spray pan with butter-flavored nonstick cooking spray and eliminate oil.

Deviled Green Beans ⓠⓜ

Serves: 6 to 8 (½ cup = 1 serving)

2 tablespoons salt-free chicken
  broth, defatted
½ onion, chopped
½ green pepper, seeded and
  chopped
1 garlic clove, minced

8-ounce can salt-free tomato sauce
2 teaspoons Dijon mustard
4-ounce jar chopped pimiento,
  drained
20-ounce package frozen French-cut
  green beans, defrosted

1. Place chicken broth in nonstick skillet. Add onion, pepper, and garlic and sauté until limp.
2. Add tomato sauce, mustard, pimiento, and green beans. Bring to a simmer.
3. Place in 1-quart casserole and bake for 20 minutes at 350°. Let stand for 3 minutes before serving.

In Microwave: Bake covered on high for 10 minutes.

Per serving: 44 calories; 1.9 gm protein; 0.3 gm fat; 9.9 gm carbohydrate; 1.6 gm fiber; 0 mg cholesterol; 22 mg sodium

Green Beans Aubergine ⓠ

Serves: 8 (½ cup = 1 serving)

1-pound eggplant, cut lengthwise
  into ½-inch-thick slices
½ tablespoon extra-virgin olive oil
1 teaspoon salt-free vegetable
  seasoning
1 teaspoon onion powder
2 shallots, minced
1 garlic clove, minced

½ tablespoon extra-virgin olive oil
½ pound fresh green beans, cut
  and blanched, or 10-ounce
  package frozen cut green beans
1 cup canned Italian plum
  tomatoes, drained and chopped
1 teaspoon Italian herb blend or
  1 tablespoon fresh basil, chopped

1. Place eggplant slices on nonstick baking sheet; brush both sides with oil and season with vegetable seasoning and onion powder. Broil until golden on both sides. Cut into ½-inch-wide strips.

2. Sauté shallots and garlic in olive oil in nonstick skillet for 3 to 5 minutes. (If they stick, add juice from tomatoes.)

3. Add blanched beans and eggplant strips. Stir over heat for 5 minutes.

4. Add tomatoes and basil. Heat mixture for 5 minutes more and serve. This is a delicious accompaniment to roast chicken.

Helpful Hint: Save vegetable stock from blanched beans and juice from tomatoes to make future soups.

Per serving: 52 calories; 1.7 gm protein; 1.9 gm fat; 8.7 gm carbohydrate; 1.8 gm fiber; 0 mg cholesterol; 9 mg sodium

Praised Fennel
(Finocchio)
Serves: 4 (2 halves = 1 serving)

So named because of all the raves received!

4 small fennel bulbs, trimmed and halved
Water to cover
2 tablespoons red wine vinegar
½ cup salt-free chicken broth, defatted
½ cup dry white wine

1 garlic clove, minced
1 teaspoon salt-free vegetable seasoning
Freshly ground black pepper
Few drops hot pepper sauce
1 tablespoon grated Parmesan cheese (optional)

1. Place fennel in 10-inch skillet; cover with cold water and add vinegar. Bring to a boil and drain.

2. Place blanched fennel in 2-quart shallow flameproof baking dish (8 x 11 inches) and add remaining ingredients except cheese.

3. Cover dish with parchment paper or foil and braise in preheated 350° oven for 20 to 30 minutes, or until tender.

4. Sprinkle with Parmesan and place under broiler briefly before serving.

To Serve: May be used as a garnish with chicken or fish entrées, served as a vegetable, or chilled and served as a first course.

Per serving: 49 calories; 2.6 gm protein; 0.4 gm fat; 5.7 gm carbohydrate; 0.5 gm fiber; 0 mg cholesterol; 11 mg sodium

Easy Stuffed Green Peppers ⓠⓜ

Serves: 6 (1 pepper = 1 serving)

6 green peppers
1 small onion, minced
2 teaspoons extra-virgin olive oil
1 cup frozen corn, defrosted
1 cup frozen lima beans, defrosted

1 cup salt-reduced tomato sauce
1 cup whole-wheat bread crumbs
Freshly ground black pepper
1 tablespoon grated Parmesan
cheese

1. Remove stem end of peppers and seed. Cook in boiling water for 5 minutes and drain.

2. Sauté onion in oil until lightly browned; add corn, lima beans, tomato sauce, bread crumbs, and pepper.

3. Fill peppers with blended mixture; sprinkle with Parmesan.

4. Arrange in glass baking dish and bake in preheated 350° oven for 30 minutes.

To Serve: Serve as a vegetable accompaniment to fish or chicken or part of a vegetarian plate.

In Microwave: Cover with plastic and bake on high for 12 minutes.

Per serving: 151 calories; 6.0 gm protein; 2.7 gm fat; 27.9 gm carbohydrate; 2.5 gm fiber; 1 mg cholesterol; 81 mg sodium

Lima Bean Puree ⓠ

Serves: 4 (⅔ cup = 1 serving)

If you are bored with the usual steamed vegetables, try this recipe.

1 small onion, sliced
2 10-ounce packages frozen lima
beans
1½ cups boiling water

½–⅔ cup nonfat evaporated milk
1–2 tablespoons white horseradish
1 teaspoon mild soy sauce

1. Add onion and lima beans to boiling water.

2. Simmer until tender and drain. (Save liquid for future soups.)

3. Puree mixture in food processor or blender.

4. Add milk, horseradish, and soy sauce; blend.

5. Return to saucepan and heat before serving.

Variation: Two 10-ounce packages of frozen chopped broccoli may be substituted for the beans.

Per serving: 177 calories; 11.5 gm protein; 0.5 gm fat; 32.4 gm carbohydrate; 2.9 gm fiber; 1 mg cholesterol; 115 mg sodium

Swiss Onion Pie

Serves: 8 (1 slice = 1 serving)

2½ pounds thinly sliced Spanish onions, sautéed in 1 tablespoon cold-pressed safflower oil, or 2 cups Onion Magic (page 36)

2 10-ounce packages frozen chopped spinach, defrosted and drained

2 cups steamed brown rice

1 cup 1% cottage cheese

¼ teaspoon freshly grated nutmeg

2 teaspoons Dijon mustard

3 egg whites plus 1 whole egg

1½ cups nonfat milk

¼ teaspoon white pepper

1 teaspoon salt-free vegetable seasoning

1 teaspoon Worcestershire sauce

1 tablespoon grated Parmesan cheese

1. Sauté onions in oil in nonstick skillet until transparent.

2. Spray 10-inch glass pie plate with butter-flavored nonstick cooking spray.

3. Combine spinach, rice, cottage cheese, and nutmeg; mix thoroughly with fork. Press into bottom and sides of pie plate as a shell.

4. Spread shell with mustard and add onions or Onion Magic.

5. Beat eggs, milk, pepper, vegetable seasoning, and Worcestershire sauce together and pour over onions. Sprinkle with Parmesan cheese.

6. Bake in preheated 425° oven for 10 minutes; reduce heat and bake at 325° for 20 minutes longer, or until knife inserted in center comes out clean.

To Serve: Cut into 8 wedges and complete meal with sliced tomato salad, Pritikin whole-wheat bread, and Pantry-Fresh Fruit Cup (page 322).

Per serving: 196 calories; 12.6 gm protein; 4.0 gm fat; 29.6 gm carbohydrate; 2.8 gm fiber; 37 mg cholesterol; 250 mg sodium

Curried Okra ⓠ

Serves: 6 as an entrée, 12 as an accompaniment

A delicious, underused vegetable. Okra originated in West Africa; it is also the Bantu name for gumbo.

1 medium onion, finely chopped
1 tablespoon cold-pressed safflower oil
1 small green pepper, seeded and chopped
1 tablespoon curry powder or to taste
Freshly ground black pepper

2 cups frozen corn
28-ounce can Italian plum tomatoes, chopped
1½ pounds okra, rinsed and stem ends removed, or 2 10-ounce packages frozen okra
3 cups cooked brown rice or bulgur wheat (optional)

1. Sauté onion in oil in nonstick sauté pan until transparent.
2. Add green pepper, curry powder, and pepper. Cook for 2 minutes.
3. Add corn, tomatoes, and okra.
4. Bring to a boil, reduce heat, cover, and simmer for 20 to 25 minutes, or until tender.

To Serve: Spoon hot mixture over steamed brown rice or bulgur.

Variation: 1 pound ground turkey may be added in Step 2.

Helpful Hint: Trim tip and stem ends of okra carefully. If sac inside pod is pierced, liquid escapes during cooking.

Per accompaniment serving: 74 calories; 2.8 gm protein; 1.5 gm fat; 14.3 gm carbohydrate; 1.8 gm fiber; 0 mg cholesterol; 15 mg sodium

Marinated Vegetable Platter Ⓠ Ⓜ

Serves: 6 to 8

This colorful cold dish would be perfect for a buffet.

¼ pound mushroom caps, cleaned
  and stems removed
¼ pound fresh green beans
½ pound fresh broccoli spears,
  peeled

½ pound fresh cauliflowerets
4 carrots, sliced diagonally ½-inch
  thick

Marinade:
½ cup white wine vinegar or
  tarragon vinegar
¼ cup frozen unsweetened apple
  juice concentrate
1 shallot, chopped
1 tablespoon Dijon mustard
1 teaspoon salt-free vegetable
  seasoning

⅛ teaspoon white pepper
Juice of ½ lemon
1 cup salt-free chicken broth,
  defatted
2 teaspoons extra-virgin olive oil
Freshly ground black pepper

1. Place vegetables on steamer rack and cook over boiling water for 6 to 8 minutes, or until tender-crisp.

2. Combine marinade ingredients. Pour marinade over hot vegetables in shallow dish, cover, and refrigerate overnight.

Variation: You may also use frozen vegetables cooked until tender-crisp if fresh are not available.

In Microwave: Vegetables may be placed on plate, covered with plastic, and microwaved on high for 6 minutes.

Per serving: 50 calories; 2.0 gm protein; 0.6 gm fat; 10.7 gm carbohydrate; 1.5 gm fiber; 0 mg cholesterol; 25 mg sodium

Peas à la Française Ⓠⓜ

Serves: 6 (⅔ cup = 1 serving)

Here is an elegant dish done in the microwave.

1 pound frozen peas
1 head butter lettuce, washed and
  shredded
1 shallot, minced
2 tablespoons water
Freshly ground black pepper

1 teaspoon salt-free vegetable
  seasoning

2-ounce jar chopped pimiento,
  drained, for garnish

1. Place frozen peas, lettuce, shallot, and water in 1½-quart nonmetal casserole.
2. Cover and cook in microwave on high for 6 minutes. (Stir halfway through cooking.)*
3. Season with pepper and vegetable seasoning.
To Serve: Garnish with chopped pimiento and serve immediately.

Variations: One quarter of a small head of iceberg lettuce may be substituted for butter lettuce and 1 pound fresh sugar snap peas or snow peas may be substituted for frozen peas.

Per serving: 67 calories; 4.4 gm protein; 0.3 gm fat; 12.4 gm carbohydrate; 3.1 gm fiber; 0 mg cholesterol; 68 mg sodium

---

* To cook these vegetables in the traditional manner, place ingredients in covered saucepan or skillet and cook 12 minutes.

Ratatouille ⓜ
(A Vegetable Stew)

Yield: 7 to 8 cups (½ cup = 1 serving)

This pungent stew tastes even better the next day, when the flavors have had a chance to blend.

1 tablespoon extra-virgin olive oil
2 garlic cloves, minced
¼ cup chopped onion
1 stalk celery, sliced
1 medium eggplant, unpeeled, cubed
4 medium zucchini, cut in ¾-inch slices
½ teaspoon each Italian herb blend and dried oregano, crushed

1 teaspoon salt-free vegetable seasoning
2 small green peppers, seeded and cubed
4 large tomatoes, seeded and chopped
1 cup quartered artichoke hearts
3 tablespoons chopped parsley

1. Heat oil in nonstick sauté pan. Add garlic and onion and sauté for 1 to 2 minutes. Add celery, eggplant, zucchini, herb blend, oregano, and vegetable seasoning. Stir-fry for 3 to 4 minutes.

2. Add green peppers, tomatoes, artichoke hearts, and parsley. Cover and simmer for 25 to 30 minutes. Uncover and cook a few additional minutes to evaporate excess liquid, if necessary.

To Serve: Place in serving bowl and serve hot, or chill overnight and serve at room temperature. This is delicious with fish, chicken, or veal.

Helpful Hint: If your vegetables seem to stick while stir-frying, add a bit of salt-free chicken broth or tomato juice—*no more oil.*

In Microwave: Proceed as in Step 1. Cover and microwave for 5 minutes on high. Stir, add remaining ingredients, and bake on high for 15 minutes.

Per serving: 35 calories; 1.5 gm protein; 0.8 gm fat; 6.9 gm carbohydrate; 1.4 gm fiber; 0 mg cholesterol; 10 mg sodium

Santa Barbara Potatoes ⓠ

Serves: 4

My friend Ann prepares simply delicious potatoes. The potatoes' natural
sweetness complements the piquancy of the yogurt.

¾ cup nonfat yogurt
4 green onions, thinly sliced
⅛ teaspoon white pepper

1 teaspoon fines herbes (optional)
8 small unpeeled new potatoes,
  steamed and halved

1. Mix yogurt, onions, and pepper together.
2. Add warm potatoes and mix lightly with fork.
To Serve: Serve potatoes with Barbecued Salmon Steaks (page 158)
and a mixture of crisp salad greens.

Per serving: 78 calories; 3.6 gm protein; 0.2 gm fat; 15 gm carbohydrate; 0.7 gm fiber;
1 mg cholesterol; 36 mg sodium

Scalloped Potatoes and Corn ⓠⓜ

Serves: 8 (⅔ cup = 1 serving)

Two high-fiber vegetables combine to make a delicious casserole.

2 pounds unpeeled baking potatoes,
  scrubbed and sliced ¼ inch thick
3 tablespoons grated Parmesan
  cheese
2 teaspoons salt-free vegetable
  seasoning
White pepper
1½ cups frozen corn

2–2½ cups buttermilk mixed with
  3 tablespoons whole-wheat blend
  flour
Hungarian paprika

2 whole green onions, thinly sliced,
  for garnish

1. Spray 2-quart rectangular baking dish with butter-flavored nonstick
cooking spray.
2. Line pan with half the potato slices. Sprinkle with 1½ tablespoons
Parmesan cheese and half vegetable seasoning, pepper, and corn. Repeat.

3. Pour buttermilk over entire mixture.

4. Sprinkle with paprika and bake in preheated 375° oven for 1 to 1½ hours.

To Serve: Sprinkle with sliced green onions and serve hot.

In Microwave: Bake potatoes on high for 10 minutes, or until *almost* tender. Let stand for 5 minutes and slice. Proceed as in Steps 1, 2, and 3. Cover with plastic wrap. Cook on medium for 10 to 12 minutes. Let stand for 5 minutes before serving.

Per serving: 183 calories; 6.4 gm protein; 1.3 gm fat; 38.2 gm carbohydrate; 1.5 gm fiber; 4 mg cholesterol; 110 mg sodium

Stuffed Sweet Potatoes Ⓠ Ⓜ

Serves: 8 (½ potato = 1 serving)

4–6 ounces sweet potatoes
½ cup orange juice
¼ cup sugar-free apricot preserves

1 tablespoon grated orange rind
½ teaspoon ground cinnamon
¼ cup chopped pecans

1. Scrub potatoes thoroughly and bake on high in microwave oven for 12 minutes (or in preheated 425° oven for 45 minutes).

2. Cut in half; scoop out pulp and reserve shells.

3. Mash potatoes, add remaining ingredients except nuts, and blend.

4. Fill shells with potato mixture and sprinkle with pecans.*

5. Place on baking sheet and return to 375° oven for 8 to 10 minutes (or microwave on high for 3 to 5 minutes).

Per serving: 136 calories; 1.9 gm protein; 2.1 gm fat; 27.7 gm carbohydrate; 2.3 gm fiber; 0 mg cholesterol; 9 mg sodium

---

* May be prepared ahead earlier in the day to this point. If refrigerated, reheat for 15 to 20 minutes.

Larry's Oven-Fried Potatoes

Serves: 4

As some of you may remember from *Deliciously Low,* my son Larry is a potato lover. These crisp potatoes are delicious served with anything, even as a snack.

3 large unpeeled baking potatoes
 or sweet potatoes
 (about 2 pounds), scrubbed
2 tablespoons cold-pressed safflower
 oil
2 teaspoons salt-free vegetable
 seasoning

1½ teaspoons onion powder
Freshly ground black pepper
Hungarian paprika
½ teaspoon chili powder (optional
 if you like a spicy flavor)
1 tablespoon grated Parmesan
 cheese (optional)

1. Cut potatoes into ⅛-inch-thick slices.
2. Place potatoes in bowl with oil and mix thoroughly.
3. Spread potato slices on nonstick baking sheet, sprinkle with half the seasonings (except Parmesan if used).
4. Roast in preheated 450° oven for 10 minutes, turn potatoes, season with remaining seasonings, and continue roasting for about 5 to 10 minutes, or until golden brown.
5. Remove potatoes from oven and sprinkle with Parmesan cheese if desired. Serve immediately.

Variation: These crispy potato slices may be served with a chive–yogurt dip or salsa as a nibble before dinner.

Per serving: 194 calories; 3.6 gm protein; 5 gm fat; 33 gm carbohydrate; 1.0 gm fiber; 0.6 mg cholesterol; 27 mg sodium

Twice-Baked Potatoes ⓆⓂ

Serves: 8 (½ potato = 1 serving)

The average American eats more potatoes than any other vegetable—about 12 pounds per year. Their generally low price is a bargain for a food so high in Vitamin C, potassium, and Vitamin B$_6$.

4 6-ounce baking potatoes, scrubbed

1 cup buttermilk, 1% fat cottage cheese, or nonfat yogurt

1 teaspoon Worcestershire sauce

¼ teaspoon white pepper

½ teaspoon dried basil, crushed

⅓ cup thinly sliced whole green onions

1 teaspoon Hungarian paprika

1. Pierce potatoes with fork and bake on high in microwave oven for 12 minutes (or 45 minutes in preheated 425° oven).

2. Cut in half and scoop out centers, leaving ¼-inch shell.

3. Mash potatoes, add buttermilk, Worcestershire, pepper, basil, and green onions. Stir well.

4. Mound shells with potato mixture and sprinkle with paprika.*

5. Return to preheated 450° oven for 10 minutes, or until reheated and lightly browned.

Variations: For a variety of flavors, try adding a 10-ounce package frozen chopped spinach or broccoli, cooked briefly and drained, or 1 cup Onion Magic (page 36).

Helpful Hint: If desired, lightly grease the potato skins with safflower oil to shorten baking time of the potato and crisp the skin.

Per serving: 108 calories; 3.1 gm protein; 0.4 gm fat; 23.6 gm carbohydrate; 0.8 gm fiber; 1 mg cholesterol; 45 mg sodium

---

* May be prepared ahead earlier in the day to this point or frozen for future use.

Simply Stuffed Onions Ⓠ Ⓜ

Serves: 4 (1 stuffed onion = 1 serving)

In defense of onions, they are inexpensive, always available, and interesting in flavor. Try them as a main dish, here done in the microwave.

4 large onions (2 pounds), peeled*
¼ cup salt-free chicken broth, defatted
½ pound ground raw turkey
½ green pepper, seeded and chopped
8-ounce can salt-reduced tomato sauce
1½ cups steamed brown rice
1 teaspoon chili powder
1 teaspoon salt-free vegetable seasoning
¼ teaspoon white pepper
1 tablespoon grated Parmesan cheese

1. Place onions and broth in 2-quart nonmetal casserole. Cover and cook in microwave on high for 9 minutes, or until tender. Save broth.
2. Drain onions, scoop out centers, leaving ⅓-inch shell.
3. Chop onion pulp to make ½ cup.** Combine chopped onion, green pepper, and turkey in nonstick skillet and cook, stirring, until opaque.
4. Add half the can of tomato sauce and the remaining ingredients except Parmesan. Stir well.
5. Stuff onions with mixture and mound high. Return onions to casserole and surround with any excess mixture.
6. Combine remaining 4 ounces tomato sauce with drained broth and pour over all. Sprinkle with Parmesan and cover.
7. Cook covered in microwave on high for 8 to 10 minutes. Let stand for 5 minutes before serving.

To Serve: Complete meal with Ever-Ready Red Cabbage Slaw (page 108), Harriet's Quick and Crusty Multi-Grain Bread (page 343), and Lemony Cheese Pie (page 321) for dessert.

Per serving: 260 calories; 18.1 gm protein; 3.9 gm fat; 39.1 gm carbohydrate; 2.2 gm fiber; 33 mg cholesterol; 81 mg sodium

* Cut ½-inch slice off root end to sit flat.
** Save extra onion for future soups, sauces, or meat mixture.

Spinach with Corn ⓠ

Serves: 4 (½ cup = 1 serving)

1 garlic clove, minced
1 shallot, minced
½ cup salt-free chicken broth, defatted
1 cup frozen corn
2 10-ounce packages frozen leaf spinach, defrosted, or 1½ pounds fresh spinach, wilted*

3 tablespoons chopped fresh basil or 1 teaspoon Italian herb blend, crushed
1 teaspoon salt-free vegetable seasoning

1. Sauté garlic and shallot in broth in nonstick skillet until soft.
2. Add corn, cover, and steam for 3 minutes.
3. Add drained spinach, herb blend, and vegetable seasoning; cover and cook for 2 additional minutes.

Per serving: 89 calories; 6.4 gm protein; 0.5 gm fat; 19.4 gm carbohydrate; 4.4 gm fiber; 0 mg cholesterol; 127 mg sodium

* Cooked for 2 to 3 minutes in covered saucepan until limp.

Ever-Popular Spinach Casserole Ⓠ Ⓜ

Serves: 10

5 10-ounce packages frozen spinach,
  defrosted and well drained
16 ounces 1% fat cottage cheese
½ cup nonfat evaporated milk
2 egg whites, slightly beaten
1 bunch green onions, thinly sliced
½ teaspoon onion powder
1 teaspoon freshly grated nutmeg

1 teaspoon salt-free vegetable
  seasoning
1 teaspoon Worcestershire sauce
1½ cups shredded skim-milk
  mozzarella cheese
2 tablespoons grated Parmesan
  cheese (optional)

1. Combine spinach, cottage cheese, milk, and egg whites, and mix until blended thoroughly.
2. Add green onions, seasonings, and mozzarella. Mix.
3. Place mixture in 13 x 9 x 2-inch baking dish coated with nonstick cooking spray.
4. Sprinkle with Parmesan cheese if desired and bake in preheated 350° oven for 30 minutes, or until bubbly.

In Microwave: Bake covered on medium for 15 minutes.

Per serving: 112 calories; 13.4 gm protein; 3.0 gm fat; 9.9 gm carbohydrate; 2.7 gm fiber; 10 mg cholesterol; 346 mg sodium

Sweet Potato Pie

Serves: 8 (⅔ cup = 1 serving)

2 pounds cooked, peeled yams,
  mashed (about 2 cups)
¾ cup unsweetened pineapple
  juice*
4 egg whites, slightly beaten

1 teaspoon ground cinnamon
¼ teaspoon mace
13-ounce can nonfat evaporated
  milk
¼ cup chopped pecans

1. Mash potatoes by hand or in food processor with pineapple juice.
2. Add egg whites and spices.

* 1 large, ripe pear, pureed, may be substituted for pineapple juice.

3. Add milk gradually while mixing or blending in food processor.

4. Pour into 9-inch pie plate or 2-quart casserole coated with nonstick cooking spray.

5. Sprinkle with nuts and bake in preheated 350° oven for 25 to 35 minutes, depending on the size of the baking dish used.

Per serving: 119 calories; 5.8 gm protein; 2.7 gm fat; 18.5 gm carbohydrate; 0.2 gm fiber; 2 mg cholesterol; 77 mg sodium

Special Succotash Ⓠ Ⓜ

Serves: 4

A high-fiber savory accompaniment to chicken or fish.

10-ounce package frozen corn, separated
10-ounce package frozen lima beans, separated
⅓ cup seeded, diced green pepper
⅓ cup diced red onion
2 tablespoons salt-free chicken broth, defatted

Salt-free vegetable seasoning and freshly ground black pepper to taste
1 cup shredded radicchio or red cabbage (optional)

1. Place corn, lima beans, green pepper, onion, and chicken broth in 2½-quart nonmetal casserole. Cover and microwave on high for 6 to 7 minutes. Stir halfway through cooking.

2. Remove from oven, add seasonings, and, if desired, radicchio or cabbage. Stir and let stand for 3 to 4 minutes before serving.

Per serving: 149 calories; 7.6 gm protein; 0.4 gm fat; 31.9 gm carbohydrate; 3.4 gm fiber; 0 mg cholesterol; 28 mg sodium

Tomato–Lima Bean Mélange ⓠ

Serves: 4 (⅔ cup = 1 serving)

1 tablespoon mild soy sauce
10-ounce package frozen lima
  beans, cooked and drained (save
  liquid)
½ onion, chopped
1½ cups cleaned and sliced
  mushrooms

2 medium tomatoes or 3 canned
  Italian plum tomatoes, cut in
  wedges
1 teaspoon salt-free vegetable
  seasoning
2 green onions, thinly sliced

1. Add soy sauce and 3 tablespoons cooking juice from beans to non-stick skillet and heat.

2. Add onion and mushrooms and stir until tender, about 5 to 7 minutes.

3. Add tomatoes and heat about 3 minutes.

4. Stir in hot lima beans, vegetable seasoning, and green onions.

5. Heat, taste, and adjust seasonings.

Per serving: 108 calories; 6.6 gm protein; 0.6 gm fat; 20.6 gm carbohydrate; 2.5 gm fiber;
0 mg cholesterol; 174 mg sodium

Vegetable—Potato Pancakes

Yield: 16 pancakes (2 pancakes = 1 serving as an accompaniment;
4 pancakes = 1 serving as an entrée)

These pancakes are special for several reasons. They are not fried in oil or butter, and they are higher in fiber and food value than ordinary potato pancakes because of the corn and zucchini that are added.

1 tablespoon rapid-rise dry yeast
1 cup salt-free chicken broth,
   defatted, or water, warmed to
   115°*
¼ small onion, cubed
10 ounces baking potatoes
   unpeeled, scrubbed and cubed
1 cup coarsely shredded zucchini
1 cup frozen corn
2 egg whites

1 tablespoon cold-pressed safflower
   oil
¾ cup matzo meal or dry bread
   crumbs
⅛ teaspoon white pepper
¼ teaspoon salt (optional—
   remember, it adds 500 mg of
   sodium to your recipe)

1. Dissolve yeast in warm chicken broth in a bowl.
2. Process onion and potatoes in food processor or blender until minced.
3. Add zucchini, corn, egg whites, oil, matzo meal, flour, and pepper, and process briefly just to blend.
4. Add potato mixture to dissolved yeast and mix briefly.
5. Cover bowl with towel and let rise for 15 to 20 minutes.
6. Stir down lightly.
7. Coat nonstick skillet with butter-flavored nonstick cooking spray and heat. Add spoonsful of mixture to hot pan. Brown until golden on each side.

To Serve: Serve pancakes with choice of applesauce or plain yogurt, marinated kidney bean salad, and fresh melon slices.

Variation: If you have the time and patience, these make super little pancakes to pass as hot hors d'oeuvres with a yogurt and chive dip.

For 2 pancakes: 112 calories; 3.9 gm protein; 2.0 gm fat; 20.9 gm carbohydrate; 1.4 gm fiber; 0 mg cholesterol; 13 mg sodium

* If no thermometer is handy, you can always test liquid on the inside of your wrist. It should feel hot, but not scalding.

Best-Ever Zucchini–Corn Casserole ⓠ

Serves: 8 (⅔ cup = 1 serving)

Here again, baby food combines with corn, zucchini, and spices for a flavorful vegetable dish.

1 cup finely chopped onion
1 teaspoon extra-virgin olive oil
3 zucchini, cut in slices ¼ inch thick (2 cups)
¼ teaspoon each celery seed and chili powder
1 teaspoon salt-free vegetable seasoning
Few drops hot pepper sauce (optional)

1 tablespoon grated Parmesan cheese
3 4½-ounce jars strained creamed corn (baby food)
10½-ounce can salt-free corn, drained
2 tablespoons whole-wheat bread crumbs
Hungarian paprika

1. Sauté onions in oil in nonstick skillet for 2 to 3 minutes.
2. Add zucchini, cover, and sauté for 3 to 4 minutes.
3. Add next 6 ingredients; mix lightly.
4. Pour into 9-inch pie plate or baking dish coated with nonstick cooking spray. Sprinkle with bread crumbs and paprika.
5. Bake in preheated 375° oven for 20 to 25 minutes.

Per serving: 81 calories; 2.8 gm protein; 1.6 gm fat; 15.5 gm carbohydrate; 1.8 gm fiber; 0 mg cholesterol; 40 mg sodium

Easy Zucchini with Peas ⓠ

Serves: 4 (1 cup = 1 serving)

A shallot, chopped and added to the zucchini during sautéing, adds a delicious flavor to this recipe.

3 tablespoons salt-free chicken broth, defatted

1 pound zucchini, cut in slices ¼-inch thick

1 teaspoon salt-free vegetable seasoning

1½ cups frozen peas

2-ounce jar sliced pimiento, drained, or ½ sweet red pepper, thinly sliced

1. Place broth and zucchini in nonstick sauté pan. Sprinkle with vegetable seasoning and cook for 3 minutes. Cover and cook for 2 minutes.

2. Add peas and pimiento, cover, and cook for 5 minutes longer.

Per serving: 69 calories; 4.6 gm protein; 0.4 gm fat; 13.0 gm carbohydrate; 3.0 gm fiber; 0 mg cholesterol; 60 mg sodium

Skillet Zucchini Parmesan

Serves: 6 (⅔ cup = 1 serving)

Preparation in an iron skillet results in a little extra iron in the food.

1 onion, thinly sliced, or
  ½ cup Onion Magic (page 36)
16-ounce can salt-free stewed
  tomatoes, chopped
3 tablespoons salt-free tomato paste
1 garlic clove, minced
½ teaspoon Italian herb blend,
  crushed
3 tablespoons whole-wheat bread
  crumbs

1 tablespoon grated Parmesan
  cheese
1 pound zucchini, cut in slices
  ¼ inch thick

Chopped parsley for garnish

1. Place onions in iron or nonstick skillet, cover, and steam for 3 to 4 minutes. (If using Onion Magic, heat for 3 minutes in skillet.) Uncover and sauté 3 minutes more.

2. Add tomatoes and tomato paste; cook for 2 minutes.

3. Add garlic, herb blend, bread crumbs, Parmesan, and zucchini. Simmer gently for 5 to 10 minutes.

To Serve: Place in serving dish and garnish with chopped fresh parsley.

Variation: Instead of simmering, as in Step 3, place in ovenproof baking dish, sprinkle with 2 tablespoons skim-milk mozzarella cheese, and bake for 15 to 20 minutes in preheated 350° oven.

Per serving: 53 calories; 2.8 gm protein; 0.8 gm fat; 10.4 gm carbohydrate; 1.2 gm fiber; 1 mg cholesterol; 42 mg sodium

Pastas and Grains

FOR BREAKFAST OR BRUNCH,
FOR SUPPER OR LUNCH

Pastas

Cannelloni
Green Peppers with Pasta
Corn Pasta Noodles and Cottage
  Cheese
Italian Macaroni and Cheese
Main-Dish Macaroni Salad
Ruth's Noodle Pudding
Pasta Shells with Herbed Tomato
  Sauce
Cold Pasta Orientale
Pasta Perfect

Pasta Primavera
Pronto Pasta Primavera
Baked Polenta
Salmon–Pasta Salad
Nanette's Skillet-Baked Pasta with
  Salmon and Vegetables
Simply Savory Pasta Salad
Spinach Pasta Salad Supreme
Sunday Night Supper Spaghetti
Three-Vegetable Pasta
Quick Tomato Sauce

Grains

Bulgur and Buckwheat Pilaf
Mexican Red Rice
Curried Rice
Chinese Stir-Fried Brown Rice

Jan's Microwaved Rice with
  Vegetables
Pilaf of Wild Rice
Wild Rice Salad

Grains are the seeds of food grasses. They are very low in fat, sugar, and sodium and high in complex carbohydrate and fiber. When prehistoric man learned to plant crops for food, his nomadic life changed and farming started. Grain that grew best in various parts of the world became the food staple indigenous to the area, i.e., rice in the Far East, corn in Mexico and Africa, oats in Scotland, and wheat in the United States.

Food costs are constantly rising, and so is the awareness of the need for high-complex carbohydrate, high-fiber diets. While visiting in Kenya, Africa, I discovered that diseases common to urban societies (like cancer of the colon and rectum, diabetes, heart disease, gallstones, hemorrhoids, and intestinal diseases) were almost unknown in rural areas. Africans outside the cities have very little meat or fat. Their diets are high in fiber, complex carbohydrate grains, vegetables, and fruits.

Although fiber has little or no nutritional value, it does have a nutritional impact. A high-fiber diet provides bulk or roughage which helps the intestines to move their contents during the digestive process. Soluble fiber may also help to stabilize blood sugars in diabetic patients and reduce high cholesterol levels.

You should avoid refined cereals, flours, and cereal products. Eat only whole grains. People today are realizing the importance of eating whole foods, whether whole fruits instead of fruit juices or whole-grain products as opposed to refined or highly processed ones. People today not only want to live longer lives but also want to feel healthier. They are interested in the role that diet plays in the pursuit of good health and the practice of preventive medicine. Remember again, pastas and grains are not highly caloric. It is the sauce, rich in cream and cheeses, that you add to pasta, or the butter, sugar, syrup, or cream that you add to pancakes or cereals that puts on the pounds. Pastas and grains are one of the few food categories that can be suitably prepared for breakfast or brunch, supper or lunch.

Pastas

Cannelloni ⓠ

*Serves: 6 to 12 (1 crêpe = 1 serving as accompaniment or appetizer;
2 crêpes = 1 serving as an entrée)*

Cannelloni is a delicious accompaniment to chicken or veal.

10-ounce package frozen chopped
spinach, defrosted and squeezed
dry
16 ounces skim-milk ricotta cheese
1 teaspoon salt-free vegetable
seasoning
½ teaspoon Italian herb blend,
crushed

2 egg whites
2 whole green onions, thinly sliced
2 cups salt-reduced tomato sauce
12 Basic Crêpes (page 32)
1 tablespoon grated Parmesan
cheese

1. Place first 6 ingredients in mixing bowl and stir thoroughly.
2. Spread ½ cup of the tomato sauce on bottom of 13 x 9 x 12-inch
glass baking dish or shallow casserole.
3. Spoon ¼ cup of the spinach–cheese mixture into center of each
crêpe. Fold into thirds and place seam side down in baking dish.
4. Top with remaining tomato sauce and sprinkle with Parmesan.
5. Bake in preheated 375° oven for 20 minutes.
To Serve: To use as an entrée, start with Hot and Cold Mixed Green
Salad (page 118), serve steamed broccoli spears and petite carrots with
the cannelloni, and finish with Amaretto Peach Crème (page 314) as
dessert.

For 1 Cannelloni: 101 calories; 7.6 gm protein; 3.3 gm fat; 10.7 gm carbohydrate; 0.9 gm fiber;
12 mg cholesterol; 105 mg sodium

Green Peppers with Pasta ⓠ

Serves: 4 (½ stuffed pepper = 1 serving)

Pasta, sprinkled with vegetables and cooked in chicken broth, adds a wonderful flavor to stuffed peppers. If you use sweet red peppers instead of green, you will increase the amount of Vitamin A eightfold.

1 teaspoon extra-virgin olive oil
½ onion, minced
1 small garlic clove, minced
⅓ cup small elbow macaroni
2 medium carrots, coarsely
　shredded
1 small zucchini, diced
1 cup salt-free chicken broth,
　defatted
1 teaspoon salt-free vegetable
　seasoning

½ teaspoon dried thyme, crushed
1 cup salt-free chicken broth,
　defatted, or water
2 green or sweet red peppers,
　halved lengthwise and seeded
½ cup salt-free tomato sauce,
　heated

1 tablespoon chopped parsley for
　garnish

1. Place oil in 2-quart nonstick saucepan.
2. Add onion, garlic, and pasta and sauté for 2 to 3 minutes, or until golden, stirring frequently.
3. Add carrots, zucchini, chicken broth, and seasonings.
4. Heat to boiling, reduce to a simmer, and cover. Cook for about 15 minutes, or until liquid is absorbed and pasta is tender.
5. Spoon hot pasta mixture into pepper shells and place in 10-inch skillet.
6. Add broth or water and heat to boiling. Lower heat to simmer, cover, and simmer for 10 minutes.
7. Remove peppers to serving platter with slotted spoon. Drizzle with heated tomato sauce and sprinkle with parsley.
To Serve: Serve as a vegetarian meal with Special Succotash (page 271), steamed cauliflower, Pritikin whole-wheat bread, and an apple for dessert.

Per serving: 116 calories; 3.5 gm protein; 1.7 gm fat; 22.1 gm carbohydrate; 1.7 gm fiber; 0 mg cholesterol; 24 mg sodium

Corn Pasta Noodles and Cottage Cheese ⓠ

Serves: 8

This pasta has a slightly sweet taste, which most people find quite pleasing.

8 ounces corn pasta noodles
16 ounces 1% fat or lowfat cottage cheese
½ cup nonfat yogurt
½ cup orange juice

¼ cup seeded muscat raisins (optional)

¼ cup toasted pine nuts for garnish

1. Cook pasta in boiling water until al dente and drain.
2. While pasta is cooking, combine cottage cheese, yogurt, orange juice, and raisins if desired.
3. Add cheese mixture to hot pasta, blend with fork, and serve immediately.

To Serve: Place hot pasta on large, warm serving platter and sprinkle with pine nuts. Surround with assorted steamed vegetables such as broccoli, squash, snow peas, carrots, or green beans. Microwaved Fresh Fruit Coupe (page 325) completes the meal.

Per serving: 154 calories; 9.6 gm protein; 2.9 gm fat; 23.0 gm carbohydrate; 1.6 gm fiber; 2 mg cholesterol; 184 mg sodium

Italian Macaroni and Cheese Ⓠ Ⓜ

Serves: 6

16-ounce can salt-reduced stewed tomatoes, crushed
6-ounce can salt-free tomato paste
½ cup water
2 teaspoons Italian herb blend, crushed
1 garlic clove, minced
Freshly ground black pepper
8 ounces whole-wheat mostaccioli or rigatoni, cooked al dente and drained

16 ounces skim-milk ricotta cheese, well mixed
1 tablespoon grated Parmesan cheese

2 tablespoons chopped Italian parsley for garnish

1. Combine stewed tomatoes, tomato paste, water, herb blend, garlic, and pepper in saucepan. Bring to a boil and turn off heat.

2. Coat 2-quart glass baking dish with nonstick cooking spray.

3. Spread thin layer of sauce in bottom of dish. Layer with half the pasta, ricotta, and sauce. Repeat, ending with sauce. Sprinkle with Parmesan cheese.

4. Bake in preheated 375° oven for 35 minutes. Garnish with parsley before serving.

In Microwave: Bake on medium for 20 minutes, or until hot and bubbly.

Per serving: 290 calories; 15.6 gm protein; 7.2 gm fat; 41.6 gm carbohydrate; 1.9 gm fiber; 24 mg cholesterol; 139 mg sodium

Main-Dish Macaroni Salad

Serves: 6 (⅔ cup = 1 serving)

Using a microwave oven for vegetables and a blender or food processor for pureeing cheese really speeds up the preparation time of this entrée.

1 cup small shell macaroni
½ onion, chopped
10-ounce package frozen mixed
   vegetables, cooked and chilled
1 cup 1% fat cottage cheese
1 tablespoon nonfat yogurt
1 teaspoon Worcestershire sauce
1 teaspoon dry mustard

1 carrot, chopped
½ green pepper, seeded and
   chopped
1 celery stalk, chopped
4 red radishes, chopped
2-ounce jar chopped pimiento,
   drained

1. Cook macaroni and onion in boiling water according to package directions. Drain and rinse with cold water.
2. Add cooked mixed vegetables and chill for 15 minutes in freezer or refrigerator.
3. Puree cottage cheese with yogurt, Worcestershire sauce, and mustard in food processor or blender until smooth.
4. Add yogurt mixture and remaining ingredients to chilled macaroni mixture. Blend gently with a fork and serve.

To Serve: For an easy, refreshing hot-weather meal, spoon macaroni salad onto romaine-lined platter, garnish with sliced beefsteak tomatoes, and, if desired, thinly sliced turkey. Sprinkle macaroni salad with chopped parsley.

Per serving: 161 calories; 9.7 gm protein; 1.0 gm fat; 28.7 gm carbohydrate; 1.6 gm fiber; 2 mg cholesterol; 194 mg sodium

Ruth's Noodle Pudding

Serves: 12 (⅔ cup = 1 serving)

This is my sister Ruth's pudding. It is lovely enough to serve as a dessert, but it is also suitable as an accompaniment for a turkey, fish, or chicken dinner.

16 ounces 1% fat cottage cheese
8 ounces nonfat yogurt
½ cup frozen unsweetened apple juice concentrate
2 teaspoons pure vanilla extract
1 teaspoon ground cinnamon
16-ounce jar unsweetened applesauce
⅔ cup dark raisins
4 egg whites, slightly beaten

12 ounces whole-wheat noodles, cooked
2 apples (McIntosh or Rome Beauty), peeled, cored, and thinly sliced
½ cup dried whole-wheat bread crumbs mixed with
¼ cup Grape-nuts, ½ teaspoon cinnamon, and freshly grated nutmeg

1. Combine cottage cheese, yogurt, apple juice concentrate, vanilla, cinnamon, applesauce, raisins, and egg whites. Stir to blend well.
2. Add noodles to cheese mixture.
3. Place half the noodle mixture in a 13 x 9 x 2-inch baking dish coated with nonstick cooking spray.
4. Layer with apple slices and top with remaining noodles.
5. Sprinkle with bread crumb mixture and bake in preheated 375° oven for about 45 minutes, or until lightly browned.

Variation: Combine cottage cheese, yogurt, apple juice concentrate, vanilla, cinnamon, raisins, and egg whites. Add to noodles. Place half of the noodle mixture in baking dish and spread with mixture of ½ cup sugar-free apricot preserves and ¼ cup apple juice. Top with remaining noodles. Sprinkle with crumb mixture and bake in preheated 375° oven for 35 minutes.

Per serving: 200 calories; 10.5 gm protein; 2.0 gm fat; 36.2 gm carbohydrate; 2.4 gm fiber; 2 mg cholesterol; 216 mg sodium

Pasta Shells
with Herbed Tomato Sauce ⓠ

Serves: 4

If you don't have an Italian herb blend on your shelf, substitute ½ teaspoon each of dried rosemary, oregano, and thyme, crushed.

8 ounces small whole-wheat pasta shells (conchiglie)

1 6-ounce can salt-free tomato paste

16-ounce can salt-free tomatoes, chopped

1½ teaspoons Italian herb blend, crushed

3 tablespoons grated Parmesan cheese

1. Add pasta to briskly boiling water and cook for 12 to 15 minutes, or according to manufacturer's directions.

2. Drain pasta well and return to pot. Add tomato sauce, tomatoes, and herbs.

3. Heat together for 2 to 3 minutes.

4. Place on heated platter and sprinkle with Parmesan cheese. Serve immediately.

To Serve: A crisp green salad with a few kidney beans, crusty sourdough rolls, and sliced fresh fruit complete a simple but delicious meal in minutes.

Per serving: 299 calories; 10.6 gm protein; 6.4 gm fat; 52.6 gm carbohydrate; 4.1 gm fiber; 3 mg cholesterol; 111 mg sodium

Cold Pasta Orientale ⓠ

Serves: 4

Here is a lovely mixture of pasta, chicken, and fresh vegetables with the cool bite of cilantro.

6 ounces vermicelli (thin spaghetti)
1 cup fresh snow peas
1 cup finely shredded red cabbage
2 teaspoons sesame oil
¼ teaspoon Chinese five-spice powder
1 tablespoon mild soy sauce
Few flakes crushed red pepper

1 cup shredded cooked chicken
3 whole green onions, cut into 2-inch slivers
¼ cup coriander leaves (cilantro), chopped
4 Napa cabbage leaves

1. Cook pasta until just tender in briskly boiling water. Drain and rinse under cold water.
2. Combine sesame oil, five-spice powder, soy sauce, and pepper; mix well.
3. In large bowl, combine pasta with sesame oil mixture; then add chicken, green onions, vegetables, and coriander. Toss lightly.

To Serve: Place in salad bowl lined with Napa cabbage.

Per serving: 275 calories; 19.7 gm protein; 5.9 gm fat; 47.9 gm carbohydrate; 3.4 gm fiber; 31 mg cholesterol; 180 mg sodium

Pasta Perfect ⓠ

Serves: 8

Certainly fresh peeled, seeded, diced tomatoes would add another dimension to this recipe, but only when they are ripe tomatoes that are in season.

1 pound fusilli
28-ounce can crushed Italian plum
   tomatoes in sauce*
3 tablespoons chopped fresh basil
   or 1 tablespoon Italian herb
   blend, crushed

4 ounces shredded skim-milk
   mozzarella cheese

1. Add pasta to briskly boiling water, slowly. Cook for 10 minutes, or until al dente.

2. Drain pasta, return to pot, and add tomatoes and basil.

3. Stir quickly to just heat; add cheese and *serve immediately.*

To Serve: Begin with an Antipasto Salad (page 101), then serve this pasta with crisp Italian bread, and end with fresh fruit for dessert.

Per serving: 266 calories; 11.5 gm protein; 3.2 gm fat; 47.5 gm carbohydrate; 2.8 gm fiber; 8 mg cholesterol; 80 mg sodium

* 1½ pounds peeled, seeded, diced Italian plum tomatoes and 1 cup canned tomato sauce may be substituted for canned tomatoes.

Pasta Primavera ❻

Serves: 4 as an entrée; 8 as an appetizer

Seasonal vegetables as a sauce for pasta provide a delightful and nutritious mélange. The important thing to remember is not to overcook the vegetables.

2 small zucchini, sliced
1½ cups broccoli flowerets
6 stalks asparagus, sliced
10 mushrooms, quartered
1 cup sliced green beans
1 cup fresh or frozen peas
8 ounces whole-wheat spaghetti or
  tofu pasta
1 tablespoon extra-virgin olive oil
2 garlic cloves, minced
¼ teaspoon crushed red pepper
  flakes

¼ cup salt-free chicken broth,
  defatted
¼ cup chopped fresh basil or
  1 tablespoon Italian herb blend,
  crushed
12 cherry tomatoes, halved

¼ cup chopped Italian parsley and
2 tablespoons grated Parmesan
cheese for garnish

1. Cook first 6 vegetables in steamer for 3 to 4 minutes, or until crisp but tender. Set aside.

2. Cook pasta in briskly boiling water for 8 to 10 minutes; drain.

3. While pasta is cooking, sauté garlic in oil in large nonstick sauté pan. Add red pepper, broth, and basil. Add steamed vegetables and tomatoes.

4. Return drained pasta to vegetable mixture and toss lightly to combine ingredients. (If it seems dry, add a little broth.) Serve immediately or chill and serve cold.

To Serve: Serve equal portions in broad soup bowls and sprinkle with parsley and cheese.

Per entrée serving: 331 calories; 12.9 gm protein; 9 gm fat; 54.5 gm carbohydrate; 7 gm fiber; 0 mg cholesterol; 57 mg sodium

Pronto Pasta Primavera ⓠ

Serves: 2

When you are really pressed for time or don't have any fresh veggies on hand, this recipe will be a super low-calorie alternative.

16-ounce package frozen mixed cauliflower, broccoli, and carrots
3 ounces angel hair pasta or spaghettini

¼ cup low-calorie, oil-free Italian dressing (at room temperature)
1 tablespoon grated Parmesan cheese (optional)

1. Add mixed vegetables to 3 quarts briskly boiling water. Return to boil and cook for 2 minutes.
2. Add pasta to boiling water and cook for 4 minutes more, or until al dente.
3. Drain pasta and vegetables thoroughly.
4. Return to pot and add salad dressing. Toss lightly to blend.
To Serve: Mound hot pasta and vegetables on heated plate, sprinkle lightly with Parmesan cheese. Serve immediately while hot. Accompany with Mandarin Waldorf Salad (page 112) and crisp whole-wheat baguettes.

Per serving: 260 calories; 10.4 gm protein; 1.5 gm fat; 50.6 gm carbohydrate; 2.8 gm fiber; 2 mg cholesterol; 107 mg sodium

Baked Polenta

Serves: 12 (1 square = 1 serving)

Although strictly speaking, this complex carbohydrate is a whole grain, it is commonly served in Italy in the area around Venice in lieu of pasta. Use stone-ground cornmeal for a rich whole-grain flavor. Remember to store cornmeal in the refrigerator or freezer; otherwise, it will turn stale because of the fat content in the germ.

2 cups water
1 cup salt-free chicken broth, defatted
4½-ounce jar strained creamed corn (baby food)
1 cup yellow stone-ground cornmeal

1 cup frozen corn
4 fresh or canned Italian plum tomatoes, chopped
3 tablespoons grated Parmesan cheese

1. Bring water, broth, and creamed corn to a boil in heavy, 4-quart nonstick saucepan.
2. *Very slowly*, add cornmeal to boiling liquid, stirring constantly with wooden spoon or whisk. Continue stirring until mixture is smooth and starts to thicken. Add corn.
3. Reduce heat and cook mixture uncovered for 30 minutes, stirring occasionally. (The polenta is done when the mixture pulls away from the sides of the pan.)
4. Immediately pour hot mixture into 9 x 13 x 2-inch shallow baking dish coated with nonstick cooking spray. Spread and smooth mixture with spatula.
5. Sprinkle with chopped tomatoes and cheese. Bake in preheated 375° oven for 20 to 30 minutes.
To Serve: Cut into squares or triangular pieces and serve with roast chicken or a stew.

Per serving: 66 calories; 2.5 gm protein; 0.9 gm fat; 12.5 gm carbohydrate; 2.3 gm fiber; 1 mg cholesterol; 33 mg sodium

Salmon–Pasta Salad ⓠ

Serves: 6

A refreshing one-dish meal for hot weather.

8 ounces fusilli, cooked al dente
and drained
8 ounces poached salmon fillet or
1 7½-ounce can red salmon,
drained, skinned, boned, and
flaked
10-ounce can quartered artichoke
hearts, rinsed and drained
1 cup frozen peas, defrosted
½ green pepper, seeded and thinly
sliced
½ sweet red pepper, seeded and
thinly sliced

3 whole green onions, thinly sliced
1 teaspoon vegetable seasoning
¼ cup chopped fresh dill or
2 tablespoons dried dill with
2 tablespoons chopped parsley
½ cup low-calorie Italian dressing
mixed with 2 teaspoons Dijon
mustard

Tomato wedges and dill for garnish

1. Place all ingredients but dressing and garnish in large serving bowl.
Toss gently with 2 forks until thoroughly combined.
2. Sprinkle with salad dressing and mix gently.
3. Chill for 20 to 30 minutes before serving.
To Serve: Garnish with tomato wedges and sprinkle with dill.

Per serving: 243 calories; 15.5 gm protein; 2.5 gm fat; 40.1 gm carbohydrate; 3.7 gm fiber;
13 mg cholesterol; 84 mg sodium

Nanette's Skillet-Baked Pasta with Salmon and Vegetables ⓠ

Serves: 8

15½-ounce can red salmon, drained, skinned, boned, and flaked (save liquid)

1 medium onion, chopped

2 garlic cloves, minced

1 cup cleaned and sliced mushrooms

10-ounce package frozen chopped broccoli, defrosted

8-ounce can salt-reduced tomato sauce

1 teaspoon dried oregano, crushed

2 teaspoons dried dill or 2 tablespoons fresh chopped dill

⅛ teaspoon white pepper

3 cups cooked fusilli

2 ounces shredded skim-milk mozzarella cheese

1 tablespoon grated Parmesan cheese (optional)

1. Place 3 tablespoons salmon liquid in 10-inch iron skillet. Add onion and garlic and sauté over moderate heat until limp.

2. Add mushrooms and broccoli. Sauté several minutes.

3. Add tomato sauce, oregano, dill, and pepper. Cook for 3 minutes.

4. Add pasta, salmon, and mozzarella cheese.

5. Blend with fork, sprinkle with Parmesan cheese, and bake in upper third of preheated 375° oven for 15 to 20 minutes, until heated through.

To Serve: Serve from skillet at table. Accompany with crisp green salad, hearty Pritikin whole-wheat bread, and a fruit cup of mixed pineapple, blueberries, and kiwi.

Per serving: 198 calories; 17.3 gm protein; 4.8 gm fat; 21.3 gm carbohydrate; 1.1 gm fiber; 23 mg cholesterol; 262 mg sodium

Simply Savory Pasta Salad Ⓠ

Serves: 6

Some like it hot, some like it cold—in my family, it starts out hot, and leftovers are then served cold.

8 ounces fusilli or vegetable pasta twists, cooked al dente and drained

3 8-ounce skinned and boned chicken breasts, poached and shredded, or 2 cups shredded cooked chicken

2 10-ounce packages frozen chopped broccoli, defrosted and drained

1 cup frozen peas or snow peas, defrosted

2 16-ounce cans salt-reduced stewed tomatoes, chopped

4 tablespoons chopped fresh basil or 1½ tablespoons Italian herb blend, crushed

½ teaspoon white pepper

2 tablespoons grated Parmesan cheese

1. Combine all ingredients in salad bowl.
2. Cover with plastic and chill for 20 minutes before serving.

Variation: To serve hot, place all ingredients in saucepan and heat for 5 to 10 minutes before serving.

Per serving: 300 calories; 24.1 gm protein; 5 gm fat; 42.5 gm carbohydrate; 5.1 gm fiber; 43 mg cholesterol; 116 mg sodium

Spinach Pasta Salad Supreme ⓠ

Serves: 6

Pasta salads are still very much in vogue because there are endless varieties, they are easy to prepare, and they have a high complex carbohydrate content.

8 ounces whole-wheat spinach
  linguine
½ pound mushrooms, cleaned and
  sliced
½ red onion, thinly sliced
1 green or sweet red pepper,
  seeded and diced
¾ cup Cucumber–Dill Dressing
  (page 137)

Red leaf lettuce
1 tablespoon toasted sesame seeds
  (optional)

10 cherry tomatoes, halved, for
  garnish

1. Cook pasta until al dente, drain, rinse under cold water, and drain again. Chill.

2. Combine mushrooms, onion, and green pepper with salad dressing in large salad bowl.

3. Add pasta to ingredients in bowl and toss. Avoid overmixing.

4. Chill until serving time.

To Serve: Mound salad on platter lined with lettuce, sprinkle with sesame seeds, and garnish with cherry tomato halves. Serve with Pritikin whole-wheat bread and offer Papaya Custard (page 324) for dessert.

Per serving: 127 calories; 5.0 gm protein; 2.3 gm fat; 22.2 gm carbohydrate; 2.0 gm fiber;
0 mg cholesterol; 26 mg sodium

Sunday Night Supper Spaghetti Ⓠ

Serves: 6

I vividly remember the spaghetti my mother served us when I was growing up. It wasn't cooked al dente, didn't have an exotic sauce, and would probably offend present-day pasta purists—but I loved it. Try it; I think you will love it too, and, besides, it's a cinch to prepare.

1 medium onion, minced
1 green pepper, seeded and diced
2 garlic cloves, minced
1 tablespoon cold-pressed safflower oil or extra-virgin olive oil
6-ounce can salt-free tomato paste plus 1 can water

3½ cups 50% salt-reduced tomato juice*
8 ounces thin spaghetti

Chopped Italian parsley and grated Parmesan cheese for garnish

1. Sauté onion, green pepper, and garlic in oil in 4-quart saucepan until limp.
2. Add tomato paste, water, and tomato juice. Mix and bring to a boil.
3. Reduce heat, add spaghetti, and finish cooking at a simmer until juice is absorbed, about 15 to 20 minutes.

To Serve: Place in a large pasta bowl and garnish with chopped parsley and grated Parmesan cheese.

Per serving: 224 calories; 7.7 gm protein; 3.1 gm fat; 43.6 gm carbohydrate; 2.0 gm fiber; 0 mg cholesterol; 36 mg sodium

* If you desire a lower sodium content, use salt-free tomato juice plus 1 teaspoon Italian herb blend, crushed.

Three-Vegetable Pasta ⓠ

Serves: 4

I'm anxious for you to try this easy recipe. I know you will enjoy it.

2 teaspoons extra-virgin olive oil
2 garlic cloves, minced
3 medium carrots, coarsely
  shredded
3 medium zucchini, coarsely
  shredded
1 sweet red pepper, seeded and
  cut into julienne strips

¼ cup salt-free chicken broth,
  defatted
8 ounces spaghetti, cooked al dente
1 tablespoon fresh basil, chopped,
  or 1 teaspoon dried thyme,
  crushed
1 tablespoon grated Parmesan
  cheese (optional)

1. Place oil, garlic, and vegetables in nonstick sauté pan.
2. Stir-fry for 2 minutes, stirring constantly.
3. Add chicken broth, cover, and steam for 2 minutes.
4. Add drained, hot pasta to vegetable mixture. Mix gently.

To Serve: Place hot pasta on serving platter, garnish with chopped basil, sprinkle with Parmesan cheese, and serve immediately. Complete meal with an Antipasto Salad (page 101), crisp Italian bread, and Fresh Strawberry Tart (page 330).

Variation: One 20-ounce package of frozen broccoli cuts, defrosted, may be substituted for carrots and zucchini.

Per serving: 274 calories; 9.0 gm protein; 3.3 gm fat; 52.6 gm carbohydrate; 3.6 gm fiber; 0 mg cholesterol; 24 mg sodium

Quick Tomato Sauce Ⓠ

Yield: 4 cups (½ cup = 1 serving)

1 small red or yellow onion,
  minced
1 large garlic clove, minced
3 tablespoons dry red or white wine
28-ounce can crushed Italian plum
  tomatoes in puree

3 tablespoons chopped fresh basil
  or 2 teaspoons Italian herb
  blend, crushed
2 tablespoons chopped Italian
  parsley
Freshly ground black pepper

1. Place onion, garlic, and wine in saucepan. Cook for 3 minutes, or until wilted.
2. Add tomatoes, bring to a boil, reduce heat, and simmer for 10 minutes.
3. Add basil, parsley, and pepper.
4. Taste and adjust seasonings.

To Serve: May be served with pasta, refrigerated for 3 to 4 days, or frozen for future use.

Per serving: 61 calories; 2.4 gm protein; 0.7 gm fat; 11.7 gm carbohydrate; 1.8 gm fiber; 0 mg cholesterol; 29 mg sodium

Grains

Bulgur and Buckwheat Pilaf Ⓠ

Serves: 12 (⅔ cup = 1 serving)

Both buckwheat and bulgur wheat have long been known for their nutritional value. They have been used by Eastern Mediterranean cultures for centuries, either boiled like rice or eaten uncooked after being soaked in water. They may also be served as a hot cereal for breakfast.

2 teaspoons extra-virgin olive oil
1 cup bulgur wheat
1¼ cup buckwheat groats (kasha)
1 onion, minced
1 green pepper, seeded and
  chopped
1 cup sliced celery
1 cup sliced mushrooms

4 cups salt-free chicken broth,
  defatted, boiling
2 teaspoons salt-free vegetable
  seasoning
Freshly ground black pepper

Chopped parsley for garnish

1. Place olive oil in nonstick skillet. Add bulgur wheat, groats, and onion and sauté for 3 to 5 minutes, or until golden.
2. Add green pepper, celery, and mushrooms; sauté briefly. Add boiling broth.
3. Place in 2-quart casserole, cover, and bake in preheated 375° oven for 25 to 30 minutes, or until tender.*

To Serve: Remove from oven, sprinkle with parsley, and serve hot from casserole.

Per serving: 116 calories; 3 gm protein; 1.3 gm fat; 22.5 gm carbohydrate; 0.8 gm fiber; 0 mg cholesterol; 12 mg sodium

* May be cooked covered on top of stove for 20 to 25 minutes, or until grains are tender.

Mexican Red Rice

Serves: 8 (⅔ cup = 1 serving)

Red rice may be served with steamed vegetables as an entrée, or as an accompaniment to Mexican-style dishes.

2 cups brown rice
2 teaspoons extra-virgin olive oil
¼ teaspoon ground cumin
½ teaspoon garlic powder
1 teaspoon salt-free vegetable seasoning
½ teaspoon freshly ground black pepper

2 cups salt-free chicken broth, defatted
2 cups salt-reduced tomato sauce or chopped canned tomatoes
6 slices green pepper rings, without seeds
3 thin slices onion

1. Sauté rice in oil in nonstick saucepan for 2 to 3 minutes. Stir constantly but do not brown.

2. Add seasonings, chicken broth, and tomato sauce or tomatoes. Mix well.

3. Bring to a boil and reduce heat to a simmer.

4. Top with green pepper and onions, cover, and cook for 45 minutes, or until all liquid has been absorbed. Do not stir while cooking.

Per serving: 94 calories; 2.1 gm protein; 1.4 gm fat; 18.1 gm carbohydrate; 0.3 gm fiber; 0 mg cholesterol; 18 mg sodium

Curried Rice

Serves: 4 (⅔ cup = 1 serving)

Brown rice takes on an interesting flavor with the addition of curry and fruit. It is delicious served with barbecued lamb or lamb stew.

1 cup brown rice
1 teaspoon cold-pressed safflower oil
1 cup thinly sliced celery
1 teaspoon curry powder or to taste
½ green pepper, seeded and thinly sliced
⅛ teaspoon white pepper

2 cups salt-free chicken broth, defatted
7½-ounce can unsweetened pineapple tidbits, drained (reserve ½ cup juice)
½ green pepper, seeded and thinly sliced

1. Sauté rice in heated oil in flameproof casserole, stirring frequently until golden.
2. Stir in celery, curry powder, ½ green pepper, chicken broth, and pineapple juice.
3. Cover and bake in preheated 350° oven for 35 minutes.
4. Stir in pineapple and remaining green pepper with fork. Cover and return to oven for 10 to 15 minutes.

Per serving: 119 calories: 2.1 gm protein; 1.9 gm fat; 23.4 gm carbohydrate; 1.2 gm fiber; 0 mg cholesterol; 33 mg sodium

Chinese Stir-Fried Brown Rice ⓠ

Serves: 2

2 teaspoons cold-pressed safflower oil

1 stalk bok choy or celery cut in ¼-inch-wide strips

2 canned water chestnuts, sliced

2 egg whites, slightly beaten

1 cup leftover cooked brown rice

1 teaspoon mild soy sauce

2 whole green onions, thinly sliced, for garnish

1. Heat oil in nonstick skillet.
2. Add bok choy or celery and water chestnuts and sauté until slightly softened.
3. Add egg whites and scramble with wooden spoon.
4. Add brown rice and soy sauce; cook until dry.

To Serve: Place hot rice mixture in serving dish and sprinkle with green onions; serve immediately.

Per serving: 183 calories; 6.6 gm protein; 5.5 gm fat; 27.0 gm carbohydrate; 0.6 gm fiber; 0 mg cholesterol; 179 mg sodium

Jan's Microwaved Rice with Vegetables ⓠⓜ

Serves: 6 (⅔ cup = 1 serving)

A gentle blend of tender rice with vegetables, some cooked and some crunchy.

2 cups salt-free chicken broth, defatted, or vegetable broth
1 cup brown rice
2 teaspoons cold-pressed safflower oil
1 teaspoon salt-free vegetable seasoning
⅛ teaspoon white pepper
1 garlic clove, minced

1 teaspoon Worcestershire sauce
½ cup chopped onion
½ cup chopped green pepper
2 cups cubed zucchini
2 small tomatoes, seeded and diced
2 whole green onions, thinly sliced
1 celery stalk, thinly sliced
1 tablespoon grated Parmesan cheese (optional)

1. Pour broth into 4-quart nonmetal casserole. Heat on high in microwave for 4½ minutes, or until boiling.

2. Sauté rice with oil in nonstick skillet for 2 minutes.

3. Add rice, seasonings, onion, green pepper, and zucchini to broth.

4. Cover and cook on high for 15 to 20 minutes, or until liquid is absorbed.

5. Add tomatoes, green onions, and celery to rice. Stir vegetables and Parmesan cheese into rice with fork, cover, and let stand for 10 minutes before serving.

Per serving: 158 calories; 3.8 gm protein; 2.4 gm fat; 30.2 gm carbohydrate; 3.2 gm fiber; 0 mg cholesterol; 24 mg sodium

Pilaf of Wild Rice

Serves: 6 (⅔ cup = 1 serving)

Although not technically a grain, this seed of wild grass is a crunchy change from the ordinary. To reduce the cost of preparation, you may substitute ⅓ cup short-grain brown rice for ⅓ cup wild rice.

2 garlic cloves, minced
1 carrot, chopped
1 stalk celery, chopped
2 teaspoons cold-pressed safflower
   oil
2¾ cups salt-free chicken broth,
   defatted
1 teaspoon salt-free vegetable
   seasoning

½ teaspoon thyme
Few flakes crushed red pepper
⅔ cup wild rice, washed and
   drained
3 green onions, sliced
¼ cup toasted, slivered almonds or
   pine nuts (optional)

1. Sauté garlic, carrot, and celery in oil briefly.
2. Add broth and seasonings. Bring to a boil, add rice and bring to a second boil.
3. Reduce heat, cover, and simmer for 40 to 45 minutes, or until rice is tender and liquid is absorbed.
4. About 15 minutes before serving add green onions and nuts.

Per serving: 98 calories; 3.2 gm protein; 3.5 gm fat; 13.7 gm carbohydrate; 1.0 gm fiber; 0 mg cholesterol; 11 mg sodium

Wild Rice Salad

Serves: 4

⅔ cup wild rice
2 cups boiling water with
  2 teaspoons mild soy sauce
1 tablespoon extra-virgin olive oil
¼ cup salt-free chicken broth,
  defatted
¼ cup lemon juice
⅔ cup chopped parsley
½ green or sweet red pepper,
  seeded and diced

½ cup chopped whole green onions
¼ cup chopped mint
Salt-free vegetable seasoning and
  pepper to taste

Green pepper rings and diced
  tomatoes for garnish

1. Wash rice and place in saucepan with boiling water and soy sauce. Bring to a boil, cover, and simmer for 30 to 40 minutes, or until tender but crunchy. Drain any remaining liquid.

2. Combine remaining ingredients except garnishes and add to cooked rice.

3. Toss lightly just to blend, cover, and chill.

To Serve: Place salad in serving bowl and garnish with green pepper rings and chopped tomatoes.

Per serving: 173 calories; 4.6 gm protein; 7.1 gm fat; 24.3 gm carbohydrate; 0.9 gm fiber; 0 mg cholesterol; 104 mg sodium

Sweets and Treats

THE GRAND FINALE

Desserts

Sherried Orange Gelatin with Fruit
California Fresh Fruit Bowl
Amaretto Peach Crème
Truly Delicious Baked Apple
Harold's Choice: Bread Pudding
Carrot Cake
Glazed Blueberries and Bananas
Hazelnut Meringue Cookies
Freda's Pecan–Carob Macaroons
Company Apricot Chiffon Torte
Lemony Cheese Pie
Pantry-Fresh Fruit Cup
Orange-Baked Alaska
Orangey Gelatin Cup

Melon in Strawberry Sauce
Papaya Custard
Microwaved Fresh Fruit Coupe
Pineapple Ambrosia
Pineapple Parfait
Middle Eastern Pudding
Pumpkin Custard
Strawberry–Banana–Yogurt Pie
Fresh Strawberries with Sabayon
    Sauce
Fresh Strawberry Tart
Special Strawberry Ice Cream
Tapioca with Mango

Quick Breads

Busy Day Griddlecakes
Country Whole-Wheat Pancakes
Fluffy Oatmeal Pancakes
Waffles
Harriet's Blueberry Coffee Cake
Corn Bread or Muffins
Banana–Nut Muffins

Everyday Muffins in Minutes
Oat–Bran Muffins
Rapid-Rise Oatmeal Bread
Harriet's Quick and Crusty
    Multi-Grain Bread
Always-Delicious Zucchini Bread

When thinking about desserts, I can't help recalling Sam Levenson's amusing story about his family. It seems that they were having unexpected guests for dinner. In order to stretch the food, his mother asked the children to hold back on helping themselves to meat and vegetables. Subsequently, when serving dessert, she proudly announced, "Now, those who didn't eat their meat and vegetables will not get dessert."

How many times do parents provide this aura of a reward serving desserts to children? (To say nothing of our own conditioned sweet tooth.) It's not unusual to hear people say that they are "saving room" for dessert. I wonder if we smiled and guarded a bowl of wonderful fresh fruit or yogurt-based ice cream with the same enthusiasm as a rich, gooey chocolate cake or coconut cream pie, we could encourage children's positive response to desserts that were nutritious as well as delicious.

If you try the wonderful Strawberry Tart (page 330), Company Apricot Chiffon Torte (page 320), or Amaretto Peach Crème (page 314), I promise you'll get rave reviews, not just accommodating nods.

A colorful bowl or basket of fresh fruit, attractively arranged, is a pleasing conclusion to almost any meal. The enormous variety in fruits now available in our markets is endless. With shipping what it is today, we can enjoy fresh fruits the year round: blueberries from New Zealand; strawberries, melons, and mangos from Mexico; peaches and grapes from Chile; to say nothing of fruits shipped throughout the United States from Washington, California, and Florida. Of course, cost is a factor because somebody has to absorb the expense of the shipping. However, there are still many locally grown fresh fruits from which we can choose— in season. Here are a few tips to help you in choosing the pick of the crop.

The Look of Good Fresh Fruit

Apples
Should be smooth, firm, and free of bruises.

Bananas
A touch of green and firm. Yellow and flecked with brown when ripe. Speed ripening in a dark place.

Berries
Blueberries—firm, uniform in size, with silvery coating.
Raspberries—plump and fresh looking, medium red color, very fragile. (Wash just before using.)
Strawberries—red color (no white shoulders), hulls attached and green, no mold. Look at the bottom of the container. Size is unimportant. Check Helpful Hints (page 10) for longer storage.

Cantaloupe
Pleasant, fruity odor. No green color to skin. Yields to pressure at end opposite stem end. Ripen at room temperature.

Cherries
Try the taste test.

Grapefruit
Well shaped, thin-skinned, and heavy (that means it's juicy).

Grapes
Compact bunches—try the taste test.

Honeydew

The bigger the better, with a fruity fragrance and pale yellow or off-white velvety skin. Ripen at room temperature.

Lemons

Yellow not green, smooth, thin-skinned, and heavy (that means it's juicy).

Mangos

Firm yet a bit giving, the more red or yellow area the better. Will ripen at room temperature.

Nectarines and Peaches

The more red area, the better; a fruity odor. Avoid bruises and hard fruit: They soften but do not sweeten at room temperature.

Oranges

Color depends on variety. Firm and heavy for size. Ripe when picked.

Papaya

Firm, the more yellow the better, and heavy. They soften, but do not ripen at room temperature.

Pears

Firm, no bruises. Will ripen at room temperature.

Pineapple

Heavy, yields to touch, with a fruity fragrance. Crown is fresh and dark green.

Plums

Color varies with variety. Choose firm yet yielding fruit. No bruises. Will soften but not ripen at room temperature.

Watermelon

It's best to buy one that is cut and see if it is red, juicy, and sweet-smelling. (When buying whole, my friend Madame T. C. Wong suggests looking for brown bee spots. She says the bees know what's sweet and juicy.)

A Word of Caution

So many pesticides are used by growers that you must always wash fruit before eating, but not before storing. Fresh fruit deteriorates more rapidly after washing.

Desserts

Sherried Orange Gelatin with Fruit Ⓠ

Serves: 10 to 12 (1 cup = 1 serving)

3 tablespoons plain, unflavored gelatin
5 cups orange juice
⅔ cup sweet sherry
2 cups orange segments
2 cups seedless grapes
½ cup canned unsweetened crushed pineapple

2 cups diced unpeeled Delicious apples
1 tablespoon apricot brandy, or 2 tablespoons frozen unsweetened apple juice concentrate

1. Mix gelatin with orange juice; stir over low heat until gelatin is dissolved.
2. Add sherry; stir.
3. Pour into a shallow pan and chill until firm.
4. Mix orange segments, grapes, pineapple, and apples. Sprinkle with brandy or apple juice. Chill.

To Serve: Cube gelatin, spoon into individual glass compotes or sherbet cups, and top with fruit mixture. A dollop of nonfat yogurt may be added before serving.

Per serving: 129 calories; 3.8 gm protein; 0.4 gm fat; 25 gm carbohydrate; 1.8 gm fiber; 0 mg cholesterol; 6 mg sodium

California Fresh Fruit Bowl ⓠ

Serves: 16 (½ cup = 1 serving)

1½ pounds black bing cherries, pitted, or 20-ounce package frozen unsweetened cherries

2 pints strawberries, washed, then hulled and halved

1 pint raspberries, blackberries, or blueberries

2 cups seedless red grapes

2 tablespoons kirsch*

The Sauce:

1 very ripe banana

1 pint fresh raspberries, or 16-ounce package frozen unsweetened raspberries

1 tablespoon lemon juice

1 tablespoon Grand Marnier*

Mint sprigs for garnish

1. Combine cherries, strawberries, raspberries, and grapes in a large glass serving bowl. Sprinkle with kirsch, cover, and marinate for 30 minutes in refrigerator.

To Make the Sauce:

2. Puree banana in blender or food processor. Add raspberries and puree.

3. Stir in lemon juice and Grand Marnier. Remove to a bowl and let chill in refrigerator until ready to serve.

To Serve: Pour raspberry sauce over fruit and mix gently. Garnish with sprigs of fresh mint.

Per serving: 89 calories; 1.5 gm protein; 0.8 gm fat; 20.8 gm carbohydrate; 4.1 gm fiber; 0 mg cholesterol; 2 mg sodium

* Orange juice may be substituted for the liqueurs.

Amaretto Peach Crème ⓠ

Serves: 10 (⅓ cup = 1 serving)

Diabetics may eliminate liqueur and raisins; the almond extract will still provide an exquisite flavor. If the fruit is not sweet enough, you may have to add frozen unsweetened apple juice concentrate.

2 small ripe bananas, frozen in
   1-inch chunks
2 cups frozen unsweetened peach
   slices
1 cup nonfat evaporated milk,
   chilled for 20 minutes in freezer
2 teaspoons pure almond extract
⅓ cup seeded muscat raisins
   soaked in 2 tablespoons amaretto
   liqueur

2–3 tablespoons frozen
   unsweetened apple juice
   concentrate (optional)

Peach slices and mint for garnish

1. Defrost fruit slightly (5 to 10 minutes) before preparing. (Peach slices may need a bit longer.)
2. Place half the bananas and peaches in food processor or blender. Process until pureed. Add remaining fruit and repeat.
3. Gradually add chilled milk and almond extract to pureed fruit as machine is in motion. Process until crème is desired consistency.
4. Add soaked raisins with liqueur, process for 2 to 3 seconds.

To Serve: May be served immediately in glass sherbet dishes or parfait glasses, or covered with plastic and frozen for future use, up to 1 month. A fresh peach slice and mint leaves make an appealing garnish.

Variation: Use 2 cups frozen strawberries, raspberries, or bananas instead of peaches and low-fat yogurt instead of nonfat evaporated milk. Omit Step 4 and add 1 to 2 teaspoons strawberry, raspberry, or banana extract instead of almond extract, amaretto, and raisins.

Per serving: 109 calories; 2.6 gm protein; 0.2 gm fat; 23.7 gm carbohydrate; 0.8 gm fiber; 1 mg cholesterol; 34 mg sodium

Truly Delicious Baked Apple Ⓠ Ⓜ
(In the Microwave)

Serves: 4 (1 apple = 1 serving)

Imagine, the flavor of a fresh apple, but the texture of apple pie. A microwave oven prepares apples in a way not even comparable to those baked in a traditional oven. You may substitute pears as a tasty alternative.

4 Rome Beauty apples (about
  2 pounds), cored and peeled
  ⅓ of way down from stem end
½ cup orange juice, apple juice, or
  unsweetened papaya juice

½ teaspoon ground cinnamon
Freshly grated nutmeg

1. Place apples in 2-quart round covered nonmetal casserole.
2. Spoon juice over apples. Sprinkle with cinnamon and nutmeg.
3. Cover and bake in microwave on high for 9 to 11 minutes. When the apples have finished baking, they will have retained their original shape but be tender.

To Serve: Serve warm apples in glass compotes or dessert dishes. Spoon sauce over apples or top with Almost Crème Anglaise (page 364).

Variation: Muscatel wine may be substituted for half the fruit juice. You may also stuff the cavity of the apple with dried raisins or dates.

Helpful Hint: For one serving, cook the prepared apple on high for 2 to 4 minutes.

Per serving: 89 calories; 0.5 gm protein; 0.5 gm fat; 22.8 gm carbohydrate; 3.0 gm fiber; 0 mg cholesterol; 0 mg sodium

Harold's Choice: Bread Pudding

Serves: 12 (½ cup = 1 serving)

My husband's preference in desserts has always been toward home-style puddings—whether they are made of rice, bread, tapioca, etc. I must admit, they can be delicious, even when prepared without being laden with sugar, egg yolks, and heavy cream. We love this bread pudding for breakfast!

5 cups cubed stale whole-wheat
   raisin bread*
4 egg whites
2 cups nonfat milk
1 cup nonfat evaporated milk
⅓ cup frozen unsweetened apple
   juice concentrate

1½ teaspoons pure vanilla extract
1 teaspoon ground cinnamon
½ teaspoon freshly grated nutmeg
¼ cup chopped pecans

1. Spray 8-inch-square glass baking dish with butter-flavored nonstick cooking spray.
2. Spread bread cubes in pan.
3. Beat egg whites, milk, apple juice concentrate, vanilla, ½ teaspoon of the cinnamon, and the nutmeg with fork until blended.
4. Pour mixture over bread and let soak for 10 to 15 minutes.
5. Sprinkle with remaining ½ teaspoon cinnamon and the chopped pecans.
6. Bake in preheated 350° oven for 45 minutes.
To Serve: Serve warm on dessert plates or in glass sherbet dishes and accompany with pitcher of nonfat milk.

Variation: In Step 3, layer half the bread cubes in pan and spread with 2 peeled, thinly sliced apples. Top with remaining bread cubes and proceed with recipe.

Per serving: 170 calories; 8.7 gm protein; 3.9 gm fat; 25.4 gm carbohydrate; 0.7 gm fiber; 37 mg cholesterol; 151 mg sodium

* Pritikin whole-wheat raisin bread is now available.

Carrot Cake

Serves: 16 (1 2¼-inch square = 1 serving)

2½ cups whole-wheat pastry flour*
1 teaspoon baking soda
1 tablespoon low-sodium baking
  powder
1 tablespoon ground cinnamon
2 teaspoons ground ginger
½ teaspoon freshly grated nutmeg
¼ teaspoon ground allspice
½ cup chopped pecans
½ cup dark raisins

3 egg whites
2 tablespoons cold-pressed
  safflower oil
1 teaspoon pure vanilla extract
6-ounce can frozen unsweetened
  apple juice concentrate
8-ounce can unsweetened crushed
  pineapple in juice
3 cups grated carrots

1. Combine dry ingredients in mixing bowl. Mix with fork.
2. Combine all remaining ingredients in separate bowl and beat well.
3. Add liquid to dry ingredients, mixing with fork until flour disappears.
4. Place batter in 9 x 9 x 2-inch pan coated with nonstick cooking spray. Bake in preheated 350° oven for 40 to 45 minutes, or until cake shrinks from sides of pan.
5. Cool on rack and remove from pan.

To Serve: Cut into squares and, if desired, top each serving with Almost Crème Anglaise (page 364).

Per serving: 151 calories; 4.1 gm protein; 3.7 gm fat; 27.1 gm carbohydrate; 2.2 gm fiber; 0 mg cholesterol; 44 mg sodium

* If you substitute regular whole-wheat flour, use 1¾ cups.

Glazed Blueberries and Bananas ⓠ

Serves: 8

4 ripe bananas, cut lengthwise in
  half, then quartered
⅓ cup frozen unsweetened apple
  juice concentrate
⅔ cup fresh or frozen blueberries

1 tablespoon banana liqueur
2 whole papayas, seeded and
  quartered

Mint or lemon leaf for garnish

1. Place bananas in nonstick skillet with apple juice concentrate. Baste
bananas with juice. Cover and simmer for 3 minutes.
2. Cook uncovered for 3 minutes more. Add blueberries and liqueur
and baste fruit with sauce.
To Serve: Serve immediately while hot on quartered papaya garnished
with mint or lemon leaf.

Per serving: 109 calories; 1.1 gm protein; 0.5 gm fat; 26.5 gm carbohydrate; 1.7 gm fiber;
0 mg cholesterol; 6 mg sodium

Hazelnut Meringue Cookies

Yield: 24 cookies (1 cookie = 1 serving)

3–4 extra-large egg whites (½ cup)
  at room temperature
1 teaspoon brown rice vinegar
2 teaspoons Frangelica liqueur or
  almond extract
¼ cup date sugar, frozen
  unsweetened apple juice
  concentrate, or, if permitted,
  sugar

½ cup toasted, finely chopped
  hazelnuts, almonds, or a mixture
  of both
3 tablespoons cornstarch

1. Beat egg whites until frothy. Add vinegar and beat egg whites until
soft peaks form. Beat in liqueur or extract.
2. Beat in date sugar a little at a time until meringue is glossy and
stiff. (If apple juice is used, mixture will not be as stiff.)

3. Combine nuts with cornstarch. Fold into meringue.

4. Spoon tablespoons of meringue onto nonstick baking sheet or parchment paper and bake in preheated 200° oven for 25 to 30 minutes, or until very lightly colored and firm to the touch. Turn off heat and let cool in oven with door slightly ajar.

5. Remove to rack, cool, and store in container (not airtight).

Variation: *Meringue Shells for Fruit.* Meringues may be shaped into 5-inch circles and baked as above. When cool, arrange on dessert dishes, cover with sliced strawberries or peaches, and top with Almost Crème Anglaise (page 364) or Strawberry Sauce (page 324).

Per serving: 28 calories; 0.8 gm protein; 1.5 gm fat; 2.8 gm carbohydrate; 0.1 gm fiber; 0 mg cholesterol; 8 mg sodium

Freda's Pecan–Carob Macaroons

Yield: 48 cookies (1 cookie = 1 serving)

Freda's interest and testing of delicious, healthy food has finally produced a cookie that's tasty, without added fat and sugar.

⅔ cup frozen unsweetened apple
   juice concentrate
⅔ cup carob powder
2 teaspoons pure vanilla extract

6 extra-large egg whites (⅔ cup),
   at room temperature
1 cup chopped pecans

1. Mix apple juice concentrate and carob together in saucepan. Bring to a boil and allow to simmer for 5 minutes. (Stir occasionally so that it does not stick.) Add vanilla and cool before using.

2. Beat egg whites until stiff.

3. Add syrup and nuts to beaten whites, folding in carefully.

4. Drop by teaspoonfuls onto nonstick baking sheet. Bake in preheated 300° oven for 20 to 30 minutes.

5. Cool on rack and store in container (not airtight). May be frozen for future use.

Per serving: 32 calories; 0.9 gm protein; 1.7 gm fat; 3.5 gm carbohydrate; 0 gm fiber; 0 mg cholesterol; 11 mg sodium

Company Apricot Chiffon Torte

Serves: 12

Although this preparation takes a bit of time, your guests' pleasure will make it all worthwhile. Prepare the crust in a 9- or 10-inch springform pan and add the chiffon filling.

1 Basic Tart Crust (page 35)
1½ envelopes unflavored gelatin dissolved in ½ cup cold white unsweetened grape juice*
Juice of 2 lemons plus white grape juice to equal 1 cup
¼ cup frozen unsweetened apple juice concentrate
1 pound fresh, ripe apricots, pitted, plus ½ cup white grape juice, or 8 ounces sun-dried apricots plus 1⅓ cups white grape juice

1 teaspoon grated lemon rind
1 tablespoon apricot liqueur
1 cup nonfat evaporated milk, well chilled
1 teaspoon pure vanilla extract

2 kiwi, peeled and sliced, and ¼ cup toasted, chopped hazelnuts, for garnish

1. Make the tart crust. Dissolve gelatin in cold grape juice.
2. Bring lemon juice plus grape juice and apple juice to a boil. Add dissolved gelatin and stir until liquefied. Chill in freezer until consistency of unbeaten egg whites.
3. Place apricots and juice in saucepan. Simmer for 5 to 10 minutes, or until tender. Cool 10 minutes and puree in a blender or food processor until nearly smooth.
4. Add lemon rind and apricot liqueur.
5. Beat chilled evaporated milk *in chilled bowl* until stiff. Add vanilla.
6. Fold chilled gelatin mixture into apricot mixture; then fold fruit mixture into whipped milk.
7. Spoon fruited milk mixture into tart crust in springform pan. Chill for 2 hours or overnight. Remove sides of springform pan and place torte on platter.
To Serve: Garnish with fresh kiwi slices and chopped nuts.

Per serving: 119 calories; 4.9 gm protein; 3.3 gm fat; 18.4 gm carbohydrate; 0.8 gm fiber; 1 mg cholesterol; 46 mg sodium

* Apple juice may be substituted for white grape juice in this recipe.

Lemony Cheese Pie

Serves: 10

Mr. Imoos is the executive pastry chef I worked with at the Holiday Inn Golden Mile in Hong Kong. His expertise and creativity helped produce the following dessert.

1 Basic Tart Crust (page 35)
1 envelope unflavored gelatin
⅓ cup orange juice
2 cups lowfat cottage cheese
¼ cup frozen unsweetened apple juice concentrate
3 egg whites
Grated rind of ½ lemon

1–1½ tablespoons lemon juice
1½ teaspoons pure vanilla extract

Sliced fresh strawberries, blueberries, and kiwi for garnish

Strawberry Sauce (page 324)

1. Make the tart crust.
2. Sprinkle gelatin over orange juice and let stand for 1 minute. Stir constantly over low heat until dissolved. Remove from heat.
3. Process cottage cheese in food processor or blender until creamy and smooth.
4. Add dissolved gelatin, apple juice concentrate, egg whites, rind, lemon juice, and vanilla, and process briefly until blended.
5. Pour cheese mixture into tart crust in springform pan, cover, and chill for 30 minutes, or until set.*

To Serve: Garnish with sliced fresh strawberries, blueberries, and kiwi fruit and pass Strawberry Sauce to be used as desired.

Per serving: 114 calories; 9.4 gm protein; 4.2 gm fat; 10 gm carbohydrate; 0.4 gm fiber; 1.8 mg cholesterol; 220 mg sodium

* At this point, 1 cup fresh blueberries may be sprinkled over the top of cheesecake before chilling.

Pantry-Fresh Fruit Cup ⓠ

Serves: 8 (½ cup = 1 serving)

A simple dessert that always provides a nice ending to a meal.

16-ounce can unsweetened fruit
   cocktail in fruit juice
2 apples, unpeeled, cored and diced
1 pear, unpeeled, cored and diced
1 ripe banana, peeled and sliced

1 tablespoon apricot or banana
   liqueur (optional)

Mint sprig for garnish

1. Combine all ingredients except mint in bowl. Mix gently with fork.
2. Cover and chill for 20 minutes before serving.

To Serve: Place in white serving bowl and garnish with sprig of fresh mint.

Variations: A combination of 2 cups of fresh seasonal fruit such as cherries, apricots, nectarines, plums, or seedless grapes may be substituted for canned fruit cocktail. If all fresh fruit is used, add ½ cup orange juice.

Per serving: 71 calories; 0.6 gm protein; 0.3 gm fat; 18.4 gm carbohydrate; 1.7 gm fiber; 0 mg cholesterol; 2 mg sodium

Orange Baked Alaska ⓠ

Serves: 8 (1 orange = 1 serving)

8 navel oranges
1 ripe banana, diced
2 tablespoons Grand Marnier or
   papaya juice

3 extra-large egg whites
¼ teaspoon cream of tartar
2 teaspoons pure vanilla extract

1. Cut 1 inch off top of each orange.
2. Cut around flesh close to skin and remove all orange meat.
3. Dice fruit into bite-sized pieces and mix with banana and Grand Marnier.

4. Fill orange cups with the diced fruit. Dry outside and rim of orange cup.

5. Beat egg whites until foamy, add cream of tartar, and beat until stiff (does not slide in bowl). Add vanilla and mix gently.

6. Spread meringue over each orange and place on baking sheet.

7. Bake in preheated 475° oven for 2 to 3 minutes, or until lightly browned. Serve immediately.

Helpful Hint: Cut thin slice from bottom of orange so that it does not rock.

Per serving: 100 calories; 3.4 gm protein; 0.3 gm fat; 20.2 gm carbohydrate; 2.8 gm fiber; 0 mg cholesterol; 36 mg sodium

Orangey Gelatin Cup ⓠ

Serves: 6 (⅔ cup = 1 serving)

A low-calorie dessert that is high in potassium because of the oranges and bananas.

1 package unflavored gelatin
¾ cup orange juice, boiling
½ cup orange juice, cold plus ice
   cubes to equal 1¼ cups

1½ cups orange segments
½ banana, sliced

1. Dissolve gelatin in boiling orange juice.

2. Combine remaining ½ cup orange juice and ice cubes to measure 1¼ cups.

3. Add mixture to dissolved gelatin and stir until slightly thickened. (Remove any unmelted ice.)

4. Add oranges and bananas.

5. Pour into glass dessert cups.

6. Chill for 20 minutes, or until set.

Variation: Unsweetened white grape juice may be substituted for orange juice and fresh red and green grapes added instead of oranges.

Per serving: 65 calories; 2.3 gm protein; 0.2 gm fat; 14.9 gm carbohydrate; 1.2 gm fiber; 0 mg cholesterol; 3 mg sodium

Melon in Strawberry Sauce ℚ

Serves: 8 (½ cup = 1 serving)

Depending on the season, 4 cups cubed pineapple may be substituted for melon.

1 ripe casaba or crenshaw melon,
  peeled and cubed
2 tablespoons lemon juice
4 cups strawberries, washed and
  hulled

¼ cup frozen unsweetened apple
  juice concentrate
2 tablespoons Grand Marnier or
  kirsch (optional)

1. Place cubed melon in serving bowl and sprinkle with lemon juice.
2. Puree 3 cups strawberries in blender or food processor. Add apple juice and Grand Marnier. Taste and adjust seasonings.
3. Pour strawberry puree over cubed melon, mix, and top with remaining 1 cup whole strawberries. Cover and chill for 15 minutes before serving.

Per serving: 75 calories; 1.6 gm protein; 0.4 gm fat; 15.7 gm carbohydrate; 1.8 gm fiber; 0 mg cholesterol; 13 mg sodium

Papaya Custard

Serves: 8 (⅔ cup = 1 serving)

My husband loves both papaya and custard, so I tried combining them, with a delicious result.

2½–3 cups peeled, seeded, and
  mashed ripe papaya (2 large
  papayas)
3 cups nonfat milk
⅓ cup frozen unsweetened apple
  juice concentrate

4 egg whites
Grated rind of 2 oranges
½ cup fresh orange juice
2 teaspoons pure vanilla extract
½ teaspoon ground cinnamon
Freshly grated nutmeg

1. Spread papaya on bottom of 1½-quart baking dish.
2. In bowl, beat together milk, apple juice, egg whites, orange rind and juice, and vanilla. Pour over fruit.

3. Sprinkle with cinnamon and nutmeg.

4. Set dish in hot water bath. Bake in preheated 350° oven for 40 to 45 minutes, or until knife comes out clean near the edges.

5. Cool on rack and serve warm or, if desired, chill before serving.

Per serving: 105 calories; 5.6 gm protein; 0.4 gm fat; 20.6 gm carbohydrate; 0.8 gm fiber; 2 mg cholesterol; 79 mg sodium

Microwaved Fresh Fruit Coupe Ⓠ Ⓜ

Serves: 6 (1 cup = 1 serving)

Served warm, at room temperature, or chilled—any way, it tastes delicious.

2 ripe peaches or nectarines, pitted and cut into ½-inch-thick lengthwise slices

1 ripe pear cored and cut into ½-inch-thick lengthwise slices

1 Rome Beauty apple, cored and cut into ½-inch-thick lengthwise slices

1 cup frozen, pitted, unsweetened black cherries

¼ cup fresh orange juice or ¼ cup apple juice

1 banana cut into ½-inch-thick slices

1 tablespoon banana cordial or frozen unsweetened apple juice concentrate

1. Combine peaches, pear, apple, cherries, and juice in 2-quart casserole.

2. Cover with lid and cook in microwave on high for 3 minutes. Stir and cook for 2 more minutes.

3. Add bananas and banana cordial; mix well. Cover and let stand for 5 minutes before serving.

To Serve: Spoon into glass brandy snifters and, if desired, top with Almost Crème Anglaise (page 364).

Per serving: 87 calories; 1.0 gm protein; 0.5 gm fat; 22.1 gm carbohydrate; 2.5 gm fiber; 0 mg cholesterol; 2 mg sodium

Pineapple Ambrosia ⓠ

Serves: 6 (⅔ cup = 1 serving)

A light and refreshing dessert. If fresh pineapple is not available, use chunks canned in juice instead.

1½ cups cubed ripe pineapple
2 oranges, peeled and thinly sliced
1 banana, sliced
1 cup washed, hulled, and sliced strawberries

3 tablespoons orange juice or 1 tablespoon banana brandy

Fresh mint leaves for garnish

1. Combine fruit and sprinkle with orange juice.
2. Cover with plastic wrap and refrigerate until serving time.
To Serve: Garnish bowl with fresh mint leaves.

Per serving: 72 calories; 1.0 gm protein; 0.5 gm fat; 17.8 gm carbohydrate; 2.2 gm fiber; 0 mg cholesterol; 1 mg sodium

Pineapple Parfait ⓠ

Serves: 6 (½ cup = 1 serving)

This dessert may also be placed in a 1½-pint ring mold and served as a jellied salad with dinner.

2 tablespoons lemon juice
2 tablespoons pineapple juice (drained from canned pineapple below)
1½ teaspoons unflavored gelatin
15½-ounce can unsweetened crushed pineapple, drained
2 small ripe bananas, mashed

1 cup lowfat yogurt
1 teaspoon pure vanilla extract
1 tablespoon banana liqueur (optional)

Fresh pineapple wedges or strawberries and fresh mint leaves for garnish

1. Combine lemon juice and pineapple juice in small cup. Sprinkle gelatin over juice and dissolve.

2. Liquefy gelatin mixture over heat or in microwave; cool slightly.

3. Combine pineapple, bananas, yogurt, and vanilla; stir well.

4. Add dissolved gelatin to fruit-and-yogurt mixture; mix thoroughly.

5. Divide mixture among 6 parfait glasses or small dessert dishes and chill.

To Serve: Garnish with fresh mint and pineapple wedges or strawberries and fresh mint.

Variation: Canned peaches in juice may be substituted for pineapple.

Per serving: 88 calories; 3.2 gm protein; 1.0 gm fat; 18.1 gm carbohydrate; 1.3 gm fiber; 2 mg cholesterol; 28 mg sodium

Middle Eastern Pudding

Serves: 4 (½ cup = 1 serving)

¼ cup rice or barley flour (available in health food stores or Middle Eastern markets)

¼ cup frozen unsweetened apple juice concentrate

1½ cups low-fat milk

½ teaspoon orange flower water or pure vanilla extract

2 tablespoons dark raisins for garnish

2 tablespoons chopped pistachios and ⅛ teaspoon ground cinnamon, mixed together, for garnish

1. Stir rice or barley flour and apple juice together in heavy saucepan. Add ½ cup of the milk and stir until smooth.

2. Scald remaining 1 cup milk. Stir hot milk into rice mixture until smooth.

3. Cook mixture over medium heat, stirring constantly, for 2 minutes, or until thick and smooth. When mixture boils, reduce heat and simmer for 1 minute.

4. Remove from heat and stir in orange water or vanilla. Cool slightly. Pour into glass dessert dishes.* Refrigerate several hours before serving.

To Serve: Serve pudding very cold. Sprinkle with raisins and nut-and-cinnamon mixture as garnish.

Per serving: 119 calories; 3.7 gm protein; 1.9 gm fat; 21.7 gm carbohydrate; 0.3 gm fiber; 7 mg cholesterol; 51 mg sodium

* To prevent skin from forming, press waxed paper directly onto surface of pudding when refrigerating.

Pumpkin Custard

Serves: 6

This is an easy dessert whose flavor is reminiscent of pumpkin pie. Of course, you have no crust, but there are fewer calories and a lower fat content also.

½ cup frozen unsweetened apple
   juice concentrate or date sugar
3 egg whites, slightly beaten
1½ cups canned pumpkin
12-ounce can nonfat evaporated
   milk, scalded

½ teaspoon each ground ginger
   and freshly grated nutmeg
1 teaspoon ground cinnamon
½ cup Grape-nuts

1. Combine all ingredients except Grape-nuts in mixing bowl and stir thoroughly.
2. Pour into 1½-quart soufflé dish or 9-inch glass pie plate, sprayed with nonstick cooking spray. Sprinkle with Grape-nuts.
3. Bake for 35 to 45 minutes in preheated 400° oven, or until knife inserted near center comes out clean.

To Serve: Serve warm with pitcher of skim milk, Almost Crème Anglaise (page 364), or whipped nonfat milk.

Per serving: 151 calories; 8.2 gm protein; 0.5 gm fat; 29.7 gm carbohydrate; 1.5 gm fiber; 2 mg cholesterol; 170 mg sodium

Strawberry–Banana–Yogurt Pie

Serves: 10 (1 slice = 1 serving)

A flavorful way to add some calcium to your diet. One cup of yogurt supplies about one fourth of your daily requirement for calcium.

1 package unflavored gelatin
1 cup boiling frozen unsweetened apple juice concentrate
2 cups nonfat strawberry yogurt*
1 ripe banana, sliced
1 cup sliced strawberries

1 9-inch Basic Tart Crust (page 35)

½ cup halved strawberries for garnish

1. Dissolve gelatin in boiling apple juice concentrate and cool in freezer or refrigerator.
2. Blend in yogurt and banana.
3. Arrange 1 cup sliced strawberries on bottom of crust.
4. Pour in gelatin mixture and garnish with halved berries.
5. Chill for several hours or overnight until firm.

Per serving: 153 calories; 5.8 gm protein; 4.0 gm fat; 24.8 gm carbohydrate; 1.0 gm fiber; 0.9 mg cholesterol; 62 mg sodium

* If you are diabetic, use plain nonfat yogurt that contains no sugar.

Fresh Strawberries with Sabayon Sauce ⓠ

Serves: 6 (⅔ cup strawberries plus 2 tablespoons sauce = 1 serving)

Fresh, seasonal berries topped with a delicate sauce with a tinge of liqueur.

2 pints fresh strawberries, washed   Sabayon Sauce (page 368)
    and *then* hulled and halved

1. Arrange berries in glass bowl.
2. Place sauce in small, footed dish.
To Serve: Pass fruit and sauce and let guests serve themselves.

Variation: Fresh blueberries may be substituted for strawberries.

Per serving: 76 calories; 2.2 gm protein; 0.8 gm fat; 15.4 gm carbohydrate; 3.0 gm fiber; 0 mg cholesterol; 17 mg sodium

Fresh Strawberry Tart ⓠ

Serves: 8 (1 slice = 1 serving)

Guests always have room for this special dessert, no matter how sated they claim to be. Different seasonal berries may be substituted for variety.

1 9-inch Chocolate Lover's Tart   1 tablespoon cornstarch
    Shell (page 360)   1 teaspoon lemon juice
2 pints fresh strawberries, washed   1 teaspoon strawberry extract
    and *then* hulled   2 tablespoons sliced almonds,
2 tablespoons frozen unsweetened   toasted lightly in oven
    apple juice concentrate
    (optional)

1. Prepare the crust.
2. Place 1 pint strawberries into 1-quart saucepan; mash with potato masher.

3. Add apple juice concentrate as needed, depending on sweetness of strawberries.

4. Add cornstarch, blend, and cook over moderate heat, stirring constantly until shiny.

5. Add lemon juice and extract. Cool slightly.

6. Halve remaining pint of strawberries and arrange on cool tart.

7. Cover berries with strawberry glaze, sprinkle with almonds.

To Serve: Serve with whipped nonfat milk or Almost Crème Anglaise (page 364).

Per serving: 87 calories; 2.5 gm protein; 4.0 gm fat; 11.6 gm carbohydrate; 1.5 gm fiber; 0 mg cholesterol; 20.9 mg sodium

Special Strawberry Ice Cream ⓠ

Serves: 10 (½ cup = 1 serving)

If you freeze this dessert, defrost it at room temperature about 15 minutes before serving.

2 small ripe bananas, frozen in 1-inch chunks

2 cups frozen unsweetened strawberries

1 cup nonfat evaporated milk, chilled for 20 minutes in freezer

2 teaspoons pure vanilla extract

2 tablespoons framboise liqueur or 2 teaspoons pure strawberry extract

10 strawberries with stems for garnish

1. Remove fruit from freezer 10 minutes before preparing.

2. Place half of each fruit in food processor or blender. Process until pureed. Add remaining half of fruits and repeat.

3. Gradually add chilled milk, vanilla, and liqueur or strawberry extract to pureed fruit as machine is in motion. Process until crème is desired consistency.

To Serve: May be served immediately in glass sherbet cups or mounded in ½ cup soufflé dishes covered with plastic and frozen for future use, up to 1 month. Garnish with stemmed strawberry for an elegant presentation.

Per serving: 50 calories; 2.2 gm protein; 0.2 gm fat; 10.1 gm carbohydrate; 0.5 gm fiber; 1 mg cholesterol; 30 mg sodium

Tapioca with Mango ◎

Serves: 4 (⅔ cup = 1 serving)

Tapioca is a starchy substance from cassava roots. It is used in pies as a thickener and also in puddings and fruit desserts.

⅓ cup minute tapioca
⅓ cup frozen unsweetened apple
  juice concentrate
2 cups nonfat milk
2 egg whites, slightly beaten
1 teaspoon pure vanilla extract

Freshly grated nutmeg
1 mango, peeled and sliced
  (2 peaches, 2 nectarines, or 1 cup
  berries may be substituted)

Mint leaves for garnish

1. Mix tapioca, apple juice, milk, and egg whites in saucepan; let stand for 5 minutes.
2. Cook tapioca mixture over medium heat to full boil, stirring constantly, about 6 to 8 minutes.
3. Add vanilla and nutmeg to tapioca. Stir to combine.
4. Cool slightly in freezer or refrigerator.
To Serve: Place several mango slices in bottom of glass sherbet dishes. Pour tapioca mixture over slices and garnish with 2 more mango slices. Serve warm or chill until serving time. At this time, fresh mint leaves may be added as a further garnish.

Per serving: 169 calories; 6.3 gm protein; 0.5 gm fat; 35.1 gm carbohydrate; 0.6 gm fiber; 2 mg cholesterol; 96 mg sodium

Quick Breads

This section is for the reader who finds breadmaking a time-consuming anathema but still loves the aromas and flavors of home-baked goods—not laden with fat, sugar, cholesterol, and salt.

Actually, American hot breads are the descendants of the crude, harsh cakes made many years ago by primitive peoples. Tiny muffins and biscuits have now had a renaissance in the bread baskets of many popular restaurants. These breads and muffins are called quick breads because of the quick-acting leavening of baking soda and buttermilk, baking powder, and now a new product called rapid-rise yeast. The Busy Day Baking Mix (page 29) will make the task even easier.

Here are recipes for muffins, breads, pancakes, waffles, and French Toast—the easiest, quickest way to make and enjoy lovely, leisurely breakfasts or brunches, teas or luncheons. But what a wonderful, nourishing snack for any time! A few hints:

1. Always preheat oven 25° higher than the recipe calls for; then lower to suggested temperature when you place the dough or batter in the oven.

2. If more convenient, make up batter or dough for quick breads 1 to 2 hours ahead, and place, covered, in refrigerator until time to bake (cold slows down leavening action).

3. If batter does not fill all cups, wipe spray from empty cups to prevent them from browning.

4. Use paper baking cups for attractive serving.

5. Serve second-day muffins and bread split or sliced and toasted, heated in the microwave,* or frozen for future use.

---

* When warming breads in a microwave oven, be *very careful.* Overheating results in doughy and tough breads. Use a medium setting for 15 to 20 seconds. Cover with white paper towel. The time depends upon the size and amount of bread being warmed.

Busy Day Griddle Cakes Ⓠ

Yield: 12 3-inch pancakes (3 pancakes = 1 serving)

Although this recipe may have a whole egg in it, it is still a wiser choice than having eggs for breakfast. You are only consuming the cholesterol of ¼ egg in each serving. Serve plain, with blueberries, or as buckwheat pancakes as a variation.

2 egg whites or 1 egg
1⅓ cups nonfat milk or yogurt
1 tablespoon frozen unsweetened
  apple juice concentrate

1 tablespoon cold-pressed safflower
  oil
1½ cups Busy Day Baking Mix
  (page 29, or see Note below)

1. Combine egg whites or egg, milk or yogurt, apple juice and oil.
2. Blend into baking mix in bowl with a fork. Avoid overmixing.
3. Cook on hot griddle* sprayed with butter-flavored nonstick cooking spray. When pancakes bubble, they should be ready to turn. Brown on each side.

To Serve: Serve hot on warm plate with sugar-free preserves, unsweetened applesauce, pancake syrup (page 14), or fresh fruit.

Variations:
1. For thinner pancakes, add more milk.
2. *Buckwheat Pancakes:* ¾ cup Busy Day Baking Mix (or ¾ cup whole-wheat flour, 1 tablespoon oat bran, 1 teaspoon low-sodium baking powder, and ½ teaspoon baking soda) and ¾ cup buckwheat flour may be used as dry ingredients for making buckwheat pancakes.
3. *Blueberry Pancakes:* ½ cup blueberries may be added for blueberry pancakes.

Per serving: 232 calories; 11.1 gm protein; 4.7 gm fat; 38.3 gm carbohydrate; 3.7 gm fiber; 2 mg cholesterol; 74 mg sodium

Note: If you do not have the mix made up, use 1½ cups whole-wheat flour, 2 tablespoons oat bran, 2 teaspoons low-sodium baking powder, and ½ teaspoon baking soda.

* When a few drops of water dance on your griddle, it is hot enough to use.

Country Whole-Wheat Pancakes ©

Yield: 12 3-inch pancakes (3 pancakes = 1 serving)

1½ cups whole-wheat flour
2 teaspoons low-sodium baking
  powder
2 egg whites or 1 large egg
1 tablespoon frozen unsweetened
  apple juice concentrate

1⅓ to 1½ cups nonfat milk or
  nonfat yogurt
1 tablespoon cold-pressed safflower
  oil

1. Stir together flour and baking powder with a fork.
2. Beat egg slightly; add apple juice concentrate, milk, and oil, and blend.
3. Add liquid to dry ingredients and stir with a fork briefly. (*Avoid overmixing.*)
4. Spoon batter onto hot* nonstick pan or griddle sprayed with butter-flavored nonstick spray. When bubbles appear, turn pancakes, only once.

To Serve: Serve hot on warm plate with fresh fruit slices, sugar-free preserves, or pancake syrup (page 14).

Helpful Hint: Use ¼ cup measure to spoon pancake mixture onto griddle.

Per serving: 229 calories; 10.8 gm protein; 4.5 gm fat; 38.7 gm carbohydrate; 4.0 gm fiber; 2 mg cholesterol; 75 mg sodium

* When a few drops of water dance on griddle it's hot enough to use.

Fluffy Oatmeal Pancakes ⑨

Serves: 4 (2 4-inch pancakes = 1 serving)

1 cup buttermilk
¾ cup rolled oats, coarsely
 chopped in blender
2 teaspoons frozen unsweetened
 apple juice concentrate
½ teaspoon pure vanilla extract
¼ cup whole-wheat flour

½ teaspoon baking soda or
 1 teaspoon low-sodium baking
 powder
1 egg white, stiffly beaten

Seasonal fruit for garnish

1. Combine buttermilk and rolled oats; add apple juice and vanilla and let stand for a few minutes.
2. Stir in flour that has been mixed with baking soda or baking powder.
3. Fold in stiffly beaten egg white.
4. Bake on nonstick griddle or skillet, using ¼ cup batter for each pancake.
To Serve: Place pancakes on plate and garnish with chopped fresh strawberries or fresh seasonal fruit of your choice.

Variation: For banana pancakes, add sliced ripe banana to pancake on griddle, turn and brown lightly on other side.

Per serving: 119 calories; 6.0 gm protein; 1.8 gm fat; 20.1 gm carbohydrate; 2.7 gm fiber; 2 mg cholesterol; 122 mg sodium

Waffles ⑨

Yield: 3 9-inch waffles (1 waffle = 1 serving)

1½ cups nonfat milk
2 tablespoons frozen unsweetened
 apple juice concentrate
1 tablespoon cold-pressed safflower
 oil

1¾ cups Busy Day Baking Mix
 (page 29, or see Note, page 29)
2 egg whites, at room temperature

Seasonal fruit for garnish

1. Coat waffle iron with nonstick cooking spray and preheat.
2. Combine milk, apple juice, and oil. Stir to blend well.

3. Add liquid to baking mix and stir until smooth.

4. Beat egg whites until stiff, not dry, and fold into batter.

5. Pour 1 cup batter on preheated waffle iron. Close lid and bake according to manufacturer's directions (about 5 minutes), or until steaming stops.

To Serve: Place hot waffle on warm plate, serve with pancake syrup (page 14), and garnish with fresh fruit such as cubed strawberries, pineapple, or melon.

Per serving: 323 calories; 14.4 gm protein; 6.2 gm fat; 55.1 gm carbohydrate; 4.9 gm fiber; 2 mg cholesterol; 95 mg sodium

Harriet's Blueberry Coffee Cake

Serves: 16 (1 2¼-inch square = 1 serving)

2 cups Busy Day Baking Mix (page 29, or see Note, page 29) — stir before measuring
1 teaspoon ground cinnamon
1 cup nonfat evaporated milk
2 tablespoons cold-pressed safflower oil

½ cup frozen unsweetened apple juice concentrate or ½ cup date sugar
3 egg whites
1½ teaspoons pure vanilla extract
1–1½ cups blueberries*

Topping:
⅓ cup ground nuts
⅓ cup Grape-nuts

½ teaspoon ground cinnamon

1. Preheat oven to 400°.

2. Combine baking mix and cinnamon in bowl.

3. Combine milk, oil, apple juice, egg whites, and vanilla. Mix thoroughly.

4. Add liquid to dry ingredients and stir only until flour disappears. Add blueberries and mix gently.

5. Pour into 9-inch-square pan coated with nonstick cooking spray. Sprinkle with topping, which has been mixed together first.

6. Bake in preheated 375° oven for 30 to 35 minutes, or until cake pulls away from sides of pan.

Per serving: 130 calories; 4.9 gm protein; 3.6 gm fat; 20.8 gm carbohydrate; 1.8 gm fiber; 1 mg cholesterol; 48 mg sodium

* Coat blueberries with 2 tablespoons whole-wheat blend flour to keep them from sinking in batter.

Corn Bread or Muffins ⓠ
(Everybody's Favorite)

Yield: 20 pieces (1 pie-shaped piece = 1 serving)

Adding the batter to a hot pan results in a wonderful crisp crust.

1½ cups yellow cornmeal
½ cup whole-wheat blend or
   whole-wheat flour
¾ teaspoon baking soda*
¼ teaspoon salt (optional)

1⅓ cups buttermilk*
3 egg whites
1½ tablespoons cold-pressed
   safflower oil

1. Preheat oven to 450°.
2. Combine first 3 ingredients (plus salt if desired) in a bowl. Mix well with a fork.
3. Beat buttermilk and eggs with a fork.
4. Add oil to 10-inch glass pie plate coated with nonstick cooking spray. Heat in oven for 3 minutes.
5. Add liquid ingredients including hot oil to dry ingredients. Beat thoroughly with fork until batter is smooth and pour into heated pie plate.
6. Place in oven and lower temperature to 425°. Bake for 25 to 30 minutes, or until bread pulls away from sides of plate and is lightly browned.

To Serve: Cool plate slightly on rack and cut into 20 pie-shaped pieces for serving.

Variation: *Blueberry Corn Mini-Muffins*—Add 1 cup fresh or frozen blueberries after batter is smooth in Step 5. Fill 24 1½-inch muffin cups coated with nonstick cooking spray. Bake in preheated 400° oven for 12 minutes.

Per serving: 57 calories; 2.3 gm protein; 1.6 gm fat; 8.3 gm carbohydrate; 1.7 gm fiber; 1 mg cholesterol; 67 mg sodium

* If you substitute 2 tablespoons low-sodium baking powder for the baking soda and nonfat milk for the buttermilk, the sodium content of the corn bread will be much lower.

Banana–Nut Muffins ⓠ

Yield: 12 medium muffins (1 muffin = 1 serving)

These muffins are great for Sunday breakfast, afternoon tea, or as a dessert.

⅓ cup slivered almonds, chopped
1⅓ cups whole-wheat flour
½ cup oat bran
3 tablespoons date sugar or
  2 tablespoons sugar
1 tablespoon low-sodium baking
  powder
½ teaspoon baking soda
1 teaspoon ground cinnamon

2–3 very ripe bananas (1 cup),
  mashed
2 egg whites
1 tablespoon cold-pressed safflower
  oil
⅓ cup nonfat yogurt
⅓ cup frozen unsweetened apple
  juice concentrate
½ teaspoon vanilla extract

1. Preheat oven to 425° and coat muffin tins with nonstick cooking spray.
2. Place dry ingredients in mixing bowl and blend with fork.
3. Beat liquid ingredients, including bananas, together and add to dry. Stir with fork *only* until all flour is moistened. (The batter will look lumpy.)
4. Fill prepared muffin tins three quarters full, place in oven, and lower temperature to 400°.
5. Bake for 17 to 20 minutes, or until lightly browned. Cool slightly on rack before serving.

Per serving: 140 calories; 4.0 gm protein; 3.8 gm fat; 24.3 gm carbohydrate; 2.3 gm fiber; 0 mg cholesterol; 46 mg sodium

Everyday Muffins in Minutes ⊙

Yield: 12 medium muffins (1 muffin = 1 serving)

You don't have to wait until Sunday morning to prepare these delicious muffins.

1½ cups Busy Day Baking Mix
 (page 29, or see Note below) —
 stir before measuring
½ cup frozen unsweetened apple
 juice concentrate*
2 tablespoons cold-pressed
 safflower oil

2 egg whites
¾ cup nonfat milk or nonfat
 evaporated milk
1½ teaspoons pure vanilla extract

1. Coat muffin tins with butter-flavored nonstick cooking spray and preheat oven to 425°.
2. Place baking mix in mixing bowl.
3. Combine remaining liquid ingredients and stir to blend.
4. Add liquid to dry ingredients; stir only until dry ingredients are moistened. *Do not overmix.*
5. Fill muffin cups two thirds full. Lower oven to 400° and bake muffins for 20 to 25 minutes, or until golden brown.
To Serve: Serve warm with sugar-free preserves.

Variations:
Apple Muffins—Add ½ teaspoon ground cinnamon and ⅓ cup finely chopped pecans to dry ingredients and 1 grated apple with skin to liquid ingredients. Proceed as above.
Wheat Flake Muffins—Use only 1 cup baking mix and gently fold in 1½ cups sugar-free wheat flakes at the end of the recipe.

Per serving: 103 calories; 3.2 gm protein; 2.7 gm fat; 16.9 gm carbohydrate; 1.2 gm fiber; 0 mg cholesterol; 19 mg sodium

Note: If you do not have the mix made up, use 1½ cups whole-wheat flour, 3 tablespoons oat bran, and 1 tablespoon low-sodium baking powder.

* Date sugar or syrup (page 5) may be substituted for apple juice concentrate.

Oat–Bran Muffins ⓠ

Yield: 12 medium muffins (1 muffin = 1 serving)

Recent findings have shown that soluble fiber may help to lower cholesterol. Oat bran is high in soluble fiber.

1¾ cups oat bran
½ cup whole-wheat flour
1½ tablespoons low-sodium baking powder
⅓ cup date sugar* or 3 tablespoons sugar
3 egg whites

1 cup nonfat milk
⅓ cup frozen unsweetened apple juice concentrate
1 tablespoon cold-pressed safflower oil
¼ cup dark raisins (optional)
¼ cup chopped almonds (optional)

1. Preheat oven to 425° and coat muffin tins with nonstick cooking spray.
2. Place dry ingredients in mixing bowl and blend with fork.
3. Beat liquid ingredients together in separate bowl.
4. Add liquid to dry ingredients and stir with fork until flour is moistened. Add raisins and nuts.
5. Fill muffin tin three quarters full, place in oven, and lower temperature to 400°.
6. Bake for 17 to 20 minutes, or until lightly browned. Cool slightly on rack before serving.

Per serving: 112 calories; 4.5 gm protein; 2.5 gm fat; 18.1 gm carbohydrate; 3.5 gm fiber; 0 mg cholesterol; 24 mg sodium

* Frequently I use date sugar in baking. If, however, you have difficulty finding it, I suggest you use a small amount of sugar rather than artificial sweetener. Of course, for diabetics, sugar is not acceptable.

Rapid-Rise Oatmeal Bread

Yield: 2 small 8½ x 4½ x 2-inch loaves, 32 slices (1 slice = 1 serving)

If you wonder what a yeast bread is doing in a quick and easy book, the answer is the new rapid-rise yeast, which cuts preparation time in half.* This very light bread is marvelous for sandwiches and is especially delicious toasted and spread with your favorite unsweetened jam.

3 cups whole-wheat flour
1 cup unbleached white flour
1 envelope rapid-rise dry yeast
1 teaspoon salt
1 cup rolled oats
¼ cup oat bran
2 cups boiling water or
   1 cup boiling nonfat milk plus
   1 cup water

½ cup frozen unsweetened apple juice concentrate (at room temperature)
1 tablespoon cold-pressed safflower oil
About ½ cup additional whole-wheat blend flour as necessary for kneading
¼ cup rolled oats for coating pan

1. Mix flours, yeast, and salt together.
2. Pour boiling water over oats and bran, let stand for 10 minutes.
3. Add apple juice and oil and mix.
4. Stir hot oatmeal into dry ingredients. Knead 7 to 8 minutes in mixer with dough hook or by hand. Use additional whole-wheat blend flour with dough if it's too sticky. Cover and let rest for 10 minutes.
5. Punch down and shape dough. Place in loaf pans coated with butter-flavored nonstick cooking spray and sprinkled with ¼ cup rolled oats. Cover and let rest in a warm place for 20 minutes, or until doubled or to the top of the pan.
6. Bake in preheated 375° oven for 40 to 45 minutes, or until bread sounds hollow when removed from tins and tapped on bottom.
7. Cool on rack before slicing. Each loaf yields 16 slices.

Note: The average bread recipe calls for 1 tablespoon of salt. By adding only 1 teaspoon of salt, 1 slice of this bread contains only 72 mg of sodium!

Per serving: 75 calories; 2.3 gm protein; 0.9 gm fat; 15 gm carbohydrate; 1.3 gm fiber; 0 mg cholesterol; 72 mg sodium

* When using undissolved rapid-rise yeast mixed with dry ingredients, heat liquids to 130° before adding.

Harriet's Quick and Crusty Multi-Grain Bread

Yield: 1 large 9¼ x 5¼ x 3-inch loaf (1 slice = 1 serving)

Did you ever think that a yeast bread could be considered a quick bread? With the new rapid-rise yeast the preparation time is cut in half. This bread recipe is simple, delicious, and healthy. It can easily be prepared by any beginner cook.

3 tablespoons sesame seeds
  (optional)
3½ cups whole-wheat flour
1 cup 7-grain cereal
¼ cup date sugar

1 envelope rapid-rise yeast
1 teaspoon salt
2 cups *hot* water or nonfat milk
  (130°)

1. Preheat oven to 425°.
2. Coat pan with butter-flavored nonstick cooking spray. Sprinkle with half the sesame seeds, if desired.
3. Place dry ingredients in mixing bowl and stir with fork.
4. Add liquid to dry ingredients and stir with wooden spoon until all flour is moistened.
5. Put in prepared pan. Sprinkle with remaining sesame seeds. Cover and allow to rise in warm place for 20 minutes, or until mixture reaches top of pan.
6. Bake in preheated 400° oven for 40 to 45 minutes.
To Serve: Remove bread from pan. Place on rack to cool before slicing.

Per serving: 90 calories; 3.3 gm protein; 1.1 gm fat; 17.9 gm carbohydrate; 1.6 gm fiber; 0 mg cholesterol; 99 mg sodium

Always-Delicious Zucchini Bread
(More Like Cake)

Yield: 18 slices (1 slice = 1 serving)

What a treat to have this excellent tea loaf to serve, without cholesterol and with minimal fat. Freeze some for future use.

½ cup nonfat powdered milk
½ cup frozen unsweetened apple
  juice concentrate
⅓ cup date sugar or 1 cup
  granulated sugar
½ cup water
2 tablespoons cold-pressed
  safflower oil
2 large egg whites
2 teaspoons pure vanilla extract

1½ cups whole-wheat flour
¼ cup oat or wheat bran
1 teaspoon baking soda
1 teaspoon low-sodium baking
  powder
2 teaspoons ground cinnamon
1¼ cups shredded zucchini
⅓ cup chopped pecans
½ cup seeded dark raisins

1. Spray a 8½ x 4½ x 2½-inch loaf pan with butter-flavored nonstick cooking spray.

2. In food processor with steel blade, add powdered milk, apple juice, date sugar, water, oil, egg whites, and vanilla. Process 4 seconds.

3. Add all dry ingredients. Process just until moistened.

4. Add zucchini, nuts and raisins; process for 3 seconds.

5. Spoon batter into pan and bake in preheated 325° oven for 50 to 60 minutes, or until toothpick comes out clean.

6. Cool on wire rack for 5 minutes. Remove from pan and finish cooling.

Variation: For lovely little tea loaves, spoon batter into 8 6-ounce cans (juice or tomato paste cans will do) sprayed with nonstick cooking spray. Fill cans half full, place on baking sheet, and bake in preheated 325° oven for 25 minutes. Cool as above.

Helpful Hint: Use a serrated knife for slicing.

Per serving: 96 calories; 4.1 gm protein; 2.4 gm fat; 16.7 gm carbohydrate; 1.2 gm fiber; 1 mg cholesterol; 46 mg sodium

Salmagundi

A FEW AFTERTHOUGHTS

Hot Mulled Apple Juice
Pita Bread Pizza
Matzoh and Egg Scramble
Frittata Loaf
My Favorite Frittata
Whole-Wheat Cheese Puffs
French Toast with Raisins
E-Z Time Pizza
Stuffed Pita Pocket
Hot Tuna Salad Sandwich
Potato Tostada
Tostada
Mother Mollie's Cheese Blintzes

Chocolate Lover's Tart Shell
Sally's Cottage Cheese Swedish
  Pancakes
Cucumber Raita
Fresh Tomato Relish
Fresh Tomato Coulis
Almost Crème Anglaise
Spicy Barbecue Sauce
Green Sauce
Horseradish–Mustard–Yogurt
  Sauce
Onion–Mustard Sauce
Sabayon Sauce

Here again are the leftovers—left over in the sense that they didn't seem to fit into any of my other chapters. A mixture of recipes from Hot Mulled Apple Juice to Almost Crème Anglaise, from pita pockets to pizza. When you start talking or writing about food, beginning is easy, but there never seems to be an end.

Hot Mulled Apple Juice ⓠ

Serves: 8 (½ cup = 1 serving)

You need not wait until Halloween to enjoy this warm and spicy drink. Any brisk afternoon or evening will do.

12 whole cloves
4 cinnamon sticks, broken up
½ nutmeg, cracked
⅛ teaspoon allspice

1 quart unsweetened apple juice
½ cup Calvados
8 cinnamon sticks (optional)

1. Tie cloves, cinnamon sticks, nutmeg, and allspice in cheesecloth bag.
2. Place spice bag and apple juice in large saucepan and slowly bring to boil.
3. Reduce heat, cover, and simmer for 20 minutes.
4. Add Calvados and heat to simmer; do not boil.
5. Remove spice bag and serve in heatproof glass cups. Use cinnamon sticks as stirrers if desired.

Per serving: 93 calories; 0.1 gm protein; 0.1 gm fat; 14.5 gm carbohydrate; 0.3 gm fiber; 0 mg cholesterol; 4 mg sodium

Pita Bread Pizza ⓠ

Serves: 4 as an entrée, 12 as an appetizer

2 large whole-wheat pita breads, split
1½ cups salt-free tomato sauce, blended with ½ teaspoon Italian herb blend, crushed
1 cup coarsely shredded zucchini

1 small red onion, thinly sliced
½ cup sliced mushrooms
½ cup sliced artichoke hearts
½ cup diced green pepper
2 ounces shredded skim-milk mozzarella cheese

1. Place pita bread smooth side down on nonstick baking sheet.
2. Spread bread with seasoned tomato sauce.
3. Divide next 5 ingredients evenly over each piece of bread.

4. Sprinkle with mozzarella cheese and bake in preheated 425° oven until bubbling and hot, approximately 7 minutes.

To Serve: Pizza may be served as an entrée with Red and Green Slaw (page 120) or Almost Santo Pietro's Salad (page 130) and a wedge of fresh melon for dessert.

Per serving: 74 calories; 2.8 gm protein; 1.2 gm fat; 12.8 gm carbohydrate; 0.3 gm fiber; 3 mg cholesterol; 34 mg sodium

Matzoh and Egg Scramble ⓠ
(Matzoh Brie)
Serves: 6

4 squares whole-wheat matzoh,
  crumbled
Nonfat milk to cover
2 whole eggs

4 egg whites
Dash ground cinnamon (optional)

Sliced fresh fruit for garnish

1. Place crumbled matzoh in bowl. Add milk to cover and let soak 10 minutes.
2. Beat eggs and egg whites with cinnamon until blended.
3. Squeeze matzoh dry* and add to eggs. Let soak 20 minutes.
4. Coat nonstick skillet with butter-flavored cooking spray, heat, and add egg mixture.
5. Scramble until cooked and serve immediately.

To Serve: Mound on serving platter and garnish with sliced fresh fruit such as kiwi, melon, or strawberries.

Per serving: 119 calories; 6.7 gm protein; 2.1 gm fat; 18.3 gm carbohydrate; 0 gm fiber; 92 mg cholesterol; 62 mg sodium

* Save drained milk to prepare hot cereal at another time.

Frittata Loaf

Serves: 8 (1 slice = 1 serving)

10-inch round sourdough or
whole-wheat bread, halved
crosswise
2 tablespoons Dijon mustard
1 roasted green pepper, peeled and
sliced
3 large tomatoes, cut into slices
½-inch thick
1 red onion, cut into slices ¼-inch
thick
2 teaspoons extra-virgin olive oil
3 whole green onions, thinly sliced
2 garlic cloves, minced
2 small zucchini, thinly sliced

6 mushrooms, cleaned and thinly
sliced
1 cup fresh bean sprouts, washed
3 whole eggs plus 7 egg whites,
beaten
1 teaspoon salt-free vegetable
seasoning
1 teaspoon fines herbes, crushed
2 tablespoons grated Parmesan
cheese

Watercress, grapes, and
strawberries for garnish

1. Remove soft center of bread, leaving a ½-inch shell.
2. Spread mustard on inside surface of bread. Arrange pepper, tomato, and onion on bottom half of bread; cover with top half and wrap in foil.
3. Place oil in 10-inch nonstick skillet* and sauté green onions, garlic, zucchini, and mushrooms for several minutes. Add bean sprouts, mix, and remove from heat.
4. Combine beaten eggs with vegetable seasoning, fines herbes, and 1 tablespoon of the Parmesan cheese.
5. Add sautéed vegetable mixture to eggs and stir.
6. Pour mixture into heated skillet and cook over medium heat until firm.
7. Sprinkle frittata with remaining 1 tablespoon Parmesan cheese and brown lightly under broiler.
8. Loosen bottom of frittata and slide onto bottom half of bread. Cover with top, and rewrap in foil to keep warm until serving time.
9. Reheat in preheated 300° oven for 10 minutes, or until warm, and cut into 8 pie-shaped pieces to serve. Garnish with crisp watercress and small bunches of grapes and strawberries.

Per serving: 129 calories; 9.2 gm protein; 4.5 gm fat; 14.5 gm carbohydrate; 1.7 gm fiber; 104 mg cholesterol; 135 mg sodium

* Use skillet with heatproof handle.

My Favorite Frittata ⓠ

Yield: 8 slices (1 slice = 1 serving)

After you try this recipe once, it will be one of your favorites too. I do use a few egg yolks in this frittata, but it serves 8.

¾ pound thinly sliced onions, sautéed in ½ tablespoon extra-virgin olive oil, or 1 cup Onion Magic (page 36)
2 garlic cloves, minced
6 mushrooms, cleaned and thinly sliced
1 small zucchini, thinly sliced
1 teaspoon salt-free vegetable seasoning

3 whole eggs
7 egg whites
1 Italian plum tomato, diced
2 whole green onions, thinly sliced
Freshly ground black pepper
2 tablespoons grated Parmesan cheese

Cherry tomatoes for garnish

1. Sauté onions and garlic with oil in 10-inch nonstick skillet,* covered, for about 10 minutes, or heat Onion Magic with garlic.
2. Add mushrooms, zucchini, and vegetable seasoning and sauté for 3 minutes.
3. Beat eggs and egg whites with fork. Add tomato, green onions, pepper, 1 tablespoon of the cheese, and sautéed vegetables. Blend well with fork.
4. Coat skillet again with nonstick cooking spray and heat.
5. When hot, pour in egg mixture. Cook over medium heat for about 5 minutes, or until bottom is browned.
6. Sprinkle with remaining 1 tablespoon Parmesan and place under preheated broiler until top is cooked and golden. Serve hot or at room temperature.

To Serve: Slide onto serving plate and cut into 8 pie-shaped pieces. Garnish with halved cherry tomatoes around the edge.

Variation: Any leftover cooked vegetables *except beets* may be added to the egg mixture.

Helpful Hint: If you wish to eliminate all cholesterol, use 10 egg whites and proceed as in recipe.

Per serving: 83 calories; 7.0 gm protein; 3.6 gm fat; 6.1 gm carbohydrate: 0.8 gm fiber; 104 mg cholesterol; 97 mg sodium

* Use skillet with heatproof handle.

Whole-Wheat Cheese Puffs ⓠ

Serves: 4 (1 sandwich = 1 serving)

A perfect brunch or supper selection. Faster than a blintz and lower in fat than a grilled cheese sandwich.

1 cup 1% fat cottage cheese
2 tablespoons nonfat yogurt
1 tablespoon frozen unsweetened apple juice concentrate
½ teaspoon ground cinnamon
1 whole egg plus 2 egg whites, beaten

⅔ cup nonfat milk plus ⅓ cup nonfat evaporated milk
2 tablespoons unsweetened apple juice
1 teaspoon pure vanilla extract
8 slices whole-wheat bread

1. Mix cottage cheese, yogurt, apple juice, and cinnamon together.
2. Beat egg and egg whites with milk, apple juice, and vanilla.
3. Coat 8- or 9-inch-square glass baking dish with nonstick cooking spray.
4. Spread 4 slices of bread with cheese filling. Top with remaining 4 slices of bread as in preparing a sandwich.
5. Dip both sides of sandwich in egg mixture and place in baking dish. Pour remaining milk mixture over sandwiches.
6. Bake in preheated 400° oven for 20 minutes, or until puffed and golden brown.

To Serve: Cut sandwiches in half and serve immediately with fresh pineapple or berries.

Per serving: 229 calories; 17.9 gm protein; 3.2 gm fat; 31.3 gm carbohydrate; 0.6 gm fiber; 73 mg cholesterol; 454 mg sodium

French Toast with Raisins ⓠ

Serves: 5 (3 halves = 1 serving)

This is an old standby in our household for Sunday morning brunch. If there happen to be any leftovers, wrap individually in plastic wrap, freeze, and reheat in a 375° oven or microwave oven.

4 egg whites
½ cup nonfat milk
¼ cup orange juice
2 tablespoons frozen unsweetened apple juice concentrate

1 teaspoon pure vanilla extract
8 slices whole-wheat raisin bread, cut in half diagonally*

1. In a shallow pan, beat first 5 ingredients with fork.
2. Soak bread in mixture until each slice is saturated.
3. Coat a 12-inch nonstick skillet with butter-flavored nonstick cooking spray. Place skillet over medium high heat, add bread, four slices at a time. Reduce to medium heat, and brown both sides.
4. Remove toast to heated serving dish or, if large amounts are prepared, keep warm in preheated 250° oven until ready to serve.

To Serve: This may be served with unsweetened preserves, unsweetened applesauce, or fresh fruit such as sliced strawberries, oranges, or mangos.

Variation: *French Toast Sandwich*—Spread 4 slices of bread with unsweetened preserves; cut in half and proceed as in Step 2.

Per serving: 164 calories; 7.6 gm protein; 2.0 gm fat; 29.4 gm carbohydrate; 1.1 gm fiber; 55 mg cholesterol; 159 mg sodium

* Sliced sourdough bread may be substituted for whole-wheat raisin bread.

E-Z Time Pizza Ⓠ

Yield: 1 10-inch Pizza (¼ pizza = 1 serving)

You can make this in less than half an hour and it has about a third the number of calories of traditional homemade pizza.

Dough:
½ cup whole-wheat flour
⅛ teaspoon salt
1½ teaspoons low-sodium baking
  powder

3–4 tablespoons water
1 tablespoon flour for rolling dough

Topping:
⅓ cup salt-free marinara sauce
¼ cup shredded skim-milk
  mozzarella cheese
2 small Italian plum tomatoes
  (10 thin slices)

4 thin green pepper rings

1 tablespoon chopped fresh basil
  for garnish

1. Place flour, salt, and baking powder in small bowl. Stir until well blended.
2. Sprinkle 3 tablespoons water over mixture and stir with a fork until dough comes together (add a bit more water, if necessary). Knead until smooth—about 2 minutes.
3. Roll dough out into 10-inch circle, using flour as needed.
4. Coat 10-inch nonstick skillet with butter-flavored nonstick cooking spray. Heat over medium heat until very hot.
5. Place dough in hot pan and cook until bottom is flecked with brown spots and top blisters and is dry.
6. Spread marinara sauce over crust. Sprinkle with cheese and top with tomato slices and green pepper rings.
7. Broil* until cheese is melted and lightly browned.
To Serve: Place pizza on round breadboard or plate. Sprinkle with basil and cut into 4 servings and serve immediately.

Per serving: 93 calories; 4.7 gm protein; 1.6 gm fat; 16.5 gm carbohydrate; 2.0 gm fiber; 4 mg cholesterol; 117 mg sodium

* If handle of skillet is not heatproof, or you make more than one pizza, transfer pizza to a cookie sheet.

Stuffed Pita Pocket ⓠ
(With Tuna Salad and Vegetables)

Serves: 4 (½ stuffed pocket = 1 serving)

Pita bread originated in the Middle East, but is becoming very popular in the United States. The ingredients we have used may be varied to suit your palate.

6½-ounce can salt-reduced tuna in water, drained

1 stalk celery, thinly sliced

1 red apple with skin, cored and chopped

6 mushrooms, cleaned and sliced

2 tablespoons slivered almonds, toasted

⅓ cup nonfat yogurt

2 whole-wheat pita breads, halved vertically

2 cups shredded romaine lettuce or alfalfa sprouts

2 Italian plum tomatoes, diced

2 carrots, coarsely grated, and 1 small green pepper, seeded and cut into rings, for garnish

1. Combine tuna, celery, apple, mushrooms, almonds, and yogurt.
2. Layer lettuce and tomato in bottom of pockets.
3. Stuff pockets with tuna mixture and sprinkle with remaining lettuce. Garnish with grated carrot and green pepper rings.

To Serve: Whether in a lunch box for children, in a brown bag for the office, or for supper at home, this salad-in-a-sandwich answers all of your nutritional needs as well as being expeditious.

Per serving: 273 calories; 20.9 gm protein; 4.1 gm fat; 36.6 gm carbohydrate; 2.0 gm fiber; 34 mg cholesterol; 55 mg sodium

356 &§ DELICIOUSLY SIMPLE

Hot Tuna Salad Sandwich @

Serves: 4 (1 open-face sandwich = 1 serving)

Not quite a tuna melt, but very tasty indeed.

6½-ounce can salt-reduced tuna in water, drained
1 tablespoon finely chopped celery
2 tablespoons finely chopped green pepper
1 whole green onion, thinly sliced
Freshly ground black pepper
½ teaspoon salt-free vegetable seasoning

2 tablespoons light mayonnaise
2 tablespoons nonfat yogurt
4 slices whole-wheat, rye, or pumpernickel bread
2 tomatoes (8 slices)
2 tablespoons shredded skim-milk mozzarella cheese or
1 tablespoon grated Parmesan cheese

1. Combine tuna, celery, green pepper, onion, pepper, vegetable seasoning, mayonnaise, and yogurt. Stir to blend well.
2. Spread each bread slice with one quarter of the mixture, 2 tomato slices, and ½ tablespoon shredded cheese.
3. Place under preheated broiler until cheese is melted and very lightly browned.

To Serve: Place open-face sandwich on each plate. Serve with Red and Green Slaw (page 120) or sliced fresh fruit.

Variation: Using 8 slices of bread, make a traditional sandwich and grill on nonstick griddle coated with butter-flavored nonstick cooking spray. Brown lightly on both sides. Before serving, cut in half; then serve immediately.

Per serving: 152 calories; 17.3 gm protein; 1.9 gm fat; 26.0 gm carbohydrate; 0.8 gm fiber; 34 mg cholesterol; 147 mg sodium

Potato Tostada Ⓠ

Serves: 8 (1 filled potato skin = 1 serving)

Instead of a corn tortilla, use a baked potato skin and save the potato pulp for hash, salmon patties, or mashed potatoes at another time.

1 teaspoon cold-pressed safflower oil

½ cup chopped red onion

1-pound can vegetarian refried beans

½ teaspoon chili powder

2 cups shredded cooked chicken

3 cups shredded romaine lettuce

3 whole green onions, thinly sliced

1 cup diced tomato

½ cup canned green chili salsa

8 halves baked potato skins, crisped in oven

Nonfat yogurt and chopped cilantro for garnish

1. Heat oil in nonstick saucepan; add onions and cook until tender. Stir in refried beans and chili powder. Heat.

2. In mixing bowl, combine chicken, romaine, green onions, tomato, and salsa.

3. Divide hot bean mixture between potato skins; top with chicken mixture. Garnish with dollop of yogurt (and a bit more salsa if you like) and chopped cilantro.

Per serving: 204 calories; 16.7 gm protein; 4.5 gm fat; 24.8 gm carbohydrate; 6.6 gm fiber; 31 mg cholesterol; 59 mg sodium

Tostada ⓠ

Serves: 4 (1 tortilla plus filling = 1 serving)

A Mexican salad served as a main dish. I use vegetarian beans, since the regular beans have lard added.

4 fresh corn tortillas, seasoned with garlic powder and paprika
1 cup canned vegetarian refried beans*
¼ red onion, chopped
⅓ cup canned green chili salsa

4 cups assorted vegetables, such as shredded romaine, diced cucumber, sliced radishes, sliced green onions, alfalfa sprouts, sliced green and sweet red peppers

Nonfat yogurt and additional salsa as garnish (optional)

1. Place tortillas on baking sheet and bake in preheated 400° oven for 3 to 5 minutes, or until crisp.
2. Combine beans, onion, and chili salsa.
3. Spread ¼ cup bean mixture on tostada shell, top with ⅔ cup various vegetables; additional salsa and a dollop of yogurt may be added as a garnish.

Variation: Shredded cooked chicken or tuna may be added.

Per serving: 230 calories; 9.7 gm protein; 2.9 gm fat; 44.3 gm carbohydrate; 8.2 gm fiber; 0 mg cholesterol; 65 mg sodium

* For a spicier bean spread, add 2 tablespoons chopped green chilies.

Mother Mollie's Cheese Blintzes ⓠ

Yield: 13 blintzes (2 blintzes = 1 serving)

Every child thinks his mother is the best cook in the world. Then he grows up, expands his horizons, and realizes that this *may* not be true. Frequently, a touching, sometimes comforting way to remember loved ones is through their legacy of food preparation, be it good or bad.

16-ounce carton 1% fat cottage cheese*

2 egg whites

1 tablespoon nonfat yogurt

3 tablespoons frozen unsweetened apple juice concentrate

½ teaspoon ground cinnamon

2 teaspoons pure vanilla extract

¼ cup seeded muscat raisins

1 recipe Basic Crêpes (page 32)

1. Place first 6 ingredients in food processor or blender. Process briefly until smooth, using pulsing action.
2. Add raisins and stir.
3. Place 2 tablespoons cheese mixture into center of each crêpe. Fold in 2 ends and roll up into thirds.**
4. Coat nonstick skillet with butter-flavored nonstick cooking spray and arrange blintzes in pan. Brown on both sides over medium heat and serve immediately.

Variations:

Blueberry Blintzes—Mix 1½ cups frozen blueberries with ¼ cup frozen pear, grape, or apple juice, 1½ teaspoons whole-wheat blend flour, and a dash of ground cinnamon. Microwave on high for 2 minutes and proceed as in cheese blintzes. Serve with yogurt.

Apple Blintzes—Mix 2 cups thinly sliced apples with 2 tablespoons orange juice and cinnamon to taste. Microwave on high for 3 minutes. Proceed as in cheese blintzes and serve with yogurt.

Per serving: 125 calories; 11.8 gm protein; 0.9 gm fat; 16.8 gm carbohydrate; 0.9 gm fiber; 3 mg cholesterol; 306 mg sodium

---

* Skim-milk ricotta cheese may be substituted for cottage cheese.
** Blintzes may be prepared in advance and kept in refrigerator until ready to heat or frozen for future use.

Chocolate Lover's Tart Shell Ⓠ

Yield: 1 9-inch tart shell, serving 10 (1 slice = 1 serving)

A delicious exception!

2¾ cups bite-sized shredded wheat squares, crushed (1 cup)
3 tablespoons frozen unsweetened apple juice concentrate

2 ounces unsweetened chocolate, melted
½ cup finely chopped pecans or almonds

1. Toast squares in oven until lightly browned. Crush. Transfer to bowl. Add apple juice concentrate and stir to blend.
2. Add nuts and melted chocolate. Stir with fork to blend.
3. Place mixture in 9-inch springform pan coated with nonstick cooking spray. Press lightly with back of spoon or hand.
4. Chill for 20 minutes before adding filling.

To Serve: May be substituted for Basic Tart Crust (page 35) and filled with fruit or an Apricot Chiffon filling (page 320).

Per serving: 112 calories; 3.1 gm protein; 5.7 gm fat; 13.8 gm carbohydrate; 0.7 gm fiber; 0 mg cholesterol; 2.5 mg sodium

Sally's Cottage Cheese Swedish Pancakes ⓠ

Yield: 8 thin pancakes (2 pancakes = 1 serving)

Although not quite a pancake or a crêpe, these are special served for Sunday breakfast or brunch.

1 cup 1% cottage cheese
1 whole egg
3 egg whites
½ cup whole-wheat blend flour
1 teaspoon pure vanilla extract
1 tablespoon frozen unsweetened
  apple juice concentrate

¼ teaspoon ground cinnamon
Unsweetened fruit preserves for
  filling

Fresh fruit for garnish

1. Place all ingredients except fruit preserve in blender or food processor.
2. Blend just until mixed, not smooth.
3. Heat a 6-inch nonstick skillet that has been coated with butter-flavored nonstick cooking spray. Pour 3 tablespoons batter into heated skillet, tilting and covering bottom of pan as you pour. When edges have browned slightly, loosen pancake around edges with metal spatula and turn over to just dry opposite side. Spread 1 teaspoon jam over pancakes and fold over pancakes from two ends so they overlap.

To Serve: Serve hot with fresh fruit garnish such as orange wedge, pineapple spear, or a few strawberries.

Per serving: 138 calories; 6.2 gm protein; 2.3 gm fat; 15.2 gm carbohydrate; 0.5 gm fiber; 71 mg cholesterol; 295 mg sodium

Cucumber Raita Ⓠ

Yield: 4 cups (2 tablespoons = 1 serving)

Delicious served with curries, tandoori game hens, or broiled fish.

2 large cucumbers, peeled, seeded,
    and cut into slices ¼ inch thick
2 cups nonfat yogurt
½ teaspoon crushed red pepper
    flakes
½ teaspoon ground cumin

¼ teaspoon white pepper
½ cup chopped parsley*

2 chopped Italian plum tomatoes
    for garnish

1. Press cucumber slices dry with paper towels.
2. Combine yogurt with remaining ingredients.
3. Add cucumbers to yogurt and mix well.
4. Cover and chill until serving time. Taste and adjust seasonings before serving.

To Serve: Place in bowl and garnish with chopped tomatoes.

Variation: A peeled, diced ripe peach may be added for a touch of sweetness.

Per serving: 11 calories; 0.9 gm protein; 0.1 gm fat; 1.7 gm carbohydrate; 0.2 gm fiber; 0 mg cholesterol; 12 mg sodium

* When used with fish, substitute fresh chopped dill for parsley.

Fresh Tomato Relish ⓠ

Yield: 2 cups (1 tablespoon = 1 serving)

This fresh relish makes a lovely accompaniment to fish or chicken.

4 ripe plum tomatoes, seeded and chopped
½ red onion, finely chopped
½ cup seeded and finely chopped sweet red and green pepper
¼ cup frozen unsweetened apple juice concentrate

¼ cup red wine vinegar
1 teaspoon mustard seeds
Freshly ground black pepper
Pinch ground cloves or allspice (optional)

1. Combine all ingredients, cover, and chill thoroughly, about 1 hour.
2. May be stored in refrigerator for 2 to 3 weeks.

Per serving: 8 calories; 0 gm protein; 0 gm fat; 2 gm carbohydrate; 0.2 gm fiber; 0 mg cholesterol; 2 mg sodium

Fresh Tomato Coulis ⓠ

Yield: 1 cup (1 tablespoon = 1 serving)

This tastes best prepared in the summer months, when tomatoes are the most plentiful and delicious.

2 ripe tomatoes
1 teaspoon extra-virgin olive oil
1 garlic clove, minced

¼ teaspoon each dried thyme, marjoram, basil, and savory, crushed, or 1 teaspoon chopped of each if fresh

1. Peel, seed, and chop tomatoes.
2. Place oil in nonstick skillet and sauté tomatoes for 2 to 3 minutes.
3. Add garlic and herbs. Sauté 1 minute, taste, and adjust flavors.

To Serve: Use as an accompaniment, either hot or cold, with chicken, fish, or All-American Chicken Sausage Patties (page 201).

Per serving: 7 calories; 0 gm protein; 0.3 gm fat; 0.8 gm carbohydrate; 0.2 gm fiber; 0 mg cholesterol; 1.5 mg sodium

Almost Crème Anglaise ⓠ

Yield: 1 cup (1 tablespoon = 1 serving)

I use this sauce as a topping on berries, fruit tarts, or bread pudding instead of either whipped or heavy cream.

½ cup nonfat powdered milk
¼ cup very cold orange juice
¼ cup very cold water

1 tablespoon Grand Marnier (optional)

1. Place all ingredients in a chilled deep bowl.
2. Beat with chilled electric hand beater until thick.
3. May be prepared several hours ahead of time if desired.

Variation: Substitute ¼ cup chilled unsweetened apple juice for orange juice and 1 tablespoon Calvados for Grand Marnier. This would be delicious with a baked apple.

Per serving: 15 calories; 1.4 gm protein; 0 gm fat; 2.4 gm carbohydrate; 0 gm fiber; 1 mg cholesterol; 20 mg sodium

Spicy Barbecue Sauce Ⓠ

Yield: 1½ cups (1 tablespoon = 1 serving)

A low-sodium sauce, delicious for basting broiled or barbecued chicken. Since tomatoes burn easily, apply the sauce to chicken the last 5 minutes of cooking; you may want to add a little more after chicken is done.

8-ounce can salt-reduced tomato sauce

1 tablespoon dehydrated onion flakes or 1 small onion, minced

1 tablespoon dehydrated celery flakes or 1 stalk celery, minced

¼ teaspoon garlic powder or 1 large garlic clove, minced

½ green pepper, seeded and minced

1 tablespoon Worcestershire sauce

1 teaspoon salt-free vegetable seasoning

1 teaspoon dry mustard

2 tablespoons lemon juice

2 tablespoons cider vinegar

2 tablespoons frozen unsweetened apple or pineapple juice concentrate

1 teaspoon liquid smoke (optional)

1. Combine all ingredients in 1-quart saucepan and bring to boil.
2. Cover, reduce heat, and simmer about 10 to 15 minutes. Stir occasionally.
3. Taste and adjust seasonings.

Note: Sauce may be refrigerated or frozen for future use.

Per serving: 9 calories; 0.2 gm protein; 0 gm fat; 2 gm carbohydrate; 0.1 gm fiber; 0 mg cholesterol; 10 mg sodium

Green Sauce Ⓠ

Yield: 1¼ cups (1 tablespoon = 1 serving)

A colorful and piquant sauce to serve with fish.

¼ cup parsley leaves
¼ cup watercress or spinach leaves
1 whole green onion, quartered
1 cup nonfat yogurt
1 tablespoon white wine vinegar

1 teaspoon frozen unsweetened
   apple juice concentrate
2 teaspoons Dijon mustard
(optional)

1. Place all ingredients in blender or food processor. Process until finely chopped and blended.
2. Taste and adjust seasonings.
3. Store in covered container in refrigerator until ready to use.

Per serving: 7 calories: 0.7 gm protein; 0 gm fat; 1.2 gm carbohydrate; 0 gm fiber;
0 mg cholesterol; 9 mg sodium

Horseradish–Mustard–
Yogurt Sauce Ⓠ

Yield: 1½ cups (1 tablespoon = 1 serving)

A tangy sauce, delicious served with turkey or chicken.

½ cup grated white horseradish*
½ cup coarse-grained mustard

½ cup nonfat yogurt

1. Combine all ingredients thoroughly. Taste and adjust seasoning, and chill.
2. Store in covered container in refrigerator for up to 10 days.

Per serving: 8 calories; 0.6 gm protein; 0.2 gm fat; 1.2 gm carbohydrate; 0.1 gm fiber;
0 mg cholesterol; 8 mg sodium

* Do not use horseradish with preservatives, oil, or creaming agent added.

Onion–Mustard Sauce ⑨

Yield: 2¼ cups (2 tablespoons = 1 serving)

If you use Onion Magic (page 36) instead of starting from scratch, you will have to brown your onions a bit more to start.

1 large onion, thinly sliced and
   browned with 2 teaspoons
   extra-virgin olive oil, or
⅔ cup Onion Magic (page 36)
1 tablespoon coarse-grained
   mustard

Freshly ground black pepper
1¼ cups salt-free chicken broth,
   defatted

1. Combine browned onion or Onion Magic with mustard and pepper and stir to blend. Add chicken broth and bring to a boil. Reduce heat and simmer uncovered for about 10 minutes.

2. Puree mixture in blender or food processor, taste, and adjust seasonings.

To Serve: May be served with All-American Chicken Sausage Patties (page 201) or broiled chicken.

Helpful Hint: Sauce may also be frozen for future use.

Per serving: 12 calories; 0.4 gm protein; 0.2 gm fat; 2.2 gm carbohydrate; 0.2 gm fiber; 0 mg cholesterol; 2 mg sodium

Sabayon Sauce ⓠ
(For Fruit)

Yield: 1¼ cups (1 tablespoon = 1 serving)

Just imagine, a sabayon sauce where you use the egg whites and discard the yolks!

3 egg whites, at room temperature   **3 tablespoons dry port or marsala**
1 small, very ripe banana, mashed

1. Beat egg whites with whisk or fork until foamy.
2. Gradually add banana as you beat vigorously.
3. Add port and beat thoroughly. The sauce will be the consistency of a medium white sauce.

To Serve: Spoon over assorted fruit, such as blueberries, raspberries, or strawberries, or use as a topping on our Fresh Strawberry Tart (page 330).

Per serving: 10 calories; 0.6 gm protein; 0 gm fat; 1.4 gm carbohydrate; 0.1 gm fiber; 0 mg cholesterol; 8 mg sodium

Bibliography

PERIODICALS

Diabetes and Nutrition News. For information write to: P.O. Box 22124, Lexington, Kentucky 40522

The Harvard Medical School Health Letter. For information write to: P.O. Box 10945, Des Moines, Iowa 50340

Healthline. For information write to: 1320 Boyport Avenue, San Carlos, Calif. 94070

Nutrition Action. For information write to: Center for Science in Public Interest, 1501 16th Street, N.W., Washington, D.C. 20036

Running and Fitness News. For information write to: AR-FA 2001 S Street N.W., Suite 540, Washington, D.C. 20009

Tufts University Diet and Nutrition Letter. Customer service: 1-800-247-5470

University of California, Berkeley, Wellness Letter. For information write to: P.O. Box 10922, Des Moines, Iowa 50340

BOOKS

Anderson, James W., *Diabetes: A Practical Guide to Healthy Living,* Arco, 1983.

Bowes and Church's, Food Values of Portions Commonly Used, J. B. Lippincott, 1983.

Brody, Jane, *Jane Brody's Nutrition Book,* Norton, 1981.

Diet, Nutrition, and Cancer. National Academy Press, 2101 Constitution Avenue N.W., Washington, D.C. 20418.

Farquhar, John W., *The American Way of Life Need Not Be Hazardous To Your Health.* Norton, 1979.

Jacobson, Michael F. *Eater's Digest and Nutrition Scoreboard,* Doubleday, 1985.

Jacobson, Michael F., *A Brand Name Guide to Salt,* Workman, 1983.

Lappe, Frances Moore, *Diet for a Small Planet,* Ballantine, 1975.

Liebman, Bonnie, and authors of Nutrition Action, *Smart Eating Guide,* CSPI.

Mayer, Jean, *A Diet for Living*, McKay, 1975.

Pritikin, Nathan, *Pritikin Permanent Weight Loss Manual*, Bantam, 1981.

Pritikin, Nathan, *The Pritikin Promise: 28 Days to a Longer, Healthier Life*, Simon & Schuster, 1983.

Sims, Dorothy, *Diabetes: Reach for Health and Freedom*, Signet, 1981.

U.S. Department of Agriculture, *Composition of Foods: Raw, Processed and Prepared*, Agricultural Handbook #8.

U.S. Department of Agriculture, *Sodium, Think About It*. U.S. Department of Health and Human Services Home and Garden Bulletin #237.

Appendix

Preferred Products

Several years ago most of these preferred products would have been available only at "health food" stores. Today many of these products are sold at local markets because of increased consumer awareness and demand. This is a partial list. Before buying any products, *remember to read the labels carefully.* Any product bearing the Pritikin label is acceptable.

Seasonings

Allspice, sweet basil, caraway seeds, chervil, chili powder, cinnamon cloves (whole), coriander, curry powder, dill weed, dehydrated vegetable flakes, fine herbes, fennel seeds, garlic powder, ginger, Italian herb blend, dry mustard, nutmeg (whole), onion powder, oregano, poppy seeds, red pepper (crushed), rosemary, saffron, sesame seeds, shallots, tarragon, thyme. Recommended brands: Wagner's, Spice Islands, Parsley Patch, Select Origins, Albert Menes, The Spice Hunter, Pocket Creek, Schillings, Lawry's Natural Choice, American Heart Association Original Herb Seasoning.

Salt-free Micro Shake.

Hungarian paprika. Recommended brands: Szeged, Kaloksa.

Gaylord Hauser Vegit, Onion Magic, and Herbal Bouquet, Select No-Salt Bar BQ Spice, Capello's Vegetable Seasoning, Nile Spices Desert Spice, Yerba Encanta Seasoning, Health Valley No-Salt Seasoning, Nature's Gourmet Lush 'n Lemon, Mrs. Dash, Wagner's Flavor Magic, Spice Time.

Bak On Herbs and Spices Salad Style.

No-salt chopped garlic. Recommended brands: Pollaner, Gilroy Farms.

Wasabi Ko Powdered Horseradish.

Dijon mustard. Recommended brands: Paul Corcillet, Amora, French's Maître Jacques, Blanchard & Blanchard, Dessaux Fils, Featherweight, Reine, Lifetone, Silver Palate.

Chinese five-spice powder.

Capers (rinsed and drained).

Mild or low-sodium soy sauce (1 tablespoon has 465 mg sodium—*use prudently*). Recommended brands: Kikkoman, San J. Tamari, Yamasi, Eden, Soken, Westbrae, Angostura.

Vinegars: brown rice, rice wine, red wine, white wine, champagne, pear, raspberry, tarragon, Italian Balsamic. Recommended brands: Paul Corcillet, Duggan's, Gourmet France, Monair Federzoni, Harry & David, Dessaux Fils, Paula's, Spice Islands, Silver Palate, Sterling Apple Cider Vinegar, Mitsukan Rice Vinegar.

Pure vanilla extract (without sugar). Recommended brands: Wagner's, Nielsen-Massey, Bickford.

Pure extracts: Bickford, Wagner's.

Angostura Aromatic Bitters.

McIlheny Tabasco, Durkee's Red Hot Pepper Sauce, Trappeys Mexi-Pep, Louisiana Hot Sauce.

French's or Lea & Perrin's Worcestershire Sauce (1 tablespoon has 150 mg sodium plus sugar—*use prudently*), or Robbie's Salt-Free Worcestershire Sauce.

Milk and Milk Products (1 percent milkfat or less)

Evaporated nonfat or skimmed milk. Recommended brands: Carnation, Pet.

Buttermilk powder. Recommended brand: Saco.

Dry curd cottage cheese. Recommended brands: Altadena, Axelrod, Borden, Breakstone, Knudsen, Lucerne, Friendship.

1% low-fat cottage cheese. Recommended brands: Weight Watchers, Friendship, A&P Look Fit, Kroger, Pathmark, Axelrod's, Reduced Salt, Sealtest, Light n Lively.

Hoop cheese. Recommended brands: Knudsen, Tuttle, Breakstone.

Nonfat yogurt. Recommended brands: Continental, Weight Watchers, Altadena, Ralph's, Johnston's.

Tomato Products

Del Monte (no salt added), Gathering Winds Spaghetti Sauce, Hunt's No Salt Spaghetti Sauce, Enrico's Spaghetti Sauce (no salt or sugar added).

Italian plum tomatoes in puree or tomato sauce. Recommended brands: Del Monte, Progresso, Contadina, Springfield (salt-free), Hunt's (salt-free), S&W 50% less salt.

Strained Fresh Tomatoes (in a box). Recommended brands: Parmalat, Bertolli.

Hunt's no-salt-added tomato products, S&W 50% salt-reduced tomato products.

Green chili salsa. Recommended brands: Enrico's, Pace, Ortega, Chunky Taco Salsa, Hot Cha-Cha Texas Salsa (no salt added).

Low-sodium tomato juice. Recommended brands: Diet Delite, Nutra Diet, Hunt's (no salt added), S&W 50% less salt.

Nutra Diet Vegetable Juice, S&W 50% less salt.

Canned Vegetables

Garbanzo and kidney beans. Recommended brands: Nutra Diet, Ralph's, S&W 50% salt-reduced.

Dennison's Chili Beans.

Rosarita Vegetarian Refried Beans.

Libby's Pumpkin.

Water chestnuts, bamboo shoots, artichokes (hearts or bottoms), hearts of palm.

Green chilis. Recommended brands: Ortega, Hot Cha-Cha.

Salt-free canned vegetables. Recommended brands: Nutra Diet, Del Monte, Libby's, Ralph's, Green Giant.

Frozen Vegetables

Recommended brand: Any brand without added salt.

Frozen Fruits

Flavorland Unsweetened Berries, Cherries, Peaches, Strawberries, Raspberries.

Overlake Blueberries.

Canned Fruits

Mott's Sugar-Free Applesauce, S&W, Appletime.

Dole Unsweetened Pineapple (crushed, chunks, slices).

Fruit in water pack or unsweetened natural fruit juice.

Knudsen's Unsweetened Cranberry or Papaya Nectar.

Hot Cereals and Grains

Brown rice, bulgur wheat, buckwheat or kasha, barley, millet, cornmeal (whole ground), rolled oats (not quick-cooking), wheat flakes, rye flakes, steel-cut oats, triticale. Recommended brands: Wheatena, Zoom, Ralston, Elams' Scotch style oatmeal, Roman Meal oats, wheat, rye, and flax, Arrowhead Mills 4-grain Cereal and 7-grain Cereal, Con Arga's Cream of Rye, Mother's Whole Wheat Hot Cereal, Kashi breakfast pilaf, Mother's Oat Bran, Sovex Oat Bran, Arrowhead Mills Oat Bran, Erewhon's Barley Plus, Mother's quick-cooking barley.

Cold Cereals
Shredded wheat (biscuit or bite-sized). Recommended brands: Nabisco, Skinners, Shredded Wheat 'n Bran.
Health Valley salt-free and sugar-free cereals, Golden Harvest, Grain-fields, Back to Nature, New Morning.
Kellogg's Nutri-Grain cereals (with or without raisins).
Uncle Sam.
Grape-Nuts (with or without raisins).
Back to Nature's 7-Grain Almond Crisp.
New Morning Oatios, Kölln Oat Bran Crunch and Crispy Oats.
Puffed rice, wheat, millet, or corn (little food value present because of processing).

Flours
Barley flour, buckwheat flour, whole-wheat flour, whole-wheat pastry flour, triticale flour, rice flour, soy flour (limited amounts because of fat content), potato flour, rye flour, stone-ground cornmeal (not de-germinated), matzo meal (in limited amounts because not whole grain), and now available, 50 percent whole wheat and 50 percent un-bleached white flour—called Gold Medal whole-wheat blend flour.
Arrowhead Mills Pancake Flour.
Health Valley 7-Sprouted Grain Pancake Mix.

Pastas
Whole-wheat ribbon noodles, whole-wheat lasagna noodles, whole-wheat macaroni shells, soba (Japanese pasta, buckwheat, and whole-wheat flours used).
De Boles Corn Pasta, Vegetable Twists, Noodles.
No Yolks Noodles.
To-Fitness Tofu Pasta.
De Ceccio Spaghetti, Lasagna, Penne, Linguine, Macaroni, Shells, Buca-tini, Whole-Wheat Spaghetti, Capellini, Fusilli, Conchiglie.

Breads and Crackers
Pritikin Whole-Wheat Bread, Rye Bread, Multi-Grain Bread, Raisin Bread, English Muffins.
Sourdough bread or rolls (without shortening), whole-wheat pita bread, corn tortillas (without preservatives and preferably without salt), Italian bread (no sugar or shortening), whole-wheat water bagels.
Wayfarer's Bread (plain or with raisins).
Edward's Baked Brown Rice Snaps.

Ry-Crisp (unseasoned).

Manischewitz whole-wheat matzo or crackers.

Finn-Crisp.

Fattorie and Pandea whole-wheat bread sticks (grissini).

Kavli whole-rye or whole-wheat flatbread (thin or thick).

Ry-Vita (unsalted).

Wasa Brod.

Hard Tack.

Ideal whole-grain flatbread.

Iverson's Slim-Rye, Pumpernickel.

Bran-a-Crisp Wheat Bran Wafers.

Rice cakes. Recommended brands: Arden, Chico San, or Hain's.

Crispy rice cakes. Recommended brand: Pacific Rice Products.

Baked corn chips. Recommended brand: Garden of Eating.

Miscellaneous

Dried fruits (in limited quantities, sun-dried or *no sulfites added*).*

Crawford's Healthy Sweetener (wheat bran and dates).

Raw trail mix (in limited quantities), a healthy snack consisting of sun-flower and pumpkin seeds, dark raisins, and raw cashews or almonds. *No salt, sugar, oil, or coconut added.* Recommended brand: Hadley's.

Natural cranberry sauce. Recommended brand: R.W. Knudsen.

Dried mushrooms (shiitake are particularly delicious).

Dehydrated vegetable flakes. Recommended brands: Durkee, Rokeach, Springfield.

Dehydrated soups (no salt or MSG). Recommended brand: Hain's tomato, cream of mushroom, cream of chicken, minestrone, hearty vegetable.

Canned soups (no salt or MSG). Recommended brands: Health Valley (minestrone, lentil, split pea, tomato, vegetable), Campbell's salt-free chicken broth. All Pritikin brand soups.

Lentil or wheat pilaf mix. Recommended brand: Near East.

---

* The Center for Science and the Public Interest, a Washington, D.C., consumer advocacy group and publishers of the Nutrition Action Health Letter, has labeled the sulfites found in foods as "the only food additive in twenty years that has actually killed people." Sulfites are added to prevent discoloration in some dried fruit, such as yellow raisins, dried peaches, and dried apricots. Read your labels and protect yourself by using sun-dried fruits or dark raisins. Sulfites are also used in many salad bars to prevent fruits and vegetables from discoloration when left exposed for extended time periods. Pre-cut potatoes frequently have sulfites added also. An F.D.A. panel has recommended a ban on the preservatives. At the time this book went to press, it has not been enacted, so be careful, particularly if you are an asthmatic or may be allergic to the chemical.

Frozen fruit juice concentrates (unsweetened): apple, orange, grape, pear, and pineapple.

Sugar-free fresh fruit popsicles.

Bottled fruit juice concentrate. Recommended brands: Jensen's, Nu-Life.

Banana flakes. Recommended brand: Kanana.

Apple butter preserves, unsweetened. Recommended brands: Westbrae, Tap'n Apple.

Sugar-free fruit preserves or conserves. Recommended brands: Poiret, Whole Earth, Sorrell Ridge, Judy & Toby's, L & A, Kozlowski Farms, Country Basket.

Low-sodium baking powder. Recommended brands: Cellu, Featherweight.

Carbonated beverages. Recommended brands: Perrier, Canada Dry, No Salt Seltzer, Hansen's Apple Lite Natural Soda.

Carob powder. Recommended brand: El Molino.

Coffee substitute. Recommended brands: Bambu, Cafix.

Teas. Recommended brands: Celestial Seasonings Herb Teas, Seelect Inc.

Pritikin No-Oil Salad Dressings (French, Russian, Vinaigrette).*

Italian salad dressings. Recommended brands: Walden Farms (no salt added), Kraft's (oil-free and reduced calorie), S&W's Nutra Diet, Tillie Lewis, Calvé.

Mayonnaise. Recommended brands: Weight Watchers, Kraft's, Best Foods (or Hellman's) Light.

Chestnuts (Marrons). Recommended brands: Minerve (roasted whole), Clement (puree, unsweetened).

Pam Nonstick Spray, Butter-Flavored Pam Spray.

Oils. Unrefined or cold-pressed if possible. Safflower oil. Recommended brands: Hain's, Hollywood. Extra-virgin olive oil. Recommended brands: Badia a Coltibuono, Old Monk, Puget, Stefanini.

Tuna. Recommended brands: Chicken of the Sea (50% salt-reduced), Starkist (60% salt-reduced).

Rapid-rise yeast. Recommended brands: Fleischmann, Red Star.

Salmon. Recommended brand: Jake's Salt-Free Coho Salmon.

Sardines. Recommended brand: Roland's Salt-Free Sardines, in tomato sauce or water.

---

* Any foods labeled Pritikin are acceptable.

IDEAL WEIGHT CHART

According to the Metropolitan Life Insurance Co., the following height-weight ratios are desirable for a longer life. Heights include one-inch heels for both men and women. Weights include five pounds of clothing for men and three pounds for women.

	MEN					WOMEN		
Height	Small Frame	Medium Frame	Large Frame		Height	Small Frame	Medium Frame	Large Frame
5'2"	128–134	131–141	138–150		4'10"	102–111	109–121	118–131
5'3"	130–136	133–143	140–153		4'11"	103–113	111–123	120–134
5'4"	132–138	135–145	142–156		5'	104–115	113–126	122–137
5'5"	134–140	137–148	144–160		5'1"	106–118	115–129	125–140
5'6"	136–142	139–151	146–164		5'2"	108–121	118–132	128–143
5'7"	138–145	142–154	149–168		5'3"	111–124	121–135	131–147
5'8"	140–148	145–157	152–172		5'4"	114–127	124–138	134–151
5'9"	142–151	148–160	155–176		5'5"	117–130	127–141	137–155
5'10"	144–154	151–163	158–180		5'6"	120–133	130–144	140–159
5'11"	146–157	154–166	161–184		5'7"	123–136	133–147	143–163
6'	149–160	157–170	164–188		5'8"	126–139	136–150	146–167
6'1"	152–164	160–174	168–192		5'9"	129–142	139–153	149–170
6'2"	155–168	164–178	172–197		5'10"	132–145	142–156	152–173
6'3"	158–172	167–182	176–202		5'11"	135–148	145–159	155–176
6'4"	162–176	171–187	181–207		6'	138–151	148–162	158–179

Metropolitan Life Insurance Co.

Recommended Daily Dietary Allowances

Beginning in 1941, committees of the National Research Council's Food and Nutrition Board have periodically reevaluated the Recommended Dietary Allowances (RDAs). The allowances have traditionally been defined as "the levels of intake of essential nutrients considered in the judgment of the Committee on the basis of available scientific knowledge to be adequate to meet the known nutritional needs of practically all healthy persons." Since an impasse has resulted from scientific differences of opinion, the National Research Council has withheld the publication of the 1985 edition until it has a more encompassing analysis of data pertaining to nutrients and health.

The chart on the facing page contains the most current recommendations.

In general, healthy people can maintain good nutrition if their diets provide safe and adequate daily amounts of the nutrients listed.*

* The commonly accepted exception is to increase the RDA of calcium to between 1000 and 1200 mg per day.

Group	Age (years)	Weight (lbs)	Height (in)	Energy (kcal)	Protein (g)	Iron (mg)	Sodium (mg)	Calcium (mg)	Phosphorus (mg)	Vitamin A (IV)	Thiamine (mg)	Riboflavin (mg)	Vitamin C (mg)	Potassium (mg)	Zinc (mg)	Niacin (mg N E)*	Vitamin B_6 (mg)	Vitamin B_{12} (µg)	Folacin (mg)
Infants	0-5	13	24	kg × 115 (95-145)	kg × 2.2	10	115-350	360	240	420	0.3	0.4	35	350-925	3	6	0.3	0.5	30
	5-10	20	28	kg × 105 (80-135)	kg × 2.0	15	250-750	540	360	400	0.5	0.6	35	425-1275	5	8	0.6	1.5	45
Children	1-3	29	35	1300 (900-1800)	23	15	325-975	800	800	400	0.7	0.8	45	550-1650	10	9	0.9	2.0	100
	4-6	44	44	1700 (1300-2300)	30	10	450-1350	800	800	500	0.9	1.0	45	775-2325	10	11	1.3	2.5	200
	7-10	62	52	2400 (1650-3300)	34	10	600-1800	800	800	700	1.2	1.4	45	1000-3000	10	16	1.6	3.0	300
Males	11-14	99	62	2700 (2000-3700)	45	18	900-2700	1200	1200	1000	1.4	1.6	50	1525-4575	15	18	1.8	3.0	400
	15-18	145	69	2800 (2100-3900)	56	18	900-2700	1200	1200	1000	1.4	1.7	60	1525-4575	15	18	2.0	3.0	400
	19-22	154	70	2900 (2500-3300)	56	10	1100-3300	800	800	1000	1.5	1.7	60	1875-5625	15	19	2.2	3.0	400
	23-50	154	70	2700 (2300-3100)	56	10	1100-3300	800	800	1000	1.4	1.6	60	1875-5625	15	18	2.2	3.0	400
	51+	154	70	2400 (2000-2800)	56	10	1100-3300	800	800	1000	1.2	1.4	60	1875-5625	15	16	2.2	3.0	400
Females	11-14	101	62	2200 (1500-3000)	46	18	900-2700	1200	1200	800	1.1	1.3	50	1525-4575	15	15	1.8	3.0	400
	15-18	120	64	2100 (1200-3000)	46	18	900-2700	1200	1200	800	1.1	1.3	60	1525-4575	15	14	2.0	3.0	400
	19-22	120	64	2100 (1700-2500)	44	18	1100-3300	800	800	800	1.1	1.3	60	1875-5625	15	14	2.0	3.0	400
	23-50	120	64	2000 (1600-2400)	44	18	1100-3300	800	800	800	1.0	1.2	60	1875-5625	15	13	2.0	3.0	400
	51+	120	64	1800 (1400-2200)	44	10	1100-3300	800	800	800	1.0	1.2	60	1875-5625	15	13	2.0	3.0	400
Pregnant				+300	+30	h		+400	+400	+200	+0.4	+0.3	+20		+5	+2	+0.6	+1.0	+400
Lactating				+500	+20	h		+400	+400	+400	+0.5	+0.5	+40		+10	+5	+0.5	+1.0	+100

Index

℗ Plume

**Buy them at your local
bookstore or use coupon
on next page for ordering.**